-1998-

Grandpa,
Hope you enjoy the wisdom
and light in this book.

Love + Light,

Philip

Conversations with God
an uncommon dialogue

Books by Neale Donald Walsch

Conversations with God, Book 1
Conversations with God, Book 1 Guidebook
Conversations with God, Book 2
Meditations from Conversations with God, Book 1
Meditations from Conversations with God, Book 2,
A Personal Journal
The Little Soul and the Sun

Conversations with God

• an uncommon dialogue •

book 3

Neale Donald Walsch

HAMPTON ROADS
PUBLISHING COMPANY, INC.

Copyright © 1998 by Neale Donald Walsch

Cover art by Louis Jones
Cover design by Marjoram Productions
Index by Leonard S. Rosenbaum

For information write:

Hampton Roads Publishing Company, Inc.
134 Burgess Lane
Charlottesville, VA 22902

Or call: (804) 296-2772
FAX: (804) 296-5096
E-mail: hrpc@hrpub.com
Website: www.hrpub.com

If you are unable to order this book from your local
bookseller, you may order directly from the publisher.
Quantity discounts for organizations are available.
Call 1-800-766-8009, toll-free.

Library of Congress Catalog Card Number: 98-71594

ISBN 1-57174-103-8

1 3 5 7 9 10 8 6 4 2

Printed on acid-free recycled paper in Canada

For

NANCY FLEMING-WALSCH

Best friend, dear companion,
passionate lover, and wonderful wife,
who has brought me and taught me
more than any human being
on Earth.

I am blessed in thee
beyond my highest dream.
You have made my soul sing again.
You have shown me love
in miracle form.
And you have given me
back to myself.

I humbly dedicate this book to you,
my greatest teacher.

Acknowledgments

As always, I wish first to thank my best friend, God. I hope one day that everyone can have a friendship with God.

Next, I acknowledge and thank my wonderful life partner, Nancy, to whom this book is dedicated. When I think of Nancy, my words of gratitude seem feeble next to her deeds, and I feel stuck with not being able to find a way to express how really extraordinary she is. This much I know. My work would not have been possible without her.

Then, I wish to acknowledge Robert S. Friedman, publisher at Hampton Roads Publishing Company, for his courage in first placing this material before the public in 1995, and in publishing all volumes of the *CWG* trilogy. His decision to accept a manuscript that was rejected by four other publishers has changed the lives of millions.

And I can't let the moment of this last installment in the *CWG* trilogy pass without acknowledging the extraordinary contribution to its publication made by Jonathan Friedman, whose clarity of vision, intensity of purpose, depth of spiritual understanding, endless well of enthusiasm, and monumental gift of creativity is in large measure the reason *Conversations with God* made its way to bookshelves when it did, how it did. It was Jonathan Friedman who recognized the enormity of this message and its importance, predicting that it would be read by millions, foreseeing that it would become a classic of spiritual literature. It was his determination which produced the timing and design of *CWG*, and his unwavering dedication which had much to do with the efffectiveness of its initial distribution. All lovers of *CWG* are forever indebted to Jonathan, as am I.

I wish to thank Matthew Friedman also, for his tireless work on this project from the beginning. The value of his co-creative efforts in design and production cannot be overstated.

Finally, I want to acknowledge some of the authors and teachers whose work has so altered the philosophical and spiritual landscape of America and the world, and who inspire me daily with their commitment to telling a larger truth regardless of the pressures and personal complications that such a decision creates.

To Joan Borysenko, Deepak Chopra, Dr. Larry Dossey, Dr. Wayne Dyer, Dr. Elisabeth Kübler-Ross, Barbara Marx Hubbard, Stephen Levine, Dr. Raymond Moody, James Redfield, Dr. Bernie Siegel, Dr. Brian Weiss, Marianne Williamson, and Gary Zukav—all of whom I have come to personally know and deeply respect—I pass on the thanks of a grateful public, and my personal appreciation and admiration.

These are some of our modern day way-show-ers, these are the pathfinders, and if I have been able to embark on a personal journey as a public declarer of eternal truth, it is because they, and others like them whom I have not met, have made it possible. Their life work stands as testimony to the extraordinary brilliance of the light in all our souls. They have *demonstrated* what I have merely talked about.

Introduction

This is an extraordinary book. I say that as someone who has had very little to do with writing it. All I did, really, was "show up," ask a few questions, then take dictation.

That is all I have done since 1992, when this conversation with God began. It was in that year that, deeply depressed, I called out in anguish: What does it take to make life work? And what have I done to deserve a life of such continuing struggle?

I wrote these questions out on a yellow legal pad, in an angry letter to God. To my shock and surprise, God answered. The reply came in the form of words whispered in my mind by a Voiceless Voice. I was fortunate enough to have written those words down.

I have done so now for over six years. And since I was told that this private dialogue would one day become a book, I sent the first batch of those words to a publisher late in 1994. They were on store shelves seven months later. At this writing that book has been on the *New York Times* bestseller list for 91 weeks.

The second installment in the dialogue became a bestseller as well, also making the *Times* list for multiple months. And now, here is the third and final portion of this extraordinary conversation.

This book took four years to write. It did not come easily. The gaps between the moments of inspiration were enormous, more than once stretching across half-a-year canyons. The words in the first book were dictated over the course of one year. The second book came through in just a little over that much time. But this final segment has had to be written with me in the public spotlight. Everywhere I've gone since 1996 all I've heard has been, "When's *Book 3* coming out?", "Where's *Book 3*?", "When can we expect *Book 3*?"

You can imagine what this did to me, and what impact this had on the process of bringing it through. I might as well have been making love on the pitcher's mound in Yankee Stadium.

Actually, that act would have afforded me more privacy. In the writing of *Book 3*, every time I picked up a pen I felt I had five million people watching, waiting, hanging on every word.

All of this is not to congratulate myself on completing this work, but rather, to simply explain why it has taken so long. My moments of mental, spiritual, and physical solitude have been, over these most recent years, very few and far between.

I began this book in the spring of 1994, and all of the early narrative was written in that time period. It then leaps across many months, ultimately jumping forward a full year, and finally culminating with closing chapters written in the spring and summer of 1998.

On this much you can depend: this book was not forced out, by any means. The inspiration either came cleanly, or I simply put the pen down and refused to write—in one case for well over 14 months. I was determined to produce no book at all, if it was to be a choice between that and a book I *had* to produce because I *said* I would. While this made my publisher a bit nervous, it went a long way toward giving me confidence in what was coming through, however long it was taking. I present it now, with confidence, to you. This book sums up the teachings in the first two installments of this trilogy. It then carries them forward to their logical, and breathtaking, conclusion.

If you've read the Foreword to either of the first two installments, you know that in each case I was a little bit apprehensive. Scared, actually, of what the response to those writings might be. I am not scared now. I have no fear whatsoever about *Book 3*. I know that it will touch many of those who read it with its insight and its truth, its warmth and its love.

I believe this to be sacred spiritual material. I see now that this is true of the entire trilogy, and that these books will be read and studied for decades, even for generations. Perhaps, for centuries. Because, taken together, the trilogy covers an amazing range of topics, from how to make relationships work to the nature of ultimate reality and the cosmology of the universe, and includes observations on life, death, romance, marriage, sex, parenting, health, education, economics, politics, spirituality and religion, life work and right livelihood, physics, time, social mores and customs, the process of creation, our relationship with God, ecology, crime and punishment, life in highly evolved societies of the cosmos, right and wrong, cultural myths and cultural ethics, the soul, soul partners, the nature of genuine love, and the way to glorious expression of the part of ourselves that knows Divinity as our natural heritage.

My prayer is that you will receive benefit from this work. Blessed be.

Neale Donald Walsch
Ashland, Oregon
September, 1998

1

It is Easter Sunday, 1994, and I am here, pen in hand, as instructed. I am waiting for God. He's promised to show up, as She has the past two Easters, to begin another yearlong conversation. The third and last—for now.

This process—this extraordinary communication—began in 1992. It will be complete on Easter, 1995. Three years, three books. The first dealt with largely personal matters—romantic relationships, finding one's right work, dealing with the powerful energies of money, love, sex, and God; and how to integrate them into our daily lives. The second expanded on those themes, moving outward to major geopolitical considerations—the nature of governments, creating a world without war, the basis for a unified, international society. This third and final part of the trilogy will focus, I am told, on the largest questions facing man. Concepts dealing with other realms, other dimensions, and how the whole intricate weave fits together.

The progression has been

Individual Truths
Global Truths
Universal Truths

As with the first two manuscripts, I have no idea where this is going. The process is simple. I put pen to paper, ask a question—and see what thoughts come to my mind. If nothing is there, if no words are given to me, I put everything away until another day. The whole process took about a year for the first book, over a year for the second. (That book is still in process as this is begun.)

I expect this will be the most important book of all.

For the first time since starting this process, I am feeling very self-conscious about it. Two months have passed since I wrote those first four or five paragraphs. Two months since Easter, and nothing has come—nothing but self-consciousness.

1

I have spent weeks reviewing and correcting errors in the typeset manuscript of the first book in this trilogy—and just this week received the final, corrected version of *Book 1*, only to have to send it back to typesetting again, with 43 separate errors to correct. The second book, meanwhile, still in handwritten form, was completed only last week—two months behind "schedule." (It was supposed to be done by Easter '94.) This book, begun on Easter Sunday in spite of the fact that *Book 2* was unfinished, has languished in its folder ever since—and, now that *Book 2* is complete—cries out for attention.

Yet for the first time since 1992, when this all began, I seem to be resisting this process, if not almost resenting it. I am feeling trapped by the assignment, and I've never liked to do anything I *have* to do. Further, having distributed to a few people uncorrected copies of the first manuscript and heard their reactions to it, I am now convinced that all three of these books will be widely read, thoroughly examined, analyzed for theological relevance, and passionately debated for dozens of years.

That has made it very difficult to come to this page; very difficult to consider this pen my friend—for while I know this material must be brought through, I know that I am opening myself up to the most scurrilous attacks, the ridicule, and perhaps even the hatred of many people for daring to put forth this information—much less for daring to announce that it is coming to me directly from God.

I think my greatest fear is that I will prove to be an inadequate, inappropriate "spokesperson" for God, given the seemingly endless series of mistakes and misdeeds which have marked my life and characterized my behavior.

Those who have known me from my past—including former wives and my own children—would have every right to step forward and denounce these writings, based on my lackluster performance as a human being in the simple, rudimentary functions of husband and father. I have failed miserably at this, and at other aspects of life having to do with friendship and integrity, industry and responsibility.

I am, in short, keenly aware that I am not worthy to represent myself as a man of God or a messenger of truth. I should be the last person to assume such a role, or to even presume to. I do an injustice to the truth by presuming to speak it, when my whole life has been a testimony to my weaknesses.

For these reasons, God, I ask that You relieve me of my duties as Your scribe, and that You find someone whose life renders them worthy of such an honor.

I should like to finish what we started here—though you are under no obligation to do so. You have no "duties," to Me or to anyone else, though I see that your thought that you do has led you to much guilt.

I have let people down, including my own children.

Everything that has happened in your life has happened perfectly in order for you—and all the souls involved with you—to grow in exactly the way you've needed and wanted to grow.

That is the perfect "out" constructed by everyone in the New Age who wishes to escape responsibility for their actions and avoid any unpleasant outcomes.

I feel that I've been selfish—incredibly selfish—most of my life, doing what pleases me regardless of its impact on others.

There is nothing wrong in doing what pleases you . . .

But, so many people have been hurt, let down—

There is only the question of what pleases you most. You seem to be saying that what now pleases you most are behaviors which do little or no damage to others.

That's putting it mildly.

On purpose. You must learn to be gentle with yourself. And stop judging yourself.

That's hard—particularly when others are so ready to judge. I feel I am going to be an embarrassment to You, to the truth;

3

that if I insist on completing and publishing this trilogy, I will be such a poor ambassador for Your message as to discredit it.

You cannot discredit truth. Truth is truth, and it can neither be proven nor disproven. It simply is.

The wonder and the beauty of My message cannot and will not be affected by what people think of you.

Indeed, you are one of the best ambassadors, because you have lived your life in a way that you call less than perfect.

People can relate to you—even as they judge you. And if they see that you are truly sincere, they can even forgive you your "sordid past."

Yet I tell you this: So long as you are still worried about what others think of you, you are owned by them.

Only when you require no approval from outside yourself can you own yourself.

My concern was more for the message than for me. I was concerned that the message would get besmirched.

If you are concerned about the message, then get the message out. Do not worry about besmirching it. The message will speak for itself.

Remember what I have taught you. It is not nearly so important how well a message is received as how well it is sent.

Remember this also: You teach what you have to learn.

It is not necessary to have achieved perfection to speak of perfection.

It is not necessary to have achieved mastery to speak of mastery.

It is not necessary to have achieved the highest level of evolution to speak of the highest level of evolution.

Seek only to be genuine. Strive to be sincere. If you wish to undo all the "damage" you imagine yourself to have done, demonstrate that in your actions. Do what you can do. Then let it rest.

That's easier said than done. Sometimes I feel so guilty.

Guilt and fear are the only enemies of man.

Guilt is important. It tells us when we've done wrong.

There is no such thing as "wrong." There is only that which does not serve you; does not speak the truth about Who You Are, and Who You Choose to Be.

Guilt is the feeling that keeps you stuck in who you are not.

But guilt is the feeling that at least lets us notice we've gone astray.

Awareness is what you are talking about, not guilt.

I tell you this: Guilt is a blight upon the land—the poison that kills the plant.

You will not grow through guilt, but only shrivel and die.

Awareness is what you seek. But awareness is not guilt, and love is not fear.

Fear and guilt, I say again, are your only enemies. Love and awareness are your true friends. Yet do not confuse the one with the other, for one will kill you, while the other gives you life.

Then I should not feel "guilty" about anything?

Never, ever. What good is there in that? It only allows you to not love yourself—and that kills any chance that you could love another.

And I should fear nothing?

Fear and caution are two different things. Be cautious—be conscious—but do not be fearful. For fear only paralyzes, while consciousness mobilizes.

Be mobilized, not paralyzed.

I was always taught to fear God.

I know. And you have been paralyzed in your relationships with Me ever since.

It was only when you stopped fearing Me that you could create any kind of meaningful relationship with Me.

If I could give you any gift, any special grace, that would allow you to find Me, it would be fearlessness.

Blessed are the fearless, for they shall know God.

That means you must be fearless enough to drop what you think you know about God.

You must be fearless enough to step away from what others have told you about God.

You must be so fearless that you can dare to enter into your *own experience* of God.

And then you must not feel guilty about it. When your own experience is violating what you thought you knew, and what everyone else has told you, about God, you must not feel guilty.

Fear and guilt are the only enemies of man.

Yet there are those who say that to do as You suggest is trafficking with the devil; that only the devil would suggest such a thing.

There is no devil.

That's something else the devil would say.

The devil would say everything that God says, is that it?

Only more cleverly.

The devil is more clever than God?

Let's say, more cunning.

6

And so the devil "connives" by saying what God would say?

With just a little "twist"—just enough to get one off the path; to lead one astray.

I think we have to have a little talk about the "devil."

Well, we talked a lot about this in *Book 1*.

Not enough, apparently. Besides, there may be those who haven't read *Book 1*. Or *Book 2*, for that matter. So I think a good place for us to begin would be to summarize some of the truths found in those books. That will set the stage for the larger, universal truths in this third book. And we'll get to the devil again, too, early on. I want you to know how, and why, such an entity was "invented."

Okay. All right. You win. I'm already into the dialogue, so apparently it's going to continue. But there's one thing people should know as I enter this third conversation: Half a *year* has passed since I wrote the first words presented here. It's now November 25, 1994—the day after Thanksgiving. It's taken 25 weeks to get this far; 25 weeks since your last words above, to my words in this paragraph. A lot has happened in those 25 weeks. But one thing that has not happened is that this book has not moved one inch forward. *Why is this taking so long?*

Do you see how you can block yourself? Do you see how you can sabotage yourself? Do you see how you can stop yourself in your tracks just when you are on to something good? You've been doing this all your life.

Hey, wait a minute! *I'm* not the one who has been stalling on this project. I can't do *anything*—can't write a single word—unless I feel moved to, unless I feel ... I hate to use the word, but I guess I have to ... *inspired* to come to this yellow legal pad and continue. And inspiration is *Your* department, not mine!

7

I see. So you think I've been stalling, not you.

Something like that, yes.

My wonderful friend, this is so much like you—and other humans. You sit on your hands for half a year, doing nothing about your highest good, actually pushing it from you, then blaming someone or something outside of yourself for you not getting anywhere. Do you not see a pattern here?

Well . . .

I tell you this: There is never a time when I am not with you; never a moment when I am not "ready."
Have I not told you this before?

Well, yes, but . . .

I am always with you, even unto the end of time.
Yet I will not impose My will on you—ever.
I choose your highest good for you, but above that, I choose your will for you. And this is the surest measure of love.
When I want for you what *you* want for you, then I truly love you. When I want for you what *I* want for you, then I am loving Me, *through* you.
So, too, by the same measure, can you determine whether others love you, and whether you truly love others. For love chooses naught for itself, but only seeks to make possible the choices of the beloved other.

That seems to directly contradict what You put in *Book 1* about love being not at all concerned with what the other is being, doing, and having, but only with what the *Self* is being, doing, and having.
It brings up other questions as well, like . . . what of the parent who shouts at the child, "Get out of the street!" Or, better yet, risks his own life to run out into swirling traffic and snatch

the child up? What of that parent? Is she not loving her child? Yet she has imposed her own will. Remember, the child was in the street because it *wanted to be*.

How do You explain these contradictions?

There is no contradiction. Yet you cannot see the harmony. And you will not understand this divine doctrine about love until you understand that My highest choice for Me is the same as your highest choice for you. And that is because you and I are one.

You see, the Divine Doctrine is also a Divine Dichotomy, and that is because life itself is a dichotomy—an experience within which two apparently contradictory truths can exist in the same space at the same time.

In this case, the apparently contradictory truths are that you and I are separate, and you and I are one. The same apparent contradiction appears in the relationship between you and everyone else.

I stand by what I said in *Book 1*: The biggest mistake people make in human relationships is to be concerned for what the other is wanting, being, doing, or having. Be concerned only for the Self. What is the Self being, doing, or having? What is the Self wanting, needing, choosing? What is the highest choice for the Self?

I also stand by another statement I made in that book: The highest choice for the Self becomes the highest choice for another when the Self realizes that there is no one else.

The mistake, therefore, is not in *choosing* what is best for you, but rather, in not *knowing* what is best. This stems from now knowing Who You Really Are, much less who you are seeking to be.

I don't understand.

Well, let me give you an illustration. If you are seeking to win the Indianapolis 500, driving 150 miles per hour might be what is best for you. If you are seeking to get to the grocery store safely, it might not.

You're saying it's all contextual.

Yes. All of *life* is. What is "best" depends on who you are, and who you seek to be. You cannot intelligently choose what is best for you until you intelligently decide who and what you are.

Now I, as God, *know* what I am seeking to be. I therefore know what is "best" for Me.

And what is that? Tell me, what is "best" for God? This ought to be interesting . . .

What is best for Me is *giving you what you decide is best for you*. Because what I am trying to be is My Self, expressed. And I am being this *through you*.

Are you following this?

Yes, believe it or not, I actually am.

Good. Now I will tell you something you may find difficult to believe.

I am always giving you what is best for you . . . though I admit that you may not always know it.

This mystery clears up a bit now that you have begun to understand what I am up to.

I am God.

I am the Goddess.

I am the Supreme Being. The All of Everything. The Beginning and The End. The Alpha and Omega.

I am the Sum and the Substance. The Question and the Answer. The Up and the Down of it. The Left and the Right, the Here and the Now, the Before and the After.

I am the Light, and I am the Darkness that creates the Light, and makes it possible. I am the Goodness Without End, and the "Badness" which makes the "Goodness" good. I am all of these things—the All of Everything—and I cannot experience any part of My Self without experiencing All of My Self.

10

And this is what you do not understand about Me. You want to make Me the one, and not the other. The high and not the low. The good, and not the bad. Yet in denying half of Me, you deny half of your Self. And in so doing, you can never be Who You Really Are.

I am the Magnificent Everything—and what I am seeking is to know Myself experientially. I am doing this through you, and through everything else that exists. And I am experiencing My Self as magnificent through the choices I make. For each choice is self creative. Each choice is definitive. Each choice represents Me—that is, re-presents Me—as Who I Choose to Be Right Now.

Yet I cannot choose to be magnificent *unless there is something to choose from.* Some part of Me must be *less* than magnificent for Me to choose the part of Me which *is* magnificent.

So, too, is it with you.

I am God, in the act of creating My Self.

And so, too, are you.

This is what your soul longs to do. This is that for which your spirit hungers.

Were I to stop you from having what you choose, I would stop My Self from having what I choose. For My greatest desire is to experience My Self as What I Am. And, as I carefully and painstakingly explained in *Book 1,* I can only do that in the space of What I Am Not.

And so, I have carefully created What I Am Not, in order that I might experience What I Am.

Yet I Am *everything* I create—therefore I Am, in a sense, What I Am *Not.*

How can someone be what they are not?

Easy. You do it all the time. Just watch your behaviors.

Seek to understand this. There is *nothing* that I am not. Therefore, I Am what I Am, and I Am What I Am Not.

11

THIS IS THE DIVINE DICHOTOMY.

This is the Divine Mystery which, until now, only the most sublime minds could understand. I have revealed it for you here in a way that more can understand.

This was the message of *Book 1*, and this basic truth you must understand—you must deeply know—if you are to understand and know the even more sublime truths to come, here, in *Book 3*.

Yet let Me now get to one of those more sublime truths—for it is contained in the answer to the second part of your question.

I was hoping we were going to get back to that part of my question. How is the parent loving the child if he says or does what is best for the child, even if he has to *thwart the child's own will* to do it? Or does the parent demonstrate the truest love by letting the child play in traffic?

This is a wonderful question. And it's the question asked by every parent, in some form or another, since parenting began. The answer is the same for you as a parent as it is for Me as God.

So *what is the answer?*

Patience, My son, patience. "All good things come to those who wait." Have you never heard of that?

Yeah, my father used to say it and I hated it.

I can understand that. But do have patience with your Self, especially if your choices are not bringing you what you think you want. The answer to the second part of your question, for example.

You say that you want the answer, but you are not choosing it. You know you are not choosing it, because you do not experience having it. In truth, you have the answer, and have had it all along. You simply are not

12

choosing it. You are choosing to believe you do not know the answer—and so you do not.

Yes, You went over this, too, in *Book 1*. I have everything I choose to have right now—including a complete understanding of God—yet I will not *experience* that I have it until I *know* that I do.

Precisely! You've put it perfectly.

But how can I *know* that I do until I *experience* that I do? How can I know something I haven't experienced? Wasn't there a great mind who said, "All knowing is experience"?

He was wrong.
Knowing does not follow experience—it precedes it.
In this, half the world has it backwards.

So You mean that I have the answer to the second part of my question, I just don't *know* that I do?

Exactly.

Yet if I don't *know* that I do, then I *don't*.

That's the paradox, yes.

I don't get it . . . except I do.

Indeed.

So how can I get to this place of "knowing that I know" something if I don't "know that I know"?

To "know that you know, act as if you do."

You mentioned something about that in *Book 1* also.

Yes. A good place to start here would be to recap what's gone before in the previous teaching. And you "just happen" to be asking the right questions, allowing Me to summarize in short form at the beginning of this book the information we discussed in prior material in some detail.

Now in *Book 1*, we talked about the Be-Do-Have paradigm, and how most people have it reversed.

Most people believe if they "have" a thing (more time, money, love—whatever), then they can finally "do" a thing (write a book, take up a hobby, go on vacation, buy a home, undertake a relationship), which will allow them to "be" a thing (happy, peaceful, content, or in love).

In actuality, they are reversing the Be-Do-Have paradigm. In the universe as it really is (as opposed to how you think it is), "havingness" does not produce "beingness," but the other way around.

First you "be" the thing called "happy" (or "knowing," or "wise," or "compassionate," or whatever), then you start "doing" things from this place of beingness—and soon you discover that what you are doing winds up bringing you the things you've always wanted to "have."

The way to set this creative process (and that's what this is . . . the process of creation) into motion is to look at what it is you want to "have," ask yourself what you think you would "be" if you "had" that, then go right straight to *being*.

In this way you reverse the way you've been using the Be-Do-Have paradigm—in actuality, set it right—and work with, rather than against, the creative power of the universe.

Here is a short way of stating this principle:

In life, you do not have to *do anything*.

It is all a question of what you are *being*.

This is one of the three messages I will touch on again at the end of our dialogue. I will close the book with it.

For now, and to illustrate this, think of a person who just knows that if he could only have a little more time, a

14

little more money, or a little more love, he'd be truly happy.

He does not get the connection between his "not being very happy" right now and his not having the time, money, or love he wants.

That's right. On the other hand, the person who is "being" happy seems to have time to do everything that's really important, all the money that's needed, and enough love to last a lifetime.

He finds he has everything he needs to "be happy" . . . by "being happy" to begin with!

Exactly. Deciding *ahead of time* what you choose to be *produces that in your experience.*

"To be, or not to be. That is the question."

Precisely. Happiness is a state of mind. And like all states of mind, it reproduces itself in physical form. There's a statement for a refrigerator magnet: "All states of mind reproduce themselves."

But how can you "be" happy to begin with, or "be" *anything* you are seeking to be—more prosperous, for instance, or more loved—if you are not having what you think you need in order to "be" that?

Act as if you are, and you will draw it to you. What you act as if you are, you become.

In other words, "Fake it until you make it."

Something like that, yes. Only you can't really be "faking." Your actions have to be sincere. *Everything you do, do out of sincerity, or the benefit of the action is lost.*

This is not because I won't "reward you." God does not "reward" and "punish," as you know. But Natural Law requires the body, mind, and spirit to be united in thought, word, and action for the process of creation to work.

You cannot fool your mind. If you are insincere, your mind knows it, and that's that. You've just ended any chance that your mind can help you in the creative process.

You can, of course, create without your mind—it's just a great deal more difficult. You can ask your body to do something your mind doesn't believe, and if your body does it long enough, your mind will begin to let go of its former thought about that, and create a New Thought. Once you have a New Thought about a thing, you're well on your way to creating it as a permanent aspect of your being, rather than something you're just acting out.

This is doing things the hard way, and even in such instances, the action must be sincere. Unlike what you can do with people, you cannot manipulate the universe.

So here we have a very delicate balance. The body does something in which the mind does not believe, yet the mind must add the ingredient of sincerity to the body's action for it to work.

How can the mind add sincerity when it does not "believe in" what the body is doing?

By taking out the selfish element of personal gain.

How?

The mind may not be able to sincerely agree that the actions of the body can bring you that which you choose, but the mind seems very clear that God will bring good things through you to another.

Therefore, whatever you choose for yourself, give to another.

Would You say that again, please?

Of course.

Whatever you choose for yourself, give to another.

If you choose to be happy, cause another to be happy.

If you choose to be prosperous, cause another to prosper.

If you choose more love in your life, cause another to have more love in theirs.

Do this sincerely—not because you seek personal gain, but because you really want the other person to have that—and all the things you give away will come to you.

Why is that so? How does that work?

The very act of your giving something away causes you to experience that you *have* it to give away. Since you cannot give to another something you do not now have, your mind comes to a new conclusion, a New Thought, about you—namely, that you must have this, *or you could not be giving it away.*

This New Thought then becomes your experience. You start "being" that. And once you start "being" a thing, you've engaged the gears of the most powerful creation machine in the universe—your Divine Self.

Whatever you are being, you are creating.

The circle is complete, and you will create more and more of that in your life. It will be made manifest in your physical experience.

This is the greatest secret of life. It is what *Book 1* and *Book 2* were written to tell you. It was all there, in far greater detail.

Explain to me, please, why sincerity is so important in giving to another what you choose for yourself.

If you give to another as a contrivance, a manipulation meant to get something to come to *you,* your mind

17

knows this. You've just given it a signal that _you do not now have this._ And since the universe is nothing but a big copying machine, reproducing your thoughts in physical form, _that will be your experience._ That is, you will continue to experience "not having it"—no matter _what_ you do!

Furthermore, that will be the experience of the person to whom you're trying to give it. They will see that you are merely seeking to get something, that you have nothing, really, to offer, and your giving will be an empty gesture, seen for all the self-serving shallowness from which it springs.

The very thing you sought to attract, you will thus push away.

Yet when you give something to another with purity of heart—because you see that they want it, need it, and should have it—then you will discover that you have it to give. And that is a grand discovery.

This is true! It really _works_ this way! I can remember once, when things were not going so well in my life, holding my head and thinking that I had no more money, and very little food, and that I didn't know when I was going to eat my next square meal, or how I could pay my rent. That very evening I met a young couple at the bus station. I'd gone down to pick up a package, and there these kids were, huddled on a bench, using their coats for a blanket.

I saw them and my heart went out to them. I remembered when I was young, how it was when we were kids, just skimming by, and on the move like that. I walked over to them and asked them if they'd like to come over to my place and sit by a hot fire, have a little hot chocolate, maybe open up the day bed and get a good night's rest. They looked up at me with eyes wide, like children on Christmas morning.

Well, we got to the house, and I made 'em a meal. We all ate better that night than any of us had for quite a while. The food had always been there. The refrigerator was loaded. I just had to reach back, and grab all the stuff I'd shoved back there. I made an "everything-in-the-fridge" stir fry, and _it was terrific!_ I remember thinking, where did all this food come from?

The next morning I even gave the kids breakfast, and sent them on their way. I reached into my pocket as I dropped them off back at the bus station and gave them a twenty-dollar bill. "Maybe this will help," I said, gave 'em a hug and sent them on their way. I felt better about my own situation all day. Heck, all *week*. And that experience, which I have never forgotten, produced a profound change in my outlook and my understandings about life.

Things got better from there, and as I looked at myself in the mirror this morning, I noticed something very important. *I'm still here.*

That's a beautiful story. And you're right. *That's exactly how it works.* So when you want something, give it away. You will then no longer be "wanting" it. You will immediately experience "having" it. From there on, it is only a question of degree. Psychologically, you will find it much easier to "add onto," than to create out of thin air.

I feel I have just heard something very profound here. Can You relate this now to the second part of my question? Is there a connection?

What I'm proposing, you see, is that you already *have* the answer to that question. Right now you are living the thought that you do not have the answer; that if you had the answer, you would have wisdom. So you come to Me for wisdom. Yet I say to you, *be* wisdom, and you will have it.

And what is the fastest way to "be" wisdom? Cause *another* to be wise.

Do you choose to have the answer to this question? *Give the answer to another.*

So, now, I'll ask *you* the question. I'll pretend that I "don't know," and you give Me the answer.

How can the parent who pulls a child out of traffic be truly loving the child, if love means that you want for the other what they want for themselves?

I don't know.

I know you don't. *But if you thought you did, what would your answer be?*

Well, I'd say that the parent *did* want for the child what the child wanted—which was to *stay alive*. I'd say that the child did not want to die, but simply did not know that wandering around in traffic could cause that. So that in running out there to get the child, the parent wasn't depriving the child of the opportunity to exercise its will at all—but simply getting in touch with the child's true choice, its deepest desire.

That would be a very good answer.

If that's true, then You, as God, should be doing nothing but *stopping us from hurting ourselves*, for it can't be our deepest desire to do damage to ourselves. Yet we do damage to ourselves all the time, and You just sit around and watch us.

I am always in touch with your deepest desire, and always I give you that.

Even when you do something that would cause you to die—if that is your deepest desire, that is what you get: the experience of "dying."

I never, ever interfere with your deepest desire.

Do You mean that when we do damage to ourselves, that is what we *wanted* to do? That is our *deepest desire?*

You cannot "do damage" to yourselves. You are incapable of being damaged. "Damage" is a subjective reaction, not an objective phenomenon. You can choose to experience "damage" to yourself out of any encounter or phenomenon, but that is entirely your decision.

Given that truth, the answer to your question is, Yes—when you have "damaged" yourself, it is because you wanted to. But I'm speaking on a very high, esoteric level, and that is not really where your question is "coming from."

In the sense that you mean it, as a matter of conscious choice, I would say that no, every time you do something that damages yourself, it is not because you "wanted to."

The child who gets hit by a car because he wandered into the street did not "want" (desire, seek, consciously choose) to get hit by a car.

The man who keeps marrying the same kind of woman—one who is all wrong for him—packaged in different forms, does not "want" (desire, seek, consciously choose) to keep creating bad marriages.

The person who hits a thumb with a hammer could not be said to have "wanted" the experience. It was not desired, sought, consciously chosen.

Yet all objective phenomena is drawn to you subconsciously; all events are created by you unconsciously; every person, place, or thing in your life was drawn to you by you—was Self-created, if you will—to provide you with the exact and perfect conditions, the perfect opportunity, to experience what you next wish to experience as you go about the business of evolving.

Nothing can happen—I say to you, nothing can occur—in your life which is not a precisely perfect opportunity for you to heal something, create something, or experience something that you wish to heal, create, or experience in order to be Who You Really Are.

And who, really, am I?

Whomever you choose to be. Whatever aspect of Divinity you wish to be—that's Who You Are. That can change at any given moment. Indeed, it often does, from moment to moment. Yet if you want your life to settle down, to stop bringing you such a wide variety of experiences, there's a way to do that. Simply stop changing your mind so often about Who You Are, and Who You Choose to Be.

That may be easier said than done!

21

What I see is that you are making these decisions at many different levels. The child who decides to go out into the street to play in traffic is not making a choice to die. She may be making a number of other choices, but dying is not one of them. The mother knows that.

The problem here is not that the child has chosen to die, but that the child has made choices that could lead to more than one outcome, including her dying. That fact is not clear to her; it is unknown to her. It is the missing data—which stops the child from making a clear choice, a better choice.

So you see, you have analyzed it perfectly.

Now, I, as God, will never interfere with your choices—but I will always know what they are.

Therefore, you may assume that if a thing happens to you, it is perfect that it did so—for nothing escapes perfection in God's world.

The design of your life—the people, places, and events in it—have all been perfectly created by the perfect creator of perfection itself: you. And Me . . . in, as, and through you.

Now We can work together in this co-creative process consciously or unconsciously. You can move through life aware, or unaware. You can walk your path asleep, or awake.

You choose.

Wait, go back to that comment about making decisions at many different levels. You said that if I wanted life to settle down, I should stop changing my mind about who I am and who I wish to be. When I said that may not be easy, You made the observation that all of us are making our choices at many different levels. Can You elaborate on that? What does that mean? What are the implications?

If all you desired is what your soul desired, everything would be very simple. If you listened to the part of you which is pure spirit, all of your decisions would be easy, and all the outcomes joyous. That is because . . .

22

. . . the choices of spirit are always the highest choices.

They don't need to be second-guessed. They don't need to be analyzed or evaluated. They simply need to be followed, acted on.

Yet you are not only a spirit. You are a Triune Being made up of body, mind, and spirit. That is both the glory and the wonder of you. For you often make decisions and choices at all three levels simultaneously—and *they by no means always coincide.*

It is not uncommon for your body to want one thing, while your mind seeks another, and your spirit desires yet a third. This can be especially true of children, who are often not yet mature enough to make distinctions between what sounds like "fun" to the body, and what makes sense to the mind—much less what resonates with the soul. So the child waddles into the street.

Now, as God, I am aware of all your choices—even those you make subconsciously. I will never interfere with them, but rather, just the opposite. It is My job to ensure that your choices are granted. (In truth, you grant them to your Self. What I have done is put a system into place that allows you to do that. This system is called the process of creation, and is explained in detail in *Book 1.*)

When your choices conflict—when body, mind, and spirit are not acting as one—the process of creation works at all levels, producing mixed results. If, on the other hand, your being is in harmony, and your choices are unified, astonishing things can occur.

Your young people have a phrase—"having it all together"—which could be used to describe this unified state of being.

There are also levels within levels in your decision making. This is particularly true at the level of the mind.

Your mind can, and does, make decisions and choices from one of at least three interior levels: logic, intuition, emotion—and sometimes from all three—producing the potential for even more inner conflict.

And within one of those levels—emotion—there are five more levels. These are the *five natural emotions*: grief, anger, envy, fear, and love.

And within these, also, there are two final levels: love and fear.

The five natural emotions include love and fear, yet love and fear are the basis of all emotions. The other three of the five natural emotions are outgrowths of these two.

Ultimately, all thoughts are sponsored by love or fear. This is the great polarity. This is the primal duality. Everything, ultimately, breaks down to one of these. All thoughts, ideas, concepts, understandings, decisions, choices, and actions are based in one of these.

And, in the end, there is really only one.

Love.

In truth, love is all there is. Even fear is an outgrowth of love, and when used effectively, expresses love.

Fear expresses *love*?

In its highest form, yes. Everything expresses love, when the expression is in its highest form.

Does the parent who saves the child from being killed in traffic express fear, or love?

Well, both, I suppose. Fear for the child's life, and love—enough to risk one's own life to save the child.

Precisely. And so here we see that fear in its highest form becomes love . . . *is* love . . . expressed as fear.

Similarly, moving up the scale of natural emotions, grief, anger, and envy are all some form of fear, which, in turn, is some form of love.

One things leads to another. Do you see?

The problem comes in when any of the five natural emotions become distorted. Then they become grotesque, and not recognizable at all as outgrowths of love, much less as God, which is what Absolute Love is.

I've heard of the five natural emotions before—from my wonderful association with Dr. Elisabeth Kübler-Ross. She taught me about them.

Indeed. And it was I who inspired her to teach about this.

So I see that when I make choices, much depends on "where I'm coming from," and that where I'm "coming from" could be several layers deep.

Yes, that is what is so.

Please tell me—I would like to hear it again, because I've forgotten much of what Elisabeth taught me—all about the five natural emotions.

Grief is a natural emotion. It's that part of you which allows you to say goodbye when you don't want to say goodbye; to express—push out, propel—the sadness within you at the experience of any kind of loss. It could be the loss of a loved one, or the loss of a contact lens.

When you are allowed to express your grief, you get rid of it. Children who are allowed to be sad when they are sad feel very healthy about sadness when they are adults, and therefore usually move through their sadness very quickly.

Children who are told, "There, there, don't cry," have a hard time crying as adults. After all, they've been told all their life not to do that. So they repress their grief.

Grief that is continually repressed becomes chronic depression, a very unnatural emotion.

People have killed because of chronic depression. Wars have started, nations have fallen.

Anger is a natural emotion. It is the tool you have which allows you to say, "No, thank you." It does not have to be abusive, and it never has to be damaging to another.

25

When children are allowed to express their anger, they bring a very healthy attitude about it to their adult years, and therefore usually move through their anger very quickly.

Children who are made to feel that their anger is not okay—that it is wrong to express it, and, in fact, that they shouldn't even experience it—will have a difficult time appropriately dealing with their anger as adults.

Anger that is continually repressed becomes rage, a very unnatural emotion.

People have killed because of rage. Wars have started, nations have fallen.

Envy is a natural emotion. It is the emotion that makes a five-year-old wish he could reach the doorknob the way his sister can—or ride that bike. Envy is the natural emotion that makes you want to do it again; to try harder; to continue striving until you succeed. It is very healthy to be envious, very natural. When children are allowed to express their envy, they bring a very healthy attitude about it to their adult years, and therefore usually move through their envy very quickly.

Children who are made to feel that envy is not okay—that it is wrong to express it, and, in fact, that they shouldn't even experience it—will have a difficult time appropriately dealing with their envy as adults.

Envy that is continually repressed becomes jealousy, a very unnatural emotion.

People have killed because of jealousy. Wars have started, nations have fallen.

Fear is a natural emotion. All babies are born with only two fears: the fear of falling, and the fear of loud noises. All other fears are learned responses, brought to the child by its environment, taught to the child by its parents. The purpose of natural fear is to build in a bit of caution. Caution is a tool that helps keep the body alive. It is an outgrowth of love. Love of Self.

Children who are made to feel that fear is not okay—that it is wrong to express it, and, in fact, that they shouldn't even experience it—will have a difficult time appropriately dealing with their fear as adults.

Fear that is continually repressed becomes panic, a very unnatural emotion.

People have killed because of panic. Wars have started, nations have fallen.

Love is a natural emotion. When it is allowed to be expressed, and received, by a child, normally and naturally, without limitation or condition, inhibition or embarrassment, it does not require anything more. For the joy of love expressed and received in this way is sufficient unto itself. Yet love which has been conditioned, limited, warped by rules and regulations, rituals and restrictions, controlled, manipulated, and withheld, becomes unnatural.

Children who are made to feel that their natural love is not okay—that it is wrong to express it, and, in fact, that they shouldn't even experience it—will have a difficult time appropriately dealing with love as adults.

Love that is continually repressed becomes possessiveness, a very unnatural emotion.

People have killed because of possessiveness. Wars have started, nations have fallen.

And so it is that the natural emotions, when repressed, produce unnatural reactions and responses. And most natural emotions are repressed in most people. Yet these are your friends. These are your gifts. These are your divine tools, with which to craft your experience.

You are given these tools at birth. They are to help you negotiate life.

Why are these emotions repressed in most people?

They have been taught to repress them. They have been told to.

By whom?

27

Their parents. Those who have raised them.

Why? Why would they do that?

Because they were taught by their parents, and their parents were told by theirs.

Yes, yes. But *why?* What is going *on?*

What is going on is that you have the wrong people doing the parenting.

What do you mean? Who are the "wrong people"?

The mother and the father.

The mother and the father are the wrong people to raise the children?

When the parents are young, yes. In most cases, yes. In fact, it's a miracle that so many of them do as good a job as they do.

No one is more ill-equipped to raise children than young parents. And no one knows this, by the way, better than young parents.

Most parents come to the job of parenting with very little life experience. They're hardly finished being parented themselves. They're still looking for answers, still searching for clues.

They haven't even discovered themselves yet, and they're trying to guide and nurture discovery in others even more vulnerable than they. They haven't even defined themselves, and they're thrust into the act of defining others. They are still trying to get over how badly they have been mis-defined by their parents.

They haven't even discovered yet Who They Are, and they're trying to tell you who you are. And the pressure is so great for them to get it right—yet they can't even get their own lives "right." So they get the whole thing wrong—their lives, and the lives of their children.

If they're lucky, the damage to their children won't be too great. The offspring will overcome it—but not, probably, before passing some on to their offspring.

Most of you gain the wisdom, the patience, the understanding, and the love to be wonderful parents *after your parenting years are over.*

Why is this? I don't understand this. I see that Your observation is in many cases correct, but why is this?

Because young child-makers were never intended to be child-raisers. Your child-raising years should really begin when they are now over.

I'm still a little lost here.

Human beings are biologically capable of creating children while they are children themselves—which, it may surprise most of you to know, they are for 40 or 50 years.

Human beings are "children themselves" *for 40 or 50 years?*

From a certain perspective, yes. I know this is difficult to hold as your truth, but look around you. Perhaps the behaviors of your race might help prove My point.

The difficulty is that in your society, you are said to be "all grown up" and ready for the world at 21. Add to this the fact that many of you were raised by mothers and fathers *who were not much older than 21 themselves* when they began raising you, and you can begin to see the problem.

If child-bearers were *meant* to be child-raisers, child bearing would not have been made possible until you were fifty!

Child *bearing* was meant to be an activity of the young, whose bodies are well developed and strong.

Child *raising* was meant to be an activity of the elders, whose minds are well developed and strong.

In your society you have insisted on making child-bearers responsible for child raising—with the result that you've made not only the process of parenting very difficult, but distorted many of the energies surrounding the sexual act as well as.

Uh . . . could You explain?

Yes.

Many humans have observed what I've observed here. Namely, that a good many humans—perhaps most —are not truly capable of raising children when they are capable of having them. However, having discovered this, humans have put in place exactly the wrong solution.

Rather than allow younger humans to enjoy sex, and if it produces children, have the elders raise them, you tell young humans not to engage in sex *until they are ready to take on the responsibility of raising children*. You have made it "wrong" for them to have sexual experiences before that time, and thus have created a taboo around what was intended to be one of life's most joyful celebrations.

Of course, this is a taboo to which offspring will pay little attention—and for good reason: *it is entirely unnatural to obey it.*

Human beings desire to couple and copulate as soon as they feel the inner signal which says they are ready. *This is human nature.*

Yet their thought about their own nature will have more to do with what you, as parents, have told them than about what they are feeling inside. Your children look to you to tell them what life is all about.

So when they have their first urges to peek at each other, to play innocently with each other, to explore each other's "differences," they will look to you for signals about this. Is this part of their human nature "good"? Is it "bad"? Is it approved of? Is it to be stifled? Held back? Discouraged?

It is observed that what many parents have told their offspring about this part of their human nature has had its origin in all manner of things: what *they* were told; what their *religion* says; what their *society* thinks—everything except the natural order of things.

In the natural order of your species, sexuality is budding at anywhere from age 9 to age 14. From age 15 onward it is very much present and expressing in most human beings. Thus begins a race against time—with children stampeding toward the fullest release of their own joyful sexual energy, and parents stampeding to stop them.

Parents have needed all the assistance and all the alliances they could find in this struggle, since, as has been noted, they are asking their offspring to *not do something* that is every bit a part of their nature.

So adults have invented all manner of familial, cultural, religious, social, and economic pressures, restrictions, and limitations to justify their unnatural demands of their offspring. Children have thus grown to accept that their own sexuality is *unnatural.* How can anything that is "natural" be so shamed, so always-stopped, so controlled, held at bay, restrained, bridled, and denied?

Well, I think You're exaggerating a bit here. Don't You think You're exaggerating?

Really? What do you think is the impact on a four- or five-year-old child when parents won't even use the correct *name* for certain of their body parts? What are you telling the child about your level of comfort with that, and what you think *theirs should be?*

Uh . . .

Yes . . . "uh . . ." indeed.

Well, "we just don't use those words," as my grammy used to say. It's just that "wee-wee" and "your bottom" *sounds* better.

31

Only because you have so much negative "baggage" attached to the actual names of these body parts that you can barely use the words in ordinary conversation.

At the youngest ages, of course, children don't know why parents feel this way, but merely are left with the impression, the often *indelible* impression, that certain body parts are "not okay," and that anything having to do with them is embarrassing—if not "wrong."

As children grow older and move into their teens, they may come to realize that this is not true, but then they are told in very clear terms about the connection between pregnancy and sexuality, and about how they will have to raise the children they create, and so they now have another reason for feeling that sexual expression is "wrong"—and the circle is complete.

What this has caused in your society is confusion and not a little havoc—*which is always the result of fooling around with nature.*

You have created sexual embarrassment, repression, and shame—which has led to sexual inhibition, dysfunction, and violence.

You will, as a society, always be inhibited about that over which you are embarrassed; always be dysfunctional with behaviors which have been repressed, and always act out violently in protest of being made to feel shame about that over which *you know in your heart you should never have felt shame at all.*

Then Freud was on to something when he said that a huge amount of the anger in the human species might be sexually related—deep-seated rage over having to repress basic and natural physical instincts, interests, and urges.

More than one of your psychiatrists has ventured as much. The human being is angry because it knows it should feel no shame over something that feels so good—and yet it does feel shame, and guilt.

First, the human becomes angry with the Self for

feeling so good about something which is supposed to be so obviously "bad."

Then, when they finally realize they've been duped—that sexuality is supposed to be a wonderful, honorable, glorious part of the human experience—they become angry with others: parents, for repressing them, religion for shaming them, members of the opposite sex for daring them, the whole society for controlling them.

Finally, they become angry with themselves, for allowing all of this to inhibit them.

Much of this repressed anger has been channeled into the construction of distorted and misguided moral values in the society in which you now live—a society which glorifies and honors, with monuments, statues, and commemorative stamps, films, pictures, and TV programs, some of the world's ugliest acts of violence, but hides—or worse yet, cheapens—some of the world's most beautiful acts of love.

And all of this—*all of this*—has emerged from a single thought: that those who bear children, bear also the sole responsibility for raising them.

But if the people who have children aren't responsible for raising them, who is?

The whole community. With special emphasis on the elders.

The elders?

In most advanced races and societies, elders raise the offspring, nurture the offspring, train the offspring, and pass on to the offspring the wisdom, teachings, and traditions of their kind. Later, when we talk about some of these advanced civilizations, I'll touch on this again.

In any society where producing offspring at a young age is not considered "wrong"—because the tribal elders raise them and there is, therefore, no sense of overwhelming responsibility and burden—sexual repression is unheard of, and so is rape, deviance, and social-sexual dysfunction.

Are there such societies on our planet?

Yes, although they have been disappearing. You have sought to eradicate them, assimilate them, because you have thought them to be barbarian. In what you have called your nonbarbarian societies, children (and wives, and husbands, for that matter) are thought of as property, as personal possessions, and child-bearers must therefore become child-raisers, because they must take care of what they "own."

A root thought at the bottom of many of your society's problems is this idea that spouses and children are personal possessions, that they are "yours."

We'll examine this whole subject of "ownership" later, when we explore and discuss life among highly evolved beings. But for now, just think about this for a minute. Is anyone really emotionally ready to raise children at the time they're physically ready to have them?

The truth is, most humans are not equipped to raise children even in their 30s and 40s—and shouldn't be expected to be. They really haven't lived enough as adults to pass deep wisdom to their children.

I've heard that thought before. Mark Twain had a take on this. He was said to have commented, "When I was 19, my father knew nothing. But when I was 35, I was amazed at how much the Old Man had learned."

He captured it perfectly. Your younger years were never meant to be for truth-teaching, but for truth-gathering. *How can you teach children a truth you haven't yet gathered?*

You can't, of course. So you'll wind up telling them the only truth you know—the truth of others. Your father's, your mother's, your culture's, your religion's.

Anything, everything, but your own truth. You are still searching for that.

And you will be searching, and experimenting, and finding, and failing, and forming and reforming your truth, your idea about yourself, until you are half a century on this planet, or near to it.

Then, you may begin at last to settle down, and settle in, with your truth. And probably the biggest truth on which you'll agree is that there is no constant truth at all; that truth, like life itself, is a changing thing, a growing thing, an evolving thing—and that just when you think that process of evolution has stopped, it has not, but only really just begun.

Yes, I've already come to that. I'm past 50, and I've arrived at that.

Good. You are now a wiser man. An elder. Now you should raise children. Or better yet, ten years from now. It is the elders who should raise the offspring—and who were intended to.

It is the elders who know of truth, and life. Of what is important and what is not. Of what is really meant by such terms as integrity, honesty, loyalty, friendship, and love.

I see the point You have been making here. It is difficult to accept, but many of us *have* barely moved from "child" to "student" when we have children of our own, and feel we have to start teaching *them*. So we figure, well, I'll teach them what my parents taught me.

Thus, the sins of the father are visited upon the son, even unto the seventh generation.

How can we change that? How can we end the cycle?

Place the raising of children in the hands of your respected Old Ones. Parents see the children whenever they wish, live with them if they choose, but are not solely responsible for their care and upbringing. The physical, social, and spiritual needs of the children are met by the entire community, with education and values offered by the elders.

Later in our dialogue, when we talk about those other cultures in the universe, we'll look at some new models for living. But these models won't work the way you've currently structured your lives.

What do You mean?

I mean it's not just parenting you're doing with an ineffective model, but your whole way of living.

Again, what do You mean?

You've moved away from each other. You've torn apart your families, disassembled your smaller communities in favor of huge cities. In these big cities there are more people, but fewer "tribes," groups, or clans whose members see their responsibility as including responsibility for the whole. So, in effect, you have no elders. None at arm's reach, in any event.

Worse than moving away from your elders, you've pushed them aside. Marginalized them. Taken their power away. And even resented them.

Yes, some members of your society are even resenting the seniors among you, claiming that they are somehow leeching on the system, demanding benefits that the young have to pay for with ever-increasing proportions of their income.

It's true. Some sociologists are now predicting a generation war, with older people being blamed for requiring more and more, while contributing less and less. There are so many more older citizens now, what with the "baby boomers" moving into their senior years, and people living longer in general.

Yet if your elders aren't contributing, it is because you have not allowed them to contribute. You have required them to retire from their jobs just when they could really do the company some good, and to retire from most active, meaningful participation in life, just when their participation could bring some sense to the proceedings.

Not just in parenting, but in politics, economics, and even in religion, where elders at least had a toehold, you have become a youth-worshipping, elder-dismissing society.

Yours has also become a singular society, rather than a plural one. That is, a society made up of individuals, rather than groups.

As you have both individualized and youthened your society, you have lost much of its richness and resource. Now you are without both, with too many of you living in emotional and psychological poverty and depletion.

I'm going to ask you again, is there any way we can end this cycle?

First, recognize and acknowledge that it's real. So many of you are living in denial. So many of you are pretending that what's so is simply not so. You are lying to yourselves, and you do not want to hear the truth, much less tell it.

This, too, we'll talk about again later, when we take that look at the civilizations of highly evolved beings, because this denial, this failure to observe and acknowledge what's so, is not an insignificant thing. And if you truly want to change things, I hope you will just allow yourself to hear Me.

The time has come for truth telling, plain and simple. Are you ready?

I am. That's why I came to You. That's how this whole conversation began.

Truth is often uncomfortable. It is only comforting to those who do not wish to ignore it. Then, truth becomes not only comforting, but inspiring.

For me, this whole three-part dialogue has been inspiring. Please, go on.

There is some good reason to be upbeat, to feel optimistic. I observe that things have begun to change. There's more emphasis among your species on creating community, and building extended families, than ever in recent years. And, more and more, you are honoring your elders, producing meaning and value in, and from, their lives. This is a big step in a wonderfully useful direction.

So things are "turning around." Your culture seems to have taken that step. Now, it's onward from there.

You cannot make these changes in one day. You cannot, for instance, change your whole way of parenting, which is how this current train of thought began, in one fell swoop. Yet you *can* change your future, step by step.

Reading this book is one of those steps. This dialogue will circle back over many important points before we are finished. That repetition will not be by accident. It is for emphasis.

Now, you have asked for ideas for the construction of your tomorrows. Let us begin by looking at your yesterdays.

2

What does the past have to do with the future?

When you know about the past, you can better know about all your possible futures. You have come to Me asking how to make your life work better. It will be useful for you to know how you got to where you are today.

I would speak to you of power, and of strength—and the difference between the two. And I would chat with you about this Satan figure you have invented, how and why you invented him, and how you decided that your God was a "He," and not a "She."

I would speak to you of Who I Really Am, rather than who you have said I am in your mythologies. I would describe to you My Beingness in such a way that you will gladly replace the mythology with the cosmology—the true cosmology of the universe, and its relationship to Me. I would have you know about life, how it works, and why it works the way it works. This chapter is about all those things.

When you know those things, then you can decide what you wish to discard of that which your race has created. For this third portion of our conversation, this third book, is about building a newer world, creating a new reality.

You have been living too long, My children, in a prison of your own devise. It is time to set yourself free.

You have imprisoned your five natural emotions, repressing them and turning them into very unnatural emotions, which have brought unhappiness, death, and destruction to your world.

The model of behavior for centuries on this planet has been: do not "indulge" your emotions. If you're feeling grief, get over it; if you're feeling angry, stuff it; if you're feeling envious, be ashamed of it; if you're feeling fear, rise above it; if you're feeling love, control it, limit it, wait with it, run from it—do whatever you have to do to stop from expressing it, full out, right here, right now.

It is time to set yourself free.

In truth, you have imprisoned your Holy Self. And it is time to set your Self free.

I'm starting to get excited here. How do we start? Where do we begin?

In our brief study of how it all got to be this way, let us go back to the time when your society reorganized itself. That is when men became the dominant species, and then decided it was inappropriate to display emotions—or in some cases to even have them.

What do You mean, "when society reorganized itself"? What are we talking about here?

In an earlier part of your history, you lived on this planet in a matriarchal society. Then there was a shift, and the patriarchy emerged. When you made that shift, you moved away from expressing your emotions. You labeled it "weak" to do so. It was during this period that males also invented the devil, and the masculine God.

Males invented the devil?

Yes. Satan was essentially a male invention. Ultimately, all of society went along with it, but the turning away from emotions, and the invention of an "Evil One," was all part of a male rebellion against the matriarchy, a period during which women ruled over everything from their emotions. They held all governmental

40

posts, all religious positions of power, all places of influence in commerce, science, academia, healing.

What power did men have?

None. Men had to justify their existence, for they had very little importance beyond their ability to fertilize female eggs and move heavy objects. They were very much like worker ants and bees. They did the heavy physical labor, and made sure that children were produced and protected.

It took men hundreds of years to find and to create a larger place for themselves in the fabric of their society. Centuries passed before males were even allowed to participate in their clan's affairs; to have a voice or a vote in community decisions. They weren't considered by women to be intelligent enough to understand such matters.

Boy, it is difficult to imagine that any society would actually prohibit one whole class of people from even voting, based simply on gender.

I like your sense of humor about this. I really do. Shall I go on?

Please.

Centuries more passed before they could think of actually holding the positions of leadership for which they finally had the chance to vote. Other posts of influence and power within their culture were similarly denied them.

When males finally obtained positions of authority within society, when they at last rose above their former place as baby-makers and virtual physical slaves, it is to their credit that they did not ever turn the tables on women, but have always accorded females the respect, power, and influence that all humans deserve, regardless of gender.

41

There's that humor again.

Oh, I'm sorry. Do I have the wrong planet?

Let's get back to our narrative. But before we go on about the invention of "the devil," let us talk a bit about power. Because this, of course, is what the invention of Satan was all about.

You're going to make the point now that men have all the power in today's society, right? Let me jump ahead of You and tell You why I think this happened.

You said that in the matriarchal period, men were very much like worker bees serving the queen bee. You said they did the difficult physical work, and made sure that children were produced and protected. And *I* felt like saying, "So what's changed? That's what they do *now!*" And I'll bet that many men would probably say that not a great deal *has* changed—except that men have extracted a price for maintaining their "thankless role." They do have more power.

Actually, most of the power.

Okay, most of the power. But the irony I see here is that both genders think they are handling the thankless tasks, while the other is having all the fun. Men resent the women who are attempting to take back some of their power, because men say they'll be damned if they'll do all that they do for the culture, and not at least have *the power it takes to do it.*

Women resent men keeping all the power, saying they'll be damned if they'll continue doing for the culture what they do, and still remain powerless.

You've analyzed it correctly. And both men and women are damned to repeat their own mistakes in an endless cycle of self-inflicted misery until one side or the other gets that life is not about power, but about strength. And until both see that it's not about separation, but unity. For it is in the *unity* that *inner strength* exists, and in the separation that it dissipates, leaving

42

one feeling weak, and powerless—and hence, struggling for power.

I tell you this: Heal the rift between you, end the illusion of separation, and you shall be delivered back to the source of your inner strength. That is where you will find true power. The power to do anything. The power to be anything. The power to have anything. For the power to create is derived from the inner strength that is produced through unity.

This is true of the relationship between you and your God—just as it is remarkably true of the relationship between you and your fellow humans.

Stop thinking of yourself as separate, and all the true power that comes from the inner strength of unity is yours—as a worldwide society, and as an individual part of that whole—to wield as you wish.

Yet remember this:

Power comes from inner strength. Inner strength does not come from raw power. In this, most of the world has it backwards.

Power without inner strength is an illusion. Inner strength without unity is a lie. A lie that has not served the race, but that has nevertheless deeply embedded itself into your race consciousness. For you think that inner strength comes from *individuality* and from *separateness*, and that is simply not so. Separation from God and from each other is the cause of all your dysfunction and suffering. Still, separation continues to masquerade as strength, and your politics, your economics, and even your religions have perpetuated the lie.

This lie is the genesis of all wars and all the class struggles that lead to war; of all animosity between races and genders, and all the power struggles that lead to animosity; of all personal trials and tribulations, and all the internal struggles that lead to tribulations.

Still, you cling to the lie tenaciously, no matter where you've seen it lead you—even as it has led you to your own destruction.

Now I tell you this: Know the truth, and the truth shall set you free.

There is no separation. Not from each other, not from God, and not from anything that is.

This truth I will repeat over and over on these pages. This observation I will make again and again.

Act as if you were separate from nothing, and no one, and you will heal your world tomorrow.

This is *the greatest secret of all time*. It is the answer for which man has searched for millennia. It is the solution for which he has worked, the revelation for which he has prayed.

Act as if you were separate from nothing, and you heal the world.

Understand that it is about power with, not power over.

Thank You. I got that. So, getting back, first it was females who had power over males, and now it is the other way around. And males invented the devil in order to wrest this power away from the female tribal or clan leaders?

Yes. They used fear, because fear was the only tool they had.

Again, not much has changed. Men do that to this day. Sometimes even before appeals to *reason* are tried, men use fear. Particularly if they are the bigger men; the stronger men. (Or the bigger or stronger nation.) Sometimes it seems actually ingrained in men. It seems *cellular*. Might is right. Strength is power.

Yes. This has been the way since the overturn of the matriarchy.

How did it get that way?

That's what this short history is all about.

Then go on, please.

What men had to do to gain control during the matriarchal period was not to convince women that men ought to be given more power over their lives, but to convince other men.

Life was, after all, going smoothly, and there were worse ways men could have to get through the day than simply doing some physical work to make themselves valued, and then have sex. So it was not easy for men, who were powerless, to convince other powerless men to seek power. Until they discovered fear.

Fear was the one thing women hadn't counted on.

It began, this fear, with seeds of doubt, sown by the most disgruntled among the males. These were usually the least "desirable" of the men; the unmuscled, the unadorned—and hence, those to whom women paid the least attention.

And I'll bet that because this was so, their complaints were discounted as the ravings of rage born of sexual frustration.

That is correct. Still, the disgruntled men had to use the only tool they had. So they sought to grow fear from the seeds of doubt. What if the women were wrong? they asked. What if their way of running the world wasn't the best? What if it was, in fact, leading the whole society—all of the race—into sure and certain annihilation?

This is something many men could not imagine. After all, didn't women have a direct line to the Goddess? Were they not, in fact, exact physical replicas of the Goddess? And was not the Goddess good?

The teaching was so powerful, so pervasive, that men had no choice but to invent a devil, a Satan, to counteract the unlimited goodness of the Great Mother imagined and worshipped by the people of the matriarchy.

How did they manage to convince anyone that there was such a thing as an "evil one"?

The one thing all of their society understood was the theory of the "rotten apple." Even the women saw and knew from their experience that some children simply turned out "bad," no matter what they did. Especially, as everybody knew, the boy children, who just could not be controlled.

So a myth was created.

One day, the myth went, the Great Mother, the Goddess of Goddesses, brought forth a child who turned out to be _not good_. No matter what the Mother tried, the child would not be good. Finally, he struggled with his Mother for her very throne.

This was too much, even for a loving, forgiving Mother. The boy was banished forever—but continued to show up in clever disguises and clever costumes, sometimes even posing as the Great Mother herself.

This myth laid the basis for men to ask, "How do we know the Goddess we worship is a Goddess at all? It could be the bad child, now grown up and wanting to fool us."

By this device, men got other men to worry, then to be angry that women weren't taking their worries seriously, then to rebel.

The being you now call Satan was thus created. It was not difficult to create a myth about a "bad child," and not difficult, either, to convince even the women of the clan of the possibility of the existence of such a creature. It was also not difficult getting anyone to accept that the bad child was male. Weren't males the inferior gender?

This device was used to set up a mythological problem. If the "bad child" was male, if the "evil one" was masculine, who would there be to overpower him? Surely, not a feminine Goddess. For, said the men cleverly, when it came to matters of wisdom and insight, of clarity and compassion, of planning and thinking, no one doubted feminine superiority. Yet in matters of brute strength, was not a male needed?

Previously in Goddess mythology, males were merely consorts—companions to the females, who acted as servants and fulfilled their robust desire for lustful celebration of their Goddess magnificence.

But now a male was needed who could do more; a male who could also protect the Goddess and defeat the enemy. This transformation did not occur overnight, but across many years. Gradually, very gradually, societies began seeing the male consort as also the male protector in their spiritual mythologies, for now that there was someone to protect the Goddess *from*, such a protector was clearly needed.

It was not a major leap from male as protector to male as *equal partner,* now standing alongside the Goddess. The *male God* was created, and, for a while, Gods and Goddesses ruled mythology together.

Then, again gradually, Gods were given larger roles. The need for protection, for strength, began to supplant the need for wisdom and love. A new kind of love was born in these mythologies. A love which protects with brute force. But it was a love which also covets what it protects; which was jealous of its Goddesses; which now did not simply serve their feminine lusts, but fought and died for them.

Myths began to emerge of Gods of enormous power, quarreling over, fighting for, Goddesses of unspeakable beauty. And so was born the *jealous God.*

This is fascinating.

Wait. We're coming to the end, but there's just a little more.

It wasn't long before the jealousy of the Gods extended not only to the Goddesses—but to all creations in all realms. We had better love Him, these jealous Gods demanded, and no other God—*or else!*

Since males were the most powerful species, and

47

Gods were the most powerful of the males, there seemed little room for argument with this new mythology.

Stories of those who did argue, and lost, began to emerge. The *God of wrath was born.*

Soon, the whole idea of Deity was subverted. Instead of being the source of all love, it became the source of all fear.

A model of love which was largely feminine—the endlessly tolerant love of a mother for a child, and yes, even of a woman for her not-too-bright, but, after all, useful man, was replaced by the jealous, wrathful love of a demanding, intolerant God who would brook no interference, allow no insouciance, ignore no offense.

The smile of the amused Goddess, experiencing limitless love and gently submitting to the laws of nature, was replaced by the stern countenance of the not-so-amused God, proclaiming power over the laws of nature, and forevermore limiting love.

This is the God you worship today, and that's how you got where you are now.

Amazing. Interesting and amazing. But what is the point of telling me all of this?

It's important for you to know that you've *made it all up.* The idea that "might is right," or that "power is strength," was born in your male-created theological myths.

The God of wrath and jealousy and anger was an imagining. Yet, something you imagined for so long, *it became real.* Some of you still consider it real today. Yet it has nothing to do with ultimate reality, or what's really going on here.

And what is that?

What's going on is that your soul yearns for the *highest experience of itself* it can imagine. It came here for that purpose—to realize itself (that is, make itself real) in its experience.

Then it discovered pleasures of the flesh—not just sex, but all manner of pleasures—and as it indulged in these pleasures, it gradually forgot the pleasures of the spirit.

These, too, are pleasures—greater pleasures than the body could ever give you. But the soul forgot this.

Okay, now we're getting away from all the history, and back into something You've touched on before in this dialogue. Could You go over this again?

Well, we're not actually getting away from the history. We're tying everything in together. You see, it's really quite simple. The purpose of your soul—its reason for coming to the body—is to be and express Who You Really Are. The soul yearns to do this; yearns to know itself and its own experience.

This yearning to know is life seeking to be. This is God, choosing to express. The God of your histories is not the God who really is. That is the point. Your soul is the tool through which I express and experience Myself.

Doesn't that pretty much *limit* Your experience?

It does, unless it doesn't. That's up to you. You get to be the expression and the experience of Me at whatever level you choose. There have been those who have chosen very grand expressions. There have been none higher than Jesus, the Christ—though there have been others who have been equally as high.

Christ is not the highest example? He is not God made Man?

Christ is the highest example. He is simply not the only example to reach that highest state. Christ is God made Man. He is simply not the only man made of God.

Every man is "God made Man." You are Me, expressing in your present form. Yet don't worry about limiting Me; about how limited that makes Me. For I am not limited, and never have been. Do you think that you are the only form that I have chosen? Do you think you are the only creatures whom I've imbued with the Essence of Me?

I tell you, I am in every flower, every rainbow, every star in the heavens, and everything in and on every planet rotating around every star.

I am the whisper of the wind, the warmth of your sun, the incredible individuality and the extraordinary perfection of every snowflake.

I am the majesty in the soaring flight of eagles, and the innocence of the doe in the field; the courage of lions, the wisdom of the ancient ones.

And I am not limited to the modes of expression seen on your planet alone. You do not know Who I Am, but only think you do. Yet think not that Who I Am is limited to you, or that My Divine Essence—this most Holy Spirit—was given to you and you alone. That would be an arrogant thought, and a misinformed one.

My Beingness is in everything. Everything. The Allness is My Expression. The Wholeness is My Nature. There is nothing that I Am Not, and something I Am Not cannot be.

My purpose in creating you, My blessed creatures, was so that I might have an experience of Myself as the Creator of My Own Experience.

Some people don't understand. Help all of us to understand.

The one aspect of God that only a very special creature could create was the aspect of Myself as The Creator.

I am not the God of your mythologies, nor am I the Goddess. I am The Creator—That Which Creates. Yet I choose to Know Myself in My Own Experience.

Just as I know My perfection of design through a snowflake, My awesome beauty through a rose, so, too, do I know My creative power—through you.

To you I have given the ability to consciously create your experience, which is the ability I have.

Through you, I can know every aspect of Me. The perfection of the snowflake, the awesome beauty of the rose, the courage of lions, the majesty of eagles, all resides in you. In you I have placed all of these things—and one thing more: the consciousness to be aware of it.

Thus have you become Self-conscious. And thus have you been given the greatest gift, for you have been aware of yourself being yourself—which is exactly what I Am.

I am Myself, aware of Myself *being* Myself.

This is what is meant by the statement, I Am That I Am.

You are that Part of Me which is the awareness, experienced.

And what you are experiencing (and what I am experiencing through you) is Me, creating Me.

I am in the continual act of creating Myself.

Does that mean God is not a constant? Does that mean You do not know what *You're* going to *be* in the next moment?

How can I know? You haven't decided yet!

Let me get this straight. *I* am deciding all this?

Yes. You are Me choosing to be Me.

You are Me, choosing to be What I Am—and choosing what I am going to be.

All of you, collectively, are creating that. You are doing it on an individual basis, as each of you decides Who You Are, and experiences that, and you are doing it collectively, as the co-creative collective being that you are.

I Am the collective experience of the lot of you!

And You really don't know who You are going to be in the next moment?

I was being lighthearted a moment ago. Of course I know. I already know all of your decisions, so I know Who I Am, Who I Have Always Been, and Who I Will Always Be.

How can You know what I am going to choose to be, do, and have in the next moment, much less what the whole human race is going to choose?

Simple. You've already done the choosing. Everything you're ever going to be, do, or have, you've already done. You're doing it right now!
Do you see? There is no such thing as time.

This, too, we have discussed before.

It is worth reviewing here.

Yes. Tell me again how this works.

Past, present, and future are concepts you have constructed, realities you have invented, in order to create a context within which to frame your present experience. Otherwise, all of your (Our) experiences would be overlapping.
They actually are overlapping—that is, happening at the same "time"—you simply don't know this. You've placed yourself in a perception shell that blocks out the Total Reality.
I've explained this in detail in _Book 2_. It might be good for you to re-read that material, in order to place what's being said here into context.
The point I am making here is that everything is happening at once. Everything. So yes, I do know what I'm

52

"going to be," what I "am," and what I "was." I know this always. That is, all ways.

And so, you see, there is no way you can surprise Me.

Your story—the whole worldly drama—was created so that you could know Who You Are in your own experience. It's also been designed to help you forget Who You Are, so that you might remember Who You Are once again, and create it.

Because I can't *create* who I am if I am already experiencing who I am. I can't create being six feet tall if I am *already* six feet tall. I'd have to be *less* than six feet tall—or at least *think that I am*.

Exactly. You understand it perfectly. And since it is the greatest desire of the soul (God) to experience Itself as The Creator, and since everything has already been created, We had no choice other than to find a way to forget all about Our creation.

I am amazed that we found a way. Trying to "forget" that we are all One, and that the One of us which we are is God, must be like trying to forget that a pink elephant is in the room. How could we be so mesmerized?

Well, you've just touched on the secret reason for all of physical life. It is life in the physical which has so mesmerized you—and rightly so, because it is, after all, an extraordinary adventure!

What We used here to help Us forget is what some of you would call the Pleasure Principle.

The highest nature of all pleasure is that aspect of pleasure which causes you to create Who You Really Are in your experience right here, right now—and to re-create, and re-create, and re-create again Who You Are at the next highest level of magnificence. That is the highest pleasure of God.

The lower nature of all pleasure is that part of pleasure which causes you to forget Who You Really Are. Do not condemn the lower nature, for without it, you could not experience the higher.

It's almost as if the pleasures of the flesh at first cause us to forget Who We Are, then become the very avenue through which we remember!

There you have it. You've just said it. And the use of physical pleasure as an avenue to remembering Who You Are is achieved by raising up, through the body, the basic energy of all life.

This is the energy which you sometimes call "sexual energy," and it is raised up along the inner column of your being, until it reaches the area you call the Third Eye. This is the area just behind the forehead between and slightly above the eyes. As you raise the energy, you cause it to course all through your body. It is like an inner orgasm.

How is this done? How do you do that?

You "think it up." I mean that, just as I said it. You literally "think it up" the inner pathway of what you have called your "chakras." Once the life energy is raised up repeatedly, one acquires a taste for this experience, just as one acquires a hunger for sex.

The experience of the energy being raised is very sublime. It quickly becomes the experience most desired. Yet you never completely lose your hunger for the lowering of the energy—for the basic passions—nor ought you try. For the higher cannot exist without the lower in your experience—as I have pointed out to you many times. Once you get to the higher, you must go back to the lower, in order to experience again the pleasure of moving to the higher.

This is the sacred rhythm of all life. You do this not only by moving the energy around inside your body. You also do this by moving around the larger energy inside the Body of God.

You incarnate as lower forms, then evolve into higher states of consciousness. You are simply raising the energy in the Body of God. You *are* that energy. And when you arrive at the highest state, you experience it fully, then you decide what next you choose to experience, and where in the Realm of Relativity you choose to go in order to experience it.

You may wish to again experience yourself becoming your Self—it is a grand experience, indeed—and so you may start all over again on the Cosmic Wheel.

Is this the same as the "karmic wheel"?

No. There is no such thing as a "karmic wheel." Not the way you have imagined it. Many of you have imagined that you are on, not a wheel, but a *treadmill*, in which you are working off the debts of past actions, and trying valiantly not to incur any new ones. This is what some of you have called "the karmic wheel." It is not so very different from a few of your Western theologies, for in both paradigms you are seen as an unworthy sinner, seeking to gain the purity to move on to the next spiritual level.

The experience which I have described here, on the other hand, I am calling the *Cosmic* Wheel, because there is nothing of unworthiness, debt-repayment, punishment, or "purification." The Cosmic Wheel simply describes the ultimate reality, or what you might call the cosmology of the universe.

It is the cycle of life, or what I sometimes term The Process. It is a picture phrase describing the no-beginning-and-no-end nature of things; the continually connected path to and from the all of everything, on which the soul joyfully journeys throughout eternity.

It is the sacred rhythm of all life, by which you move the Energy of God.

Wow, I've never had that all explained to me so simply! I don't think I've ever understood all this so clearly.

Well, clarity is what you brought yourself here to experience. That was the purpose of this dialogue. So I am glad you are achieving that.

In truth, there is no "lower" or "higher" place on the Cosmic Wheel. How can there be? It's a *wheel*, not a *ladder*.

That is excellent. That is an excellent imagery and an excellent understanding. Therefore, condemn not that which you call the lower, basic, animal instincts of man, yet bless them, honoring them as the path through which, and by which, you find your way back home.

This would relieve a lot of people of a lot of guilt around sex.

It is why I have said, play, play, *play* with sex—and with all of life!

Mix what you call the sacred with the sacrilegious, for until you see your altars as the ultimate place for love, and your bedrooms as the ultimate place for worship, you see nothing at all.

You think "sex" is separate from God? I tell you this: *I am in your bedroom every night!*

So go ahead! Mix what you call the profane and the profound—so that you can see that there is no difference, and experience All as One. Then when you continue to evolve, you will not see yourself as letting go of sex, but simply enjoying it at a higher level. For all of *life* is S.E.X.—Synergistic Energy eXchange.

And if you understand this about sex, you will understand this about everything in life. Even the end of life—what you call "death." At the moment of your death, you will not see yourself as letting go of life, but simply enjoying it at a higher level.

When at last you see that there is no separation in God's World—that is, nothing which is not God—then, at last, will you let go of this invention of man which you have called Satan.

If Satan exists, he exists as every thought you ever had of separation from Me. You cannot be separate from Me, for I Am All That Is.

Men invented the devil to scare people into doing what they wanted, under the threat of separation from God if they did not. Condemnation, being hurled into the everlasting fires of hell, was the *ultimate scare tactic*. Yet now you need be afraid no more. For nothing can, or ever will, separate you from Me.

You and I are One. We cannot be anything else if I Am What I Am: All That Is.

Why then would I condemn Myself? And how would I do it? How could I separate Myself from Myself when My Self is All There Is, and there is nothing else?

My purpose is to evolve, not to condemn; to grow, not to die; to experience, not to fail to experience. My purpose is to Be, not to cease to Be.

I have no way to separate Myself from you—or anything else. "Hell" is simply not knowing this. "Salvation" is knowing and understanding it completely. You are now saved. You needn't worry about what's going to happen to you "after death" anymore.

3

Can we talk about this death business for a minute? You said this third book was going to be about higher truths; about universal truths. Well, through all the conversation we've had, we haven't talked that much about death—and what happens after that. Let's do that now. Let's get to that.

Fine. What do you want to know?

What happens when you die?

What do you choose to have happen?

You mean that what happens is whatever we choose to have happen?

Do you think that just because you've died you stop creating?

I don't know. That's why I'm asking You.

Fair enough. (You do know, incidentally, but I see you have forgotten—which is great. Everything's gone according to plan.)

When you die, you do not stop creating. Is that definitive enough for you?

Yes.

Good.

Now the reason you do not stop creating when you die is that you don't ever die. You cannot. For you are life itself. And life cannot *not* be life. Therefore you cannot die.

So, at the moment of your death what happens is... you go on living.

This is why so many people who have "died" do not believe it—because they do not have the experience of being dead. On the contrary, they feel (because they are) very much alive. So there's confusion.

The Self may see the body lying there, all crumpled up, not moving, yet the Self is suddenly moving all over the place. It has the experience, often, of literally flying all over the room—then of being everywhere in the space, all at once. And when it desires a particular point of view, it suddenly finds itself experiencing that.

If the soul (the name we will now give to the Self) wonders, "Gee, why is my body not moving?" it will find itself right there, hovering right over the body, watching the stillness curiously.

If someone enters the room, and the soul thinks, "Who is that?"—immediately the soul is in front of, or next to, that person.

Thus, in a very short time the soul learns that it can go anywhere—with the speed of its thought.

A feeling of incredible freedom and lightness overtakes the soul, and it usually takes a little while for the entity to "get used to" all this bouncing around with every thought.

If the person had children, and should think of those children, immediately the soul is in the presence of those children, wherever they are. Thus the soul learns that not only can it be wherever it wants with the speed of its thought—it can be in two places at once. Or three places. Or five.

It can exist, observe, and conduct activities in these places simultaneously, without difficulty or confusion. Then it can "rejoin" itself, returning to one place again, simply by refocusing.

The soul remembers in the next life what it would have been well to remember in this life—that all effect is created by thought, and that manifestation is a result of intention.

What I focus on as my intention becomes my reality.

Exactly. The only difference is the speed with which you experience the result. In the physical life there might be a lapse between thought and experience. In the spirit's realm there is no lapse; results are instantaneous.

Newly departed souls therefore learn to monitor their thoughts very carefully, because whatever they think of, they experience.

I use the word "learn" here very loosely, more as a figure of speech than an actual description. The term "remember" would be more accurate.

If physicalized souls learned to control their thoughts as quickly and as efficiently as spiritualized souls, their whole lives would change.

In the creation of individual reality, thought control, or what some might call prayer—is everything.

Prayer?

Thought control is the highest form of prayer. Therefore, think only on good things, and righteous. Dwell not in negativity and darkness. And even in moments when things look bleak—especially in those moments—see only perfection, express only gratefulness, and then imagine only what manifestation of perfection you choose next.

In this formula is found tranquillity. In this process is found peace. In this awareness is found joy.

That's extraordinary. That's an extraordinary piece of information. Thanks for bringing that through me.

Thanks for letting it come through. Some times you are "cleaner" than at other times. Some moments you are more open—like a strainer which has just been rinsed. It is more "open." There are more holes open.

Good way of putting it.

I do My best.

To recap then: Souls released from the body quickly remember to monitor and control their thoughts very carefully, for whatever they think of, that is what they create and experience.

I say again, it is the same for souls still residing with a body, except the results are usually not as immediate. And it is the "time" lapse between thought and creation—which can be days, weeks, months, or even years—which creates the illusion that things are happening *to* you, not *because* of you. *This is an illusion,* causing you to *forget that you are at cause* in the matter.

As I have described now several times, this forgetting is "built into the system." It is part of the process. For you cannot create Who You Are until you forget Who You Are. So the illusion causing forgetfulness is an effect created on purpose.

When you leave the body, it will therefore be a big surprise to see the instant and obvious connection between your thoughts and your creations. It will be a shocking surprise at first, and then a very pleasant one, as you begin to remember that you are at cause in the creation of your experience, not at the effect of it.

Why is there such a delay between thought and creation *before* we die, and no delay at all after we die?

Because you are working within the illusion of time. There is no delay between thought and creation away from the body, because you are also away from the parameter of time.

In other words, as You have said so often, time does not exist.

Not as you understand it. The phenomenon of "time" is really a function of perspective.

61

Why does it exist while we are in the body?

You have caused it to by moving into, by assuming, your present perspective. You use this perspective as a tool with which you can explore and examine your experiences much more fully, by separating them into individual pieces, rather than a single occurrence.

Life is a single occurrence, an event in the cosmos that is happening *right now*. All of it is happening. Everywhere.

There is no "time" but *now*. There is no "place" but *here*.

Here and now is All There Is.

Yet you chose to experience the magnificence of here and now in its every detail, and to experience your Divine Self as the here and now creator of that reality. There were only two ways—two fields of experience—in which you could do that. Time and space.

So magnificent was this thought that you literally exploded with delight!

In that explosion of delight was created space between the parts of you, and the time it took to move from one part of yourself to another.

In this way you literally *tore your Self apart* to look at the pieces of you. You might say that you were so happy, you "fell to pieces."

You've been picking up the pieces ever since.

That's all my life is! I'm just putting together the pieces, trying to see if they make any sense.

And it is through the device called time that you have managed to separate the pieces, to divide the indivisible, thus to see it and experience it more fully, as you are creating it.

Even as you look at a solid object through a microscope, seeing that it is not solid at all, but actually a conglomeration of a million different effects—different things all happening at once and thus creating the larger

62

effect—so, too, do you use time as the microscope of your soul.

Consider the Parable of the Rock.

Once there was a Rock, filled with countless atoms, protons, neutrons, and subatomic particles of matter. These particles were racing around continually, in a pattern, each particle going from "here" to "there," and taking "time" to do so, yet going so fast that the Rock itself seemed to move not at all. It just *was*. There it lay, drinking in the sun, soaking up the rain, and moving not at all.

"What is this, inside of me, that is moving?" the Rock asked.

"It is You," said a Voice from Afar.

"Me?" replied the Rock. "Why, that is impossible. I am not moving at all. Anyone can see that."

"Yes, *from a distance*," the Voice agreed. "From way over *here* you *do* look as if you are solid, still, not moving. But when I come closer—when I look very closely at what is actually happening—I see that everything that comprises What You Are is *moving*. It is moving at incredible speed through time and space in a particular pattern which *creates* You as the thing called 'Rock.' And so, you are like magic! You are moving and *not moving* at the same time."

"But," asked the Rock, "which, then, is the illusion? The oneness, the stillness, of the Rock, or the separateness and the movement of Its parts?"

To which the Voice replied, "Which, then, is the illusion? The oneness, the stillness, of God? Or the separateness and movement of Its parts?"

And I tell you this: Upon this Rock, I will build My church. For this is the Rock of Ages. This is the eternal truth that leaves no stone unturned. I have explained it all for you here, in this little story. This is The Cosmology.

Life is a series of minute, incredibly rapid movements. These movements do not affect at all the immobility and the Beingness of Everything That Is. Yet, just as with the atoms of the rock, it is the movement which is creating the stillness, right before your eyes.

From this distance, there is no separateness. There cannot be, for All That Is is All There Is, and there *is nothing else*. I am the Unmoved Mover.

From the limited perspective with which you view All That Is, you see yourself as separate and apart, not one unmovable being, but many, many beings, constantly in motion.

Both observations are accurate. Both realities are "real."

And when I "die," I don't die at all, but simply shift into awareness of the macrocosm—where there is no "time" or "space," now and then, before and after.

Precisely. You've got it.

Let me see if I can say it back to You. Let me see if *I* can describe it.

Go ahead.

From a macro perspective, there is no separateness, and from "way back there" all the particles of everything merely look like the Whole.

As you look at the rock at your feet, you see the rock, right then and there, as whole, complete, and perfect. Yet even in the fraction of a moment that you hold that rock in your awareness, there is a lot going on within that rock—there is incredible movement, at incredible speed, of the particles of that rock. And what are those particles doing? They are making that rock what it is.

As you look at this rock, you do not see this process. Even if you are conceptually aware of it, to you it is all happening "now." The rock isn't *becoming* a rock; it *is* a rock, right here—right now.

Yet if you were the consciousness of one of the submolecular particles inside that rock, you would experience yourself moving at insane speed, first "here," then "there." And if some voice outside the rock said to you, "It is all happening at once," you would call it a liar or a charlatan.

Still, from the perspective of a distance from the rock, the idea that any part of the rock is separate from any other part, and, further, is moving around at insane speed, would appear to be the lie. From that distance could be seen what could not be seen up close—that all is One, and that all the movement *hasn't moved anything.*

You have it. You have a grasp of it. What you are saying—and you are correct—is that life is all a matter of perspective. If you continue to see this truth, you will begin to understand the macro reality of God. And you will have unlocked a secret of the whole universe: *All of it is the same thing.*

The universe is a molecule in the body of God!

That's actually not so very far off.

And it is to the macro reality that we return in consciousness when we do the thing called "die"?

Yes. Yet even the macro reality to which you return is but a *micro reality* of an *even larger macro reality,* which is a smaller part of a larger reality *still*—and so on, and on, and on, forever and ever, and even forever more, world without end.

We are God—the "It that Is"—constantly in the act of creating Our Selves, constantly in the act of being what we are now . . . until we aren't that anymore, but become something else.

Even the rock will not be a rock forever, but only what "seems like forever." Before it was a rock, it was something else. It fossilized into that rock, through a process taking hundreds of thousands of years. It was once something else, and will be something else again.

The same is true of you. You were not always the "you" that you are now. You were something else. And today, as you stand there in your utter magnificence, you truly are . . . "something else again."

Wow, that's amazing. I mean, that's absolutely amazing! I've never heard anything like that. You've taken the whole cosmology of life and put it in terms I can hold in my mind. That is amazing.

Well, thank you. I appreciate that. I'm doing My best.

You're doing a damned good job.

That's probably not the phrase you should have chosen there.

Oops.

Just kidding. Lightening things up here. Having a little fun. I cannot actually be "offended." Yet your fellow human beings often allow themselves to be offended on My behalf.

So I've noticed. But, getting back, I think I've just caught hold of something.

What's that?

This whole explanation rolled out when I asked a single question: "How come 'time' exists when we're in the body, but not when the soul is released?" And what You seem to be saying is that "time" is really *perspective;* that it neither "exists" nor "ceases to exist," but that as the soul alters its perspective, we experience ultimate reality in different ways.

That's exactly what I'm saying! You've got it!

And You were making the larger point that in the *macrocosm* the soul is *aware* of the *direct relationship* between *thought and creation*; between one's ideas and one's experience.

Yes—at the macro level, it's like seeing the rock and seeing the movement within the rock. There is no "time" between the movement of the atoms and the appearance of the rock it creates. The rock "is," even as the movements occur. Indeed, *because* the movements occur. This cause and effect is instant. The movement is occurring and the rock is "being," all at the "same time."

This is what the soul realizes at the moment of what you call "death." It is simply a change in perspective. You see more, so you understand more.

After death, you are no longer limited in your understanding. You see the rock, and you see *into* the rock. You will look at what now seem to be the most complex aspects of life and say, "Of course." It will all be very clear to you.

Then there will be new mysteries for you to ponder. As you move around the Cosmic Wheel, there will be larger and larger realities—bigger and bigger truths.

Yet if you can remember this truth—your perspective creates your thoughts, and your thoughts create everything—and if you can remember it *before you leave the body*, not after, *your whole life will change.*

And the way to control your thoughts is to change your perspective.

Precisely. Assume a different perspective and you will have a different thought about everything. In this way you will have learned to control your thought, and, in the creation of your experience, controlled thought is everything.

Some people call this constant prayer.

You've said this before, but I don't think I've ever thought of prayer in this way.

Why not see what happens if you do so? If you imagined that the controlling and directing of your thoughts is the highest form of prayer, you would think only on good things, and righteous. You would dwell not in negativity and darkness, though you may be immersed in it. And in moments when things look bleak—perhaps especially in those moments—you would see only perfection.

You have come back to that, over and over again.

I am giving you tools. With these tools you can change your life. I am repeating the most important of them. Over and over again I am repeating them, for repetition will produce re-cognition—"knowing again"—when you need it most.

Everything that occurs—everything that has occurred, is occurring, and ever will occur—is the outward physical manifestation of your innermost thoughts, choices, ideas, and determinations regarding Who You Are and Who You Choose to Be. Condemn not, therefore, those aspects of life with which you disagree. Seek instead to change them, and the conditions that made them possible.

Behold the darkness, yet curse it not. Rather, be a light unto the darkness, and so transform it. Let your light so shine before men, that those who stand in the darkness will be illumined by the light of your being, and all of you will see, at last, Who You Really Are.

Be a Bringer of the Light. For your light can do more than illuminate your own path. Your light can be the light which truly lights the world.

Shine on, then, O Illuminati! Shine on! That the moment of your greatest darkness may yet become your grandest gift. And even as you are gifted, so, too, will you gift others, giving to them the unspeakable treasure: Themselves.

Let this be your task, let this be your greatest joy: to give people back to themselves. Even in their darkest hour. Especially in that hour.

The world waits for you. Heal it. Now. In the place where you are. There is much you can do.

For My sheep are lost and must now be found. Be ye, therefore, as good shepherds, and lead them back to Me.

4

Thank You. Thank You for that call and for that challenge. Thank You for that placement of the goal before me. Thank You. For always keeping me heading in the direction You know I really want to take. That is why I come to You. That is why I have loved, and blessed, this dialogue. For it is in conversation with You that I find the Divine within me, and begin to see it within all others.

My dearly beloved, the heavens rejoice when you say that. That is the very reason I have come to you, and will come to everyone who calls to Me. Even as I have come now to those others who are reading these words. For this conversation was never intended to be with you alone. It was intended for millions around the world. And it has been placed in each person's hands just exactly when they have needed it, sometimes in the most miraculous ways. It has brought them to the wisdom they, themselves, have called forth, perfectly suited for this moment in their lives.

This is the wonder of what has been happening here: that each of you is producing this result by yourself. It "looks as if" someone else gave you this book, brought you to this conversation, opened you to this dialogue, yet *you brought your Self here*.

So let us now explore together the remaining questions which you have held in your heart.

May we, please, speak more of life after death? You were explaining what happens to the soul after death, and I so want to know as much about that as I can.

We will speak of it, then, until your yearning has been satisfied.

I said earlier that what happens is whatever you want to have happen. I meant that. You create your own reality not only when you are with the body, but when you are away from it.

At first you may not realize this, and so you may not be consciously creating your reality. Your experience will then be created by one of two other energies: your uncontrolled thoughts, or the collective consciousness.

To the degree that your uncontrolled thoughts are stronger than the collective consciousness, to that degree you will experience them as reality. To the degree that the collective consciousness is accepted, absorbed, and internalized, to that degree you will experience *it* as your reality.

This is no different from how you create what you call reality in your present life.

Always in life you have before you three choices:

1. You may allow your uncontrolled thoughts to create The Moment.

2. You may allow your creative consciousness to create The Moment.

3. You may allow the collective consciousness to create The Moment.

Here is an irony:

In your present life you find it difficult to create consciously from your individual awareness, and, indeed, often assume your individual understandings to be wrong, given all that you are seeing around you, and so, you surrender to the collective consciousness, whether it serves you to do so or not.

In the first moments of what you call the afterlife, on the other hand, you may find it *difficult* to surrender to the collective consciousness, given all that you are seeing around you (which may be unbelievable to you), and so you will be tempted to hold to your own individual understandings, whether they serve you or not.

I would tell you this: It is when you are surrounded by lower consciousness that you will benefit more from remaining with your individual understandings, and when you are surrounded by higher consciousness that you receive greater benefit from surrender.

It may, therefore, be wise to seek beings of high consciousness. I cannot overemphasize the importance of the company you keep.

In what you call the afterlife, there is nothing to worry about on this score, for you will instantly and automatically be surrounded by beings of high consciousness—and by high consciousness itself.

Still, you may not know that you are being so lovingly enveloped; you may not immediately understand. It may, therefore, seem to you as if you are having things "happen" to you; that you are at the whim of whatever fortunes are working at the moment. In truth, you experience the consciousness in which you die.

Some of you have expectations without even knowing it. All your life you've had thoughts about what occurs after death, and when you "die" those thoughts are made manifest, and you suddenly realize (make real) what you've been thinking about. And it is your strongest thoughts, the ones you've held most fervently, that, as always in life, will prevail.

Then a person _could_ go to hell. If people believed all during life that hell is a place which most certainly existed, that God will judge "the quick and the dead," that He will separate the "wheat from the chaff" and the "goats from the sheep," and that they are surely "going to hell," given all that they have done to offend God, then they _would_ go to hell! They would burn in the everlasting fires of damnation! How could they escape it? You've said repeatedly throughout this dialogue that hell does not exist. Yet You also say that we create our own reality, and have the power to create any reality at all, out of our thought about it. So hellfire and damnation _could_ and _does_ exist _for those who believe in it._

Nothing exists in Ultimate Reality save that Which Is. You are correct in pointing out that you may create any subreality you choose—including the experience

72

of hell as you describe it. I have never said at any point in this entire dialogue that you could not experience hell; I said that hell does not exist. *Most of what you experience does not exist, yet you experience it nonetheless.*

This is unbelievable. A friend of mine named Barnet Bain just produced a movie about this. I mean, about this *exactly*. It is August 7, 1998, as I write this sentence. I am inserting this in the dialogue, in between lines of a discussion of two years ago, and I have never done this before. But just before sending this to the publisher, I was re-reading the manuscript one last time, and I realized: Hold it! Robin Williams has just made a movie about *exactly what we're talking about here.* It's called *What Dreams May Come,* and it's a startling depiction on film of what You've just said.

I am familiar with it.

You are? *God goes to the movies?*

God makes movies.

Whoa.

Yes. You never saw *Oh, God?*

Well, sure, but . . .

What, you think God only writes books?

So, is the Robin Williams movie literally true? I mean, is that how it is?

No. No movie or book or other human explanation of the Divine is literally true.

Not even the Bible? The Bible is not literally true?

No. And I think you know that.

73

Well, what about *this* book? Surely *this* book is literally true!

No. I hate to tell you this, but you are bringing this through your personal filter. Now I will agree that the mesh on your filter is thinner, finer. You have become a very good filter. But you are a filter nonetheless.

I know that. I just wanted it stated again, here, because some people take books like this, and movies like *What Dreams May Come*, as literal truth. And I want to stop them from doing that.

The writers and producers of that film brought some enormous truth through an imperfect filter. The point they sought to make is that you will experience after death exactly what you expect, and choose, to experience. They made that point very effectively.

Now, shall we get back to where we were?

Yes. I'd like to know just what I wanted to know when I was watching that movie. If there is no hell, yet I am experiencing hell, *what the hell is the difference?*

There wouldn't be any, as long as you remain in your created reality. Yet you will not create such a reality forever. Some of you won't experience it for more than what you would call a "nanosecond." And therefore you will not experience, even in the private domains of your own imagination, a place of sadness or suffering.

What would stop me from creating such a place for all eternity if I believed all my life that there was such a place, and that something I'd done had caused me to deserve such a place?

Your knowledge and understanding.

Just as in this life your next moment is created out of the new understandings you've gained from your last moment, so, too, in what you call the afterlife, will you

74

create a new moment from what you've come to know and understand in the old.

And one thing you will come to know and understand very quickly is that you are at choice, always, about what you wish to experience. That is because in the afterlife results are instantaneous, and you will not be able to miss the connection between your thoughts about a thing, and the experience those thoughts create.

You will understand yourself to be creating your own reality.

This would explain why some people's experience is happy, and some people's experience is frightening; why some people's experience is profound, while other people's experience is virtually nonexistent. And why so many different stories exist about what happens in the moments after death.

Some people come back from near-death experiences filled with peace and love, and with no fear, ever again, of death, while others return very frightened, certain that they have just encountered dark and evil forces.

The soul responds to, re-creates, the mind's most powerful suggestion, producing that in its experience.

Some souls remain in that experience for a time, making it very real—even as they remained in their experiences while with the body, though they were equally as unreal and impermanent. Other souls quickly adjust, see the experience for what it is, begin to think new thoughts, and move immediately to new experiences.

Do You mean that there is no one particular way things *are* in the afterlife? Are there no eternal truths that exist outside of our own mind? Do we continue to go on creating myths and legends and make-believe experiences right past our death and into the next reality? When do we get released from the bondage? When do we come to know the truth?

When you choose to. That was the point of the Robin Williams movie. That is the point being made

75

here. Those whose only desire is to know the eternal truth of All That Is, to understand the great mysteries, to experience the grandest reality, do so.

Yes, there is a One Great Truth; there is a Final Reality. But you will always get what you choose, regardless of that reality—precisely because the reality is that you are a divine creature, divinely creating your reality even as you are experiencing It.

Yet should you choose to stop creating your own individual reality and begin to understand and experience the larger, unified reality, you will have an immediate opportunity to do that.

Those who "die" in a state of such choosing, of such desiring, of such willingness and such knowing, move into the experience of the Oneness at once. Others move into the experience only if, as, and when they so desire.

It is precisely the same when the soul is with the body.

It is all a matter of desire, of your choosing, of your creating, and, ultimately, of your creating the uncreateable; that is, of your experiencing that which has _already been created_.

This is The Created Creator. The Unmoved Mover. It is the alpha and the omega, the before and the after, the now-then-always aspect of everything, which you call God.

I will not forsake you, yet I will not force My Self upon you. I have never done so and I never will. You may return to Me whenever you wish. Now, while you are with the body, or after you have left it. You may return to the One and experience the loss of your individual Self whenever it pleases you. You may also re-create the experience of your individual Self whenever you choose.

You may experience any aspect of the All That Is that you wish, in its tiniest proportion, or its grandest. You may experience the microcosm or the macrocosm.

76

I may experience the particle or the rock.

Yes. Good. You are getting this.

When you reside with the human body, you are experiencing a smaller portion than the whole; that is, a portion of the microcosm (although by no means the smallest portion thereof). When you reside away from the body (in what some would call the "spirit world"), you have enlarged by quantum leaps your perspective. You will suddenly seem to know everything; be able to be everything. You will have a macrocosmic view of things, allowing you to understand that which you do not now understand.

One of the things you will then understand is that there is a larger macrocosm still. That is, you will suddenly become clear that All That Is is even greater than the reality you are then experiencing. This will fill you at once with awe and anticipation, wonder and excitement, joy and exhilaration, for you will then know and understand what I know and understand: that the game never ends.

Will I ever get to a place of true wisdom?

In the time after your "death" you may choose to have every question you ever had answered—and open yourself to new questions you never dreamed existed. You may choose to experience Oneness with All That Is. And you will have a chance to decide what you wish to be, do, and have next.

Do you choose to return to your most recent body? Do you choose to experience life again in human form, but of another kind?

Do you choose to remain where you are in the "spirit world," at the level you are then experiencing? Do you choose to go on, go further, in your knowing and experiencing? Do you choose to "lose your identity" altogether and now become part of the Oneness?

What do you choose? What do you choose? What do you *choose?*

77

Always, that is the question I will be asking you. Always, that is the inquiry of the universe. For the universe knows nothing except how to grant your fondest wish, your greatest desire. Indeed, it is doing that every moment, every day. The difference between you and Me is that you are not consciously aware of this.

I am.

Tell me . . . will my relatives, my loved ones, meet me after I die, and help me understand what is going on, as some people say they will? Will I be reunited with "those who have gone before"? Will we be able to spend eternity together?

What do you choose? Do you choose for these things to happen? Then they will.

Okay, I'm confused. Are You saying that all of us have free will, and that this free will extends even past our death?

Yes, that is what I am saying.

If that is true, then the free will of my loved ones would have to coincide with mine—they must have the same thought and desire that I have, when I'm having it—or they wouldn't be there for me when I die. Further, what if I wanted to spend the rest of eternity with them, and one or two of them wanted to move on? Maybe one of them wanted to move higher and higher, into this experience of Reunification with the Oneness, as You put it. Then what?

There is no contradiction in the universe. There are things that look like contradictions, but there are none in fact. Should a situation arise such as the one you describe (it is a very good question, by the way), what will happen is that you will both be able to have what you choose.

Both?

Both.

May I ask how?

You may.

Okay. How . . .

What is your thought about God? Do you think that I exist in one place, and one place only?

No. I think You exist everywhere at once. I believe God is omnipresent.

Well, you are right about that. There is nowhere that I Am Not. Do you understand this?

I think so.

Good. So what makes you think it's any different with you?

Because You're God, and I am a mere mortal.

I see. We're still hung up on this "mere mortal" thing. . . .

Okay, okay . . . suppose I assume for the sake of discussion that I, too, am God—or at least made up of the same stuff as God. Then are You saying that I, too, can be everywhere, all the time?

It is merely a matter of what the consciousness chooses to hold in its reality. In what you would call the "spirit world," what you can imagine, you can experience. Now, if you want to experience yourself being one soul, in one place, at one "time," you may do that. Yet if you wish to experience your spirit being larger than that, being in more than one place at one "time," *you may do that as well.* Indeed, you may experience your spirit as being *anywhere you wish,* any "time." That is because, in truth, there is only one "time" and one "place," and you are in all of it, always. You may thus experience any part, or *parts*, of it you wish, whenever you choose.

What if *I* want my relatives to be with *me*, but one of *them* wants to be a "part of the All" that is somewhere else? What then?

It is not possible for you and your relatives not to want the same thing. You and I, and your relatives and I—all of us—are one and the same.

The very act of your desiring something is the act of Me desiring something, since you are simply Me, acting out the experience called *desire*. Therefore, what you desire, I desire.

Your relatives and I are also one and the same. Therefore, what I am desiring, they are desiring. So it follows, then, that what you desire, your relatives are also desiring.

On Earth it is also true that all of you desire the same thing. You desire peace. You desire prosperity. You desire joy. You desire fulfillment. You desire satisfaction and self-expression in your work, love in your life, health in your body. You all desire the same thing.

You think this is a coincidence? It is not. *It is the way life works*. I am explaining that to you right now.

Now the only thing that's different on Earth from the way it is in what you call the spirit world is that on Earth, while you all desire the same thing, you all have different ideas about how to go about having it. So you're all going in different directions, seeking the same thing!

It is these differing ideas you have that produce your differing results. These ideas might be called your Sponsoring Thoughts. I have spoken to you of this before.

Yes, in *Book 1*.

One such thought which many of you share in common is your idea of insufficiency. Many of you believe at the core of your being that there is *simply not enough*. Not enough of *anything*.

There's not enough love, not enough money, not enough food, not enough clothing, not enough shelter, not enough time, not enough good ideas to go around, and certainly not enough of *you* to go around.

This Sponsoring Thought causes you to employ all sorts of strategies and tactics in seeking to acquire what you think there is "not enough" of. These are approaches you would abandon at once were you clear that there is enough for everybody . . . of *whatever* it is that you desire.

In what you call "heaven," your ideas of "not enough-ness" disappear, because you become aware that there is no separation between you and anything you desire.

You are aware that there is even more than enough of you. You are aware that you can be in more than one place at any given "time," so there is no reason not to want what your brother wants, not to choose what your sister chooses. If they want you in their space at the moment of their death, the very thought of you calls you to them—and you have no reason not to race to them, since your going there takes away nothing from whatever else you may be doing.

This state of having no reason to say No is the state in which I reside at all times.

You have heard it said before, and it is true: God never says No.

I will give you all exactly what you desire, always. Even as I have done from the beginning of time.

Are You really always *giving everyone exactly what they desire* at any given time?

Yes, My beloved, I am.

Your life is a reflection of what you desire, and what you believe you may have of what you desire. I cannot give you what you do not believe you may have—no

81

matter how much you desire it—because I will not violate your own thought about it. I cannot. That is the law.

Believing that you cannot have something is the same thing as not desiring to have it, for it produces the same result.

But on Earth we cannot have what*ever* we desire. We cannot be in two places at once, for instance. And there are many other things we may desire, but cannot have, because on Earth we are all so limited.

I know that you see it that way, and so that is the way it is for you, for one thing that remains eternally true is that you will always be given the experience you believe you will be given.

Thus, if you say that you cannot be in two places at once, then you cannot be. But if you say that you can be anywhere you wish with the speed of your thought, and can even make yourself manifest in physical form in more than one place at any given time, then you may do that.

Now, You see, that's where this dialogue leaves me. I want to believe that this information is coming straight from God—but when You say things like that, I get all crazy inside, because I just can't believe that. I mean, I just don't think what You've said there is true. Nothing in the human experience has demonstrated that.

On the contrary. Saints and sages of all religions have been said to have done both of these things. Does it take a very high level of belief? An *extraordinary* level of belief? The level of belief attained by one being in a thousand years? Yes. Does that mean it is impossible? No.

How can I create that belief? How can I get to that level of belief?

82

You cannot get there. You can only *be* there. And I am not trying to play with words. I mean that. This kind of belief—what I would call Complete Knowing—is not something you try to acquire. In fact, if you are trying to *acquire it*, you cannot have it. It is something you simply *are*. You simply *are* this Knowing. You *are* this being.

Such beingness comes out of a state of *total awareness*. It can come out of *only* such a state. If you are seeking to *become* aware, then you cannot be.

It is like trying to "be" six feet tall when you are 4-foot-9. You cannot be six feet tall. You can only "be" what you are—4-foot-9. You will "be" six feet tall *when you grow into that*. When you *are* six feet tall, you will then be able to do all the things that six-foot-tall people can do. And when you *are* in a state of total awareness, then you will be able to do all the things that beings in a state of total awareness can do.

Do not, therefore, "try to believe" that you can do these things. Try, instead, to move to a state of total awareness. Then belief will no longer be necessary. Complete Knowing will work its wonders.

Once, when I was meditating, I had the experience of total oneness, total awareness. It was wonderful. It was ecstatic. Ever since then, I have been trying to have that experience again. I sit in meditation and try to have that total awareness again. And I have never been able to. This is the reason, right? You are saying to me that as long as I am seeking to have something, I cannot have it, because my very seeking is a statement that I do not now have it. The same wisdom You have been giving me throughout this dialogue.

Yes, yes. Now you understand it. It is becoming more clear to you now. That is why we keep going around in circles here. That is why we keep repeating things, revisiting things. You get it the third, the fourth, maybe the fifth time around.

Well, I'm glad I asked the question, because this could be dangerous stuff, this business about "you can be in two places at once," or "you can do anything you want to do." This is the kind of stuff that makes people run to jump off the Empire State Building shouting "I am God! Look at me! I can fly!"

You had better be in a state of total awareness before you do that. If you have to prove yourself to be God by demonstrating it to others, then you do not know yourself to be, and this "not knowing" will demonstrate itself in your reality. In short, you will fall flat on your face.

God seeks to prove Itself to no one, for God has no need to do that. God Is, and that is what is so. Those who know themselves to be One with God, or have the experience of God within, have no need, nor do they seek, to prove that to anyone, least of all themselves.

And so it was, that when they taunted him, saying, "If you are the Son of God, come down from that cross!"—the man called Jesus did nothing.

Yet three days later, quietly and unobtrusively, when there were no witnesses and no crowds and no one to whom to prove anything, he did something a great deal more astonishing—and the world has been talking about it ever since.

And in this miracle is found your salvation, for you have been shown the truth, not only of Jesus, but of Who You Are, and may thus be saved from the lie about yourself, which you have been told, and which you have accepted as your truth.

God invites you always to your highest thought about yourself.

There are those on your planet right now who have manifested many of these higher thoughts; including causing physical objects to appear and disappear, making themselves appear and disappear, even "living forever" in the body, or coming back to the body and living again—and all of this, all of this, has been made possible because of their faith. Because of their knowing.

Because of their immutable clarity about how things are, and how they are meant to be.

And while, in the past, whenever people in earthly form have done these things, you have called the events miracles and have made the people saints and saviors, yet they are no more saints and saviors than you. For you are all saints and saviors. *Which is the very message they have been bringing you.*

How can I believe that? I want to believe that with all my heart, but I can't. I just can't.

No, you cannot believe it. You can only *know* it.

How can I know it? How can I come to that?

Whatever you choose for yourself, give to another. If you cannot come to that, help someone else come to that. *Tell* someone else that they already have. *Praise* them for it. *Honor* them for it.

This is the value in having a guru. That is the whole point. There has been a lot of negative energy in the West on the word "guru." It has almost become pejorative. To be a "guru" is to somehow be a charlatan. To give your allegiance to a guru is to somehow give your power away.

Honoring your guru is *not* giving your power away. It is *getting* your power. For when you honor the guru, when you praise your master teacher, what you say is, "I see you." And what you see in another, you can begin to see in yourself. It is outward evidence of your inner reality. It is outward proof in your inner truth. The truth of your being.

This is the truth which is being brought through you in the books you write.

I don't see myself as writing these books. I see You, *God,* as the author, and me as merely the scribe.

85

God is the author… *and so are you*. There is no difference between My writing them and you writing them. As long as you think there is, you will have missed the point of the writing itself. Yet most of humanity has missed this teaching. And so I send you new teachers, more teachers, all with the same message as the teachers of old.

I understand your reluctance to accept the teaching as your own personal truth. Were you to go around claiming to be One with God—or even a part of God—speaking or writing these words, the world would not know what to make of you.

People can make of me whatever they wish. This much I know: I do not deserve to be the recipient of the information I have been given here, and in all of these books. I do not feel worthy to be the messenger of this truth. I am working on this third book, yet I know even before its release that I, of all people, with all the mistakes I have made, all the selfish things I have done, am simply not *worthy* to be the bringer of this wonderful truth.

Yet that, perhaps, is the greatest message of this trilogy: That God stays hidden from no man, but speaks to everyone, even the least worthy among us. For if God will speak to me, God will speak directly into the heart of every man, woman, and child who seeks the truth.

There is thus hope for all of us. None of us is so horrible that God would forsake us, nor so unforgivable that God would turn away.

Is that what you believe—all of that which you have just written?

Yes.

Then so be it, and so shall it be with you.

Yet I tell you this. You *are* worthy. As is everyone else. Unworthiness is the worst indictment ever visited upon the human race. You have based your sense of worthiness on the past, while I base your sense of worthiness on the future.

The future, the future, always the future! That is where your life is, not in the past. The future. That is where your truth is, not in the past.

What you have done is unimportant compared to what you are about to do. How you have erred is insignificant compared to how you are about to create.

I forgive your mistakes. All of them. I forgive your misplaced passions. All of them. I forgive your erroneous notions, your misguided understandings, your hurtful actions, your selfish decisions. All of them.

Others may not forgive you, but I do. Others may not release you from your guilt, but I do. Others may not let you forget, allow you to go on, become something new, but I do. For I know that you are not what you were, but are, and always will be, what you are now.

A sinner can become a saint in one minute. In one second. In one breath.

In truth, there is no such thing as a "sinner," for no one can be sinned against—least of all Me. That is why I say that I "forgive" you. I use the phrase because it is one you seem to understand.

In truth, I do *not* forgive you, and will not forgive you *ever*, for *anything*. I do not have to. There is nothing to forgive. But I can release you. And I hereby do. Now. Once again. As I have done so often in the past, through the teachings of so many other teachers.

Why have we not heard them? Why have we not believed this, Your greatest promise?

Because you cannot believe in the goodness of God. Forget, then, about believing in My goodness. Believe, instead, in simple logic.

The reason I have no need to forgive you is that you cannot offend Me, nor can I be damaged or destroyed. Yet you imagine yourself capable of offending, even damaging, Me. What an illusion! What a magnificent obsession!

You cannot hurt Me, nor can I be harmed in any way. For I am the Unharmable. And that which cannot be harmed cannot, and would not, harm another.

You understand now the logic behind the truth that I do not condemn, nor shall I punish, nor have I a need to seek retribution. I have no such need, for I have not been, and cannot be, offended or damaged or hurt in any way.

The same is true of you. And of all others—though all of you imagine that you can be, and have been, hurt and damaged and destroyed.

Because you imagine damage, you require revenge. Because you experience pain, you need another to experience pain as retribution for your own. Yet what possible justification can that be for inflicting pain upon another? Because (you imagine) someone has inflicted injury upon you, you feel it right and proper to inflict injury in return? That which you say is not okay for human beings to do to each other, is okay for *you* to do, so long as you are justified?

This is insanity. And what you do not see in this insanity is that *all* people who inflict pain on others assume themselves to be justified. Every action a person takes is *understood by that person to be the right action*, given what it is they seek and desire.

By your definition, what they seek and desire is wrong. But by their definition, it is not. You may not agree with their model of the world, with their moral and ethical constructions, with their theological understandings, nor with their decisions, choices, and actions . . . but *they* agree with them, based on their values.

You call their values "wrong." But who is to say your values are "right"? Only you. Your values are "right" because you say they are. Even this might make some sense if you kept your word about it, but you, yourself, change your mind constantly about what you consider "right" and "wrong." You do this as individuals, and you do this as societies.

What your society considered "right" just a few decades ago, you consider "wrong" today. What you considered "wrong" in the not-too-distant past, you now call "right." Who can tell what is what? How do you know the players without a scorecard?

And yet we dare to sit in judgment of one another. We dare to condemn, because some other person has failed to keep up with our own changing ideas about what is permitted and what is not. Whew. We're really something. We can't even keep our own minds made up about what's "okay" and what's not.

That isn't the problem. Changing your ideas of what's "right" and "wrong" isn't the problem. You *have* to change those ideas, or you would never grow. Changing is a product of evolution.

No, the problem is not that you have changed, or that your values have changed. The problem is that so many of you insist on thinking that the values you now have are the right and perfect ones, and that everyone else should adhere to them. Some of you have become self-justified and self-righteous.

Stick to your beliefs, if that serves you. Hold tight. Do not waiver. For your ideas about "right" and "wrong" are your definitions of Who You Are. Yet do not require that others define themselves according to your terms. And do not stay so "stuck" in your present beliefs and customs that you halt the process of evolution itself.

Actually, you could not do that if you wanted to, for life goes on, with you or without you. Nothing stays the same, nor can anything remain unchanged. To be unchanged is to not move. And to not move is to die.

All of life is motion. Even rocks are filled with motion. Everything moves. *Everything.* There is nothing that is not in motion. Therefore, by the very fact of motion, nothing is the same from one moment to the next. Nothing.

Remaining the same, or seeking to, moves against the laws of life. This is foolish, because in this struggle, life will always win.

So change! Yes, change! Change your ideas of "right" and "wrong." Change your notions of this and that. Change your structures, your constructions, your models, your theories.

Allow your deepest truths to be altered. Alter them yourself, for goodness' sake. I mean that quite literally. Alter them yourself, for *goodness' sake*. Because your new idea of Who You Are is where the growth is. Your new idea of What Is So is where evolution accelerates. Your new idea of the Who, What, Where, When, How, and Why of it is where the mystery gets solved, the plot unravels, the story ends. Then you can begin a new story, and a grander one.

Your new idea about *all of it* is where the excitement is, where the creation is, where God-in-you is made manifest and becomes fully realized.

No matter how "good" you think things have been, they can be better. No matter how wonderful you think your theologies, your ideologies, your cosmologies, they can be full of even more wonder. For there are "more things in heaven and earth than are dreamt of in your philosophy."

Be open, therefore. Be OPEN. Don't close off the possibility of new truth because you have been comfortable with an old one. Life begins at the end of your comfort zone.

Yet be not quick to judge another. Rather, seek to avoid judgment, for another person's "wrongs" were your "rights" of yestermorn; another person's mistakes are your own past actions, now corrected; another person's choices and decisions are as "hurtful" and "harmful," as "selfish" and "unforgivable," as many of your own have been.

It is when you "just can't imagine" how another person could "do such a thing" that you have forgotten where you came from, and where both you and the other person are going.

And to those of you who think yourselves to be the evil ones, who think yourselves to be unworthy and irredeemable, I tell you this: There is not a one among you who is lost forever, nor will there ever be. For you are all, *all,* in the process of becoming. You are all, *all,* moving though the experience of evolution.

That is what I am up to.

Through you.

5

I remember a prayer I was taught as a child. "Lord, I am not worthy that Thou shouldst enter under my roof. Yet say but the word, and my soul shall be healed." You have said these words, and I feel healed. I no longer feel unworthy. You have a way of making me feel worthy. If I could give one gift to all human beings, that would be it.

You have given them that gift, with this dialogue.

I would like to keep on giving it when this conversation is over.

This conversation will *never* be over.

Well, when this trilogy, then, is complete.

There will be ways for you to do that.

For that, I am very happy. Because this is the gift my soul yearns to give. All of us have a gift to give. I'd like this to be mine.

Go, then, and give it. Seek to make everyone whose life you touch feel worthy. Give everyone a sense of their own worthiness as a person, a sense of the true wonder of who they are. Give this gift, and you will heal the world.

I humbly ask Your help.

You will always have it. We are friends.

Meanwhile, I am loving this dialogue, and would like to ask a question about something You said before.

I'm here.

When You were talking about life "between lives," so to speak, You said, "You may re-create the experience of your individual Self whenever you choose." What does that mean?

It means you may emerge from The All anytime you wish, as a new "Self," or the same Self you were before.

You mean I can retain, and return to, my individual consciousness, my awareness of "me"?

Yes. You may have, at all times, whatever experience you desire.

And so I can return to this life—to the Earth—as the same person I was before I "died"?

Yes.

In the flesh?

Have you heard of Jesus?

Yes, but I am not Jesus, nor would I ever claim to be like him.

Did he not say, "These things, and more, shall you also do?"

Yes, but he wasn't talking about miracles like that, I don't think.

I am sorry you don't think so. Because Jesus was not the only one to have risen from the dead.

He wasn't? Others have risen from the dead?

Yes.

My god, that's blasphemy.

It's blasphemy that someone other than Christ has risen from the dead?

Well, some people would say that it is.

Then those people have never read the Bible.

The Bible? The *Bible* says that people other than Jesus came back to the body after death?

Ever hear of Lazarus?

Oh, no fair. It was through the Christ power that he was *raised* from the dead.

Precisely. And you think that "Christ power," as you call it, was reserved only for Lazarus? One person, in the history of the world?

I hadn't thought about it that way.

I tell you this: Many have there been who have been risen from the "dead." Many have there been who have "come back to life." It's happening every day, right now, in your hospitals.

Oh, come on. No fair again. That's medical science, not theology.

Oh, I see. God has nothing to do with today's miracles, only yesterday's.

Hmph . . . okay, I'll give You the point on technical grounds. But *no one has raised himself from the dead on their own, like Jesus did!* No one has come back from the "dead" *that* way.

Are you sure?

Well . . . pretty sure . . .

Have you ever heard of Mahavatar Babaji?

I don't think we should bring Eastern mystics into this. A lot of people don't buy that stuff.

I see. Well, of course, they must be right.

Let me get this straight. Are You saying that souls can return from the so-called "dead" in spirit form or in physical form, if that's what they desire?

You're beginning to understand now.

All right, then why haven't more people done it? Why don't we hear about it every day? This kind of thing would make international news.

Actually, a lot of people do do it, in spirit form. Not many, I'll admit, choose to return to the body.

Ha! There! I gotcha! *Why not?* If this is so easy, *why don't more souls do it?*

It's not a question of ease, it's a question of desirability.

Meaning?

Meaning it's a very rare soul who desires to return to physicality in the same form as before.

If a soul chooses to return to the body, it almost always does so with another body; a different one. In this way it begins a new agenda, experiences new rememberings, undertakes new adventures.

Generally, souls leave bodies because they are finished with them. They've completed what they joined with the body to do. They've experienced the experience they were seeking.

What about people who die by accident? Were they finished with their experience, or was it "cut off"?

Do you still imagine people die by accident?

You mean they don't?

Nothing in this universe occurs by accident. There is no such thing as an "accident," nor is there any such thing as "coincidence."

If I could convince myself that was true, I would never mourn again for those who have died.

Mourning for them is the last thing they would want you to do.

If you knew where they were, and that they were there by their own higher choice, you would _celebrate_ their departure. If you experienced what you call the afterlife for one moment, having come to it with your grandest thought about yourself and God, you would smile the biggest smile at their funeral, and let joy fill your heart.

We cry at funerals for our loss. It is our sadness in knowing that we will never see them again, never hold or hug or touch or be with someone we loved.

And that is a good crying. That honors your love, and your beloved. Yet even this mourning would be short if you knew what grand realities and wondrous experiences await the joyous soul leaving the body.

What _is_ it like in the afterlife? Really. Tell me all of it.

There are some things which cannot be revealed, not because I do not choose to, but because in your present condition, at your present level of understanding, you would be unable to conceive of what is being told to you. Still, there is more which can be said.

As we discussed earlier, you may do one of three things in what you call the afterlife, just as in the life you are now experiencing. You may submit to the creations of your uncontrolled thoughts, you may create your experience consciously out of choice, or you may experience the collective consciousness of All That Is. This last experience is called Reunification, or Rejoining the One.

Should you take the first path, most of you will not do so for very long (unlike the way you behave on Earth). This is because in the moment you don't like what you are experiencing, you will choose to create a new and more pleasant reality, which you will do by simply stopping your negative thoughts.

Because of this, you will never experience the "hell" of which you are so afraid, unless you choose to. Even in that case you will be "happy," in that you will be getting what you want. (More people than you know are "happy" being "miserable.") So you will keep experiencing it until you don't choose to any more.

For most of you, the moment you even begin to experience it, you will move away from it and create something new.

You can eliminate the hell in your life on Earth exactly the same way.

Should you take the second path and consciously create your experience, you will no doubt experience going "straight to heaven," because this is what anyone who is freely choosing, and who believes in heaven, would create. If you do not believe in heaven, you will experience whatever you wish to experience—and the moment you understand that, your wishes will get better and better. And then you *will* believe in heaven!

Should you take the third path and submit to the creations of the collective consciousness, you will move very quickly into total acceptance, total peace, total joy, total awareness, and total love, for that is the consciousness of the collective. Then you will become one with the Oneness, and there will be nothing else except That

Which You Are—which is All There Ever Was, until you decide that there should be something else. This is nirvana, the "one with the Oneness" experience that many of you have had very briefly in meditation, and it is an indescribable ecstasy.

After you experience the Oneness for an infinite time-no time, you will cease to experience it, because you cannot experience the Oneness *as* Oneness unless and until That Which Is Not One also exists. Understanding this, you will create, once again, the idea and the thought of separation, or disunity.

Then you will keep traveling on the Cosmic Wheel, keep going, keep circling, keep on being, forever and ever, and even forever more.

You will return to the Oneness many times—an infinite number of times and for an infinite period each time—and you will know that you have the tools to return to the Oneness at any point on the Cosmic Wheel.

You may do so now, even as you are reading this.

You may do so tomorrow, in your meditation.

You may do so at any time.

And You've said that we do not have to stay at the level of consciousness we're at when we die?

No. You may move to another as quickly as you wish. Or take as much "time" as you like. If you "die" in a state of limited perspective and uncontrolled thoughts, you'll experience whatever that state brings you, until you don't want to anymore. Then you'll "wake up"—become conscious—and start experiencing yourself creating your reality.

You'll look back at the first stage and call it purgatory. The second stage, when you can have anything you want with the speed of your thought, you'll call heaven. The third stage, when you experience the bliss of the Oneness, you'll call Nirvana.

I have one more thing I'd like to explore along these lines. It's not about "after death," but it is about experiences outside of the body. Can You explain those to me? What is happening there?

The essence of Who You Are has simply left the physical body. This can happen during normal dreaming, often during meditation, and frequently in a sublime form while the body is in deep sleep.

During such an "excursion," your soul can be anywhere it wishes. Frequently, the person reporting such an experience has no after-memory of having made volitional decisions about this. They may experience it as "just something that happened to me." However, nothing which involves an activity of the soul is nonvolitional.

How can we be "shown" things, how can things be "revealed" to us, during one of these experiences, if all we are doing is creating as we go along? It seems to me that the only way things could be revealed to us would be if those things existed separate from us, not as part of our own creation. I need some help with this.

Nothing exists separate from you, and everything is your own creation. Even your apparent lack of understanding is your own creation; it is, literally, a figment of your imagination. You imagine that you do not know the answer to this question, and so you do not. Yet as soon as you imagine that you do, you do.

You allow yourself to do this sort of imagining so that The Process can go on.

The Process?

Life. The eternal Process.

In those moments during which you experience yourself being "revealed" to yourself—whether these are what you call out-of-body experiences, or dreams, or magic moments of wakefulness when you are greeted by crystal clarity—what has happened is that you have simply slipped into "remembering." You are remembering what you have already created. And these rememberings can be very powerful. They can produce a personal epiphany.

Once you've had such a magnificent experience, it can be very difficult to go back to "real life" in a way that blends well with what other people are calling "reality." That is because *your* reality has shifted. It has become something else. It has expanded, grown. And it cannot be shrunk again. It's like trying to get the genie back in the bottle. It can't be done.

Is that why many people who come back from out-of-body experiences, or so-called "near-death" experiences, sometimes seem very different?

Exactly. And they *are* different, because now they know so much more. Yet, frequently, the further they get from such experiences, the more time that passes, the more they revert to their old behaviors, because they have again forgotten what they know.

Is there any way to "keep remembering"?

Yes. Act out your knowingness in every moment. Keep acting on what you know, rather than what the world of illusion is showing you. Stay with it, no matter how deceiving appearances are.

This is what all masters have done, and do. They judge not by appearances, but act according to what they know.

And there is another way to remember.

Yes?

Cause another to remember. That which you wish for yourself, give to another.

That's what it feels I am doing with these books.

That is exactly what you are doing. And the longer you keep on doing it, the less you will have to do it. The more you send this message to another, the less you will have to send it to your Self.

Because my Self and the other are One, and what I give to another, I give to myself.

You see, now you are giving Me the answers. And that, of course, is how it works.

Wow. I just gave God an answer. That is cool. That is really cool.

You're telling Me.

That's what's *cool*—the fact that *I'm telling You*.

And I will tell *you* this: The day will come when we will speak as One. That day will come for all people.

Well, if that day is going to come for me, I'd like to make sure I understand exactly what it is You're saying. So I'd like to go back to something else, just one more time. I know You said this more than once, but I really want to make sure I really understand it.

Am I clear that, once we reach this state of Oneness which many call Nirvana—once we return to the Source—we don't stay there? The reason I am asking this again is that this seems to run counter to my understanding of many Eastern esoteric and mystical teachings.

To remain in the state of sublime no-thing, or Oneness with the All, would make it impossible to be there. As I've just explained, That Which Is cannot be, except in the space of That Which Is Not. Even the total bliss of Oneness cannot be experienced as "total bliss" unless something less than total bliss exists. So, something less than the total bliss of total Oneness had to be—and continually has to be—created.

But when we are in total bliss, when we have merged once more with the Oneness, when we have become Everything/No-thing, how can we even *know* that we exist? Since there is nothing else that we are experiencing... I don't know. I don't seem to understand this. This is one I can't seem to get a handle on.

You are describing what I call the Divine Dilemma. This is the same dilemma God has always had—and that God solved with the creation of that which was not God (or thought it was not).

God gave—and gives again, in every instant—a part of Itself to the Lesser Experience of not knowing Itself, so that the Rest of Itself can know Itself as Who and What It Really Is.

Thus, "God gave His only begotten son, that you might be saved." You see now from where this mythology has sprung.

I think that we are all God—and that we are constantly, every one of us, journeying from Knowing to Not Knowing to Knowing again, from being to not being to being again, from Oneness to Separation to Oneness again, in a never-ending cycle. That this *is* the cycle of life—what You call the Cosmic Wheel.

Exactly. Precisely. That is well said.

But do we all have to go back to *ground zero?* Do we always have to start over, completely? Go back to the beginning? Return to square one? Do not pass "Go," do not collect $200?

You do not *have* to do anything. Not in this lifetime, not in any other. You will have choice—*always you will have free choice*—to go anywhere you wish to go, do anything you wish to do, in your re-creation of the experience of God. You can move to any place on the Cosmic Wheel. You may "come back" as anything you wish, or in any other dimension, reality, solar system, or civilization you choose. Some of those who have reached the place of total union with the Divine have even chosen to "come back" as enlightened masters. And, yes, some were enlightened masters when they left, and then chose to "come back" as *themselves.*

You must surely be aware of reports of gurus and masters who have returned to your world over and over again, manifesting in repeated appearances throughout the decades and centuries.

You have one entire religion based on such a report. It is called the Church of Jesus Christ of Latter Day Saints, and it is based on the report of Joseph Smith that the Being calling himself Jesus returned to Earth many centuries after his apparently "final" departure, this time appearing in the United States.

So you may return to any point on the Cosmic Wheel to which it pleases you to return.

Still, even that could be depressing. Don't we ever get to *rest?* Don't we ever get to stay in nirvana, to *remain* there? Are we doomed forever to this "coming and going"—this "now you see it, now you don't" treadmill? Are we on an eternal journey to nowhere?

Yes. That's the greatest truth. There is nowhere to go, nothing to do, and no one you have to "be" except exactly who you're being right now.

The truth is that there is no journey. You are right now what you are attempting to be. You are right now where you are attempting to go.

It is the master who knows this, and thus ends the struggle. And then does the master seek to assist you in ending *your* struggle, even as you will seek to end the struggle of others when you reach mastery.

Yet this process—this Cosmic Wheel—is not a depressing treadmill. It is a glorious and continual reaffirmation of the utter magnificence of God, and all life—and there is nothing depressing about that at all.

Still seems depressing to me.

Let Me see if I can change your mind. Do you like sex?

I love it.

Most people do, except those with really weird ideas about it. So, what if I told you that beginning tomorrow you can have sex with every single person for whom you felt attraction and love. Would that make you happy?

Would this have to be against their will?

No. I would arrange it so that every one you wish to celebrate the human experience of love with in this way also wishes to do so with you. They would feel great attraction and love for you.

Wow! Hey—okaaay!

There's just one condition: You have to stop between each one. You can't just go from one to the other without interruption.

You're telling me.

So, in order to experience the ecstasy of this kind of physical union, you have to also experience *not* being united sexually with someone, if only for a while.

I think I see where you're going.

Yes. Even the ecstasy would not be ecstasy were there not a time when there was no ecstasy. This is as true with spiritual ecstasy as it is with physical.

There is nothing depressing about the cycle of life, there is only joy. Simply joy and more joy.

True masters are never less than joyful. This staying at the level of mastery is what you may now find desirable. Then you can move in and out of the ecstasy and still be joyful always. You do not need the ecstasy to be joyful. You are joyful simply knowing that ecstasy is.

6

I'd like to change the subject now, if I could, and talk about Earth changes. But before I do, I'd like to just make an observation. It seems as though there are a lot of things being said here more than once. I sometimes feel like I'm hearing the same things, over and over again.

That's good! Because you are! As I said earlier, this is by design.

This message is like a spring. When it is coiled, it circles back onto itself. One circle covers the other, and it seems to be, literally, "going around in circles." Only when the spring is uncoiled will you see that it stretches out in a spiral, farther than you could have ever imagined.

Yes, you are right. Much of what is being said has been said a number of times, in different ways. Sometimes in the *same* way. The observation is correct.

When you are finished with this message, you should be able to repeat its essential points virtually verbatim. The day may come when you may wish to.

Okay, fair enough. Now, moving *forward*, a bunch of people seem to think I have a "direct line to God," and they want to know, is our planet doomed? I know I asked this before, but now I'd really like a direct answer. Will the Earth changes occur, as so many are predicting? And if not, what are all those psychics seeing? A made-up vision? Should we be praying? Changing? Is there anything we can do? Or is it all, sadly, hopeless?

I will be happy to address those questions, but we will not be "moving forward."

We won't?

No, because the answers have already been given you, in My several previous explanations of time.

You mean the part about "everything that's ever going to happen has already happened."

Yes.

But what IS the "everything that has already happened?" How did it happen? *What* happened?

All of it happened. All of it has already happened. Every possibility exists as fact, as completed events.

How can that be? I still don't understand how that can be.

I am going to put this in terms to which you can better relate. See if this helps. Have you ever watched children use a CD-ROM to play a computerized video game?

Yes.

Have you ever asked yourself how the computer knows how to respond to every move the child makes with the joystick?

Yes, actually, I have wondered that.

It's all on the disc. The computer knows how to respond to every move the child makes because every possible move has already been placed on the disc, *along with its appropriate response.*

That's spooky. Almost surreal.

What, that every ending, and every twist and turn producing that ending, is already programmed on the disc? There's nothing "spooky" about it. It's just technology.

107

And if you think that the technology of video games is something, wait 'til you see the technology of the _universe!_

Think of the Cosmic Wheel as that CD-ROM. All the endings already exist. The universe is just waiting to see which one you choose _this time._ And when the game is over, whether you win, lose, or draw, the universe will say, "Want to play again?"

Your computer disc doesn't care whether you win or not, and you can't "hurt its feelings." It just offers you a chance to play again. All the endings already exist, and which ending you experience depends on the choices you make.

So God is nothing more than a CD-ROM?

I wouldn't put it that way, exactly. But throughout this dialogue I have been trying to use illustrations that embody concepts everyone can hold in their understanding. So I think the CD-ROM illustration is a good one.

In many ways, life _is_ like a CD-ROM. All the possibilities exist and have already occurred. Now you get to select which one you choose to experience.

This relates directly to your question about Earth changes.

What many of the psychics are saying about the Earth changes is true. They have opened a window onto the "future," and they have seen it. The question is, _which_ "future" have they seen? As with the end of the game on the CD-ROM, there is _more than one version._

In one version, the Earth will be in upheaval. In another version, it won't.

Actually, _all_ of the versions have _already happened._ Remember, time—

—I know, I know. "Time does not exist"—

—that's _right._ And so?

108

So everything's happening at once.

Right again. All that has ever happened, is happening now, and ever will happen, exists right now. Just as all the moves in the computer game exist right now on that disc. So if you think it would be interesting for the doomsday predictions of the psychics to come true, focus all your attention on that, and you can draw that to yourself. And if you think you would like to experience a different reality, focus on that, and that is the outcome you can draw to you.

So You won't tell me whether the Earth changes will occur or not, is that it?

I am waiting for you to tell Me. You will decide, by your thoughts, words, and actions.

How about the Year 2000 computer problem? There are those who are saying now that what we are now calling the "Y2K" glitch is going to be the cause of a great upheaval in our social and economic systems. Will it be?

What do you say? What do you choose? Do you think that you have nothing to do with any of this? I tell you, that would be inaccurate.

Won't You tell us how this will all turn out?

I am not here to predict your future, and I will not do that. This much I can tell you. This much *anybody* can tell you. If you are not careful, you will get exactly where you are going. If, therefore, you don't like the way you are headed, *change direction*.

How do I do that? How can I affect such a large outcome? What *should* we do in the face of all these predictions of disaster by persons of psychic or spiritual "authority"?

Go inside. Search your place of inner wisdom. See what this calls on you to do. Then do it.

If that means write your politicians and your industrialists, asking them to take action on environmental abuses that could lead to Earth changes, do it. If that means bringing your community leaders together to work on the Y2K problem, do it. And if that means just walking your path, sending out positive energy every day, and keeping those around you from falling into a panic which *brings on* a problem, do it.

Most important of all, do not be afraid. You cannot "die" in any event, so there is nothing to be afraid of. Be aware of The Process unfolding, and quietly know that everything is going to be okay with you.

Seek to get in touch with the perfection of all things. Know that you will be exactly where you have to be in order to experience exactly what you choose as you go about creating Who You Really Are.

This is the way to peace. In all things, see the perfection.

Finally, don't try to "get out" of anything. What you resist, persists. I told you that in the first book, and it's true.

People who are sad about what they "see" in the future, or what they've been "told" about the future, are failing to "stay in the perfection."

Any other advice?

Celebrate! Celebrate life! Celebrate Self! Celebrate the predictions! Celebrate God!

Celebrate! Play the game.

Bring joy to the moment, whatever the moment seems to bring, because joy is Who You Are, and Who You Will Always Be.

God cannot create anything imperfect. If you think that God can create anything imperfect, then you know nothing of God.

So celebrate. Celebrate the perfection! Smile and celebrate and see only the perfection, and that which others call the imperfection will not touch you in any way which is imperfect for you.

You mean I can avoid the Earth shifting on its axis, or being smashed by a meteor, or being crumpled by earthquakes, or being caught in a confusing and hysterical aftermath of Y2K?

You can definitely avoid being affected negatively by any of that.

That isn't what I asked You.

But it is what I answered. Face the future fearlessly, understanding The Process and seeing the perfection of all of it.

That peace, that serenity, that calmness will lead you away from most of the experiences and outcomes others would have called "negative."

What if You are wrong about all of this? What if You are not "God" at all, but just the overworkings of my fertile imagination?

Ah, back to that question, eh?

Well, what if? So what? Can you think of a better way to live?

All I am saying here is to stay calm, stay peaceful, stay serene, in the face of these dire predictions of planet-wide calamity, and you will have the best outcome possible.

Even if I'm not God, and I'm just "you," making it all up, can you get any better advice?

No, I think not.

So, as usual, it makes no difference whether I'm "God" or not.

With this, as with the information in all three books, just live the wisdom. Or, if you can think of a better way to proceed, *do that*.

Look, even if it really is just Neale Donald Walsch doing the talking in all these books, you could hardly find better advice to follow, on any of the subjects

111

covered. So look at it this way: Either I am God talking, or this Neale fellow is a pretty bright guy.
What's the difference?

The difference is, if I were convinced it was really God saying these things, I'd listen more closely.

Oh, bananas. I've sent you messages a thousand times in a hundred different forms, and you've ignored most of them.

Yeah, I suppose I have.

You suppose?

Okay, I have.

So this time, don't ignore. Who do you suppose brought you to this book? You did. So if you can't listen to God, listen to yourself.

Or my friendly psychic.

Or your friendly psychic.

You're kidding with me now, but this does bring up another subject I wanted to discuss.

I know.

You know?

Of course. You want to discuss psychics.

How did You know?

I'm psychic.

Hey, I'll bet You are. You're the Mother of all psychics. You're the *Chief Honcho*, the *Top Banana*, the *Big Cheese*.

112

You're The Man, The Boss, The Unit, The Chairman of the Board.

My man, you have got . . . it . . . right.

Gimme *five.*

Cool, brother. Right on.

So what I want to know is, what is "psychic power"?

You all have what you call "psychic power." It is, truly, a sixth sense. And you all have a "sixth sense about things."

Psychic power is simply the ability to step out of your limited experience into a broader view. To step back. To feel more than what the limited individual you have imagined yourself to be would feel; to know more than he or she would know. It is the ability to tap into the *larger truth* all around you; to sense a different energy.

How does one develop this ability?

"Develop" is a good word. It's sort of like muscles. You all have them, yet some of you choose to develop them, whereas in others they remain undeveloped, and far less useful.

To develop your psychic "muscle," you must exercise it. Use it. Every day. All the time.

Right now the muscle is there, but it's small. It's weak. It's under-used. So you'll get an intuitive "hit" now and then, but you won't act on it. You'll get a "hunch" about something, but you'll ignore it. You'll have a dream, or an "inspiration," but you'll let it pass, paying it scant attention.

Thank goodness you did pay attention to the "hit" you had about this book, or you wouldn't be reading these words now.

You think you came to these words by accident? By chance?

So the first step in developing psychic "power" is to know you have it, and to use it. Pay attention to every hunch you have, every feeling you feel, every intuitive "hit" you experience. *Pay attention.*

Then, act on what you "know." Don't let your mind talk you out of it. Don't let your fear pull you away from it.

The more that you act on your intuition fearlessly, the more your intuition will serve you. It was always there, only now you're paying attention to it.

But I'm not talking about the always-finding-a-parking-space kind of psychic ability. I'm talking about real psychic power. The kind that sees into the future. The kind that lets you know things about people you'd have no way of knowing otherwise.

That's what I was talking about, too.

How does this psychic power work? Should I listen to people who have it? If a psychic makes a prediction, can I change it, or is my future set in stone? How can some psychics tell things about you the minute you walk into the room? What if—

Wait. That's four different questions there. Let's slow down a bit and try one at a time.

Okay. How does psychic power work?

There are three rules of psychic phenomena that will allow you to understand how psychic power works. Let's go over them.

1. All thought is energy.
2. All things are in motion.
3. All time is now.

Psychics are people who have opened themselves to the experiences these phenomena produce: vibrations. Sometimes formed as pictures in the mind. Sometimes a thought in the form of a word.

The psychic becomes adept at feeling these energies. This may not be easy at first, because these energies are very light, very fleeting, very subtle. Like the slightest breeze on a summer night that you think you felt rustle your hair—but maybe didn't. Like the faintest sound in the farthest distance that you think you heard, but can't be sure. Like the dimmest flicker of an image at the corner of your eye that you swore was there, but, when you look head on, is gone. Vanished. Was it there at all?

That's the question the beginning psychic is always asking. The accomplished psychic never asks, because to ask the question sends the answer away. Asking the question engages the mind, and that's the last thing a psychic wants to do. Intuition does not reside in the mind. To be psychic, you've got to be out of your mind. Because intuition resides in the psyche. In the soul.

Intuition is the ear of the soul.

The soul is the only instrument sensitive enough to "pick up" life's faintest vibrations, to "feel" these energies, to sense these waves in the field, and to interpret them.

You have six senses, not five. They are your sense of smell, taste, touch, sight, hearing, and . . . *knowing.*

So here is how "psychic power" works.

Every time you have a thought, it sends off an energy. It *is* energy. The soul of the psychic picks up that energy. The true psychic will not stop to interpret it, but will probably just blurt out what that energy feels like. That's how a psychic can tell you what you're thinking.

Every feeling you've ever had resides in your soul. Your soul is the sum total of all your feelings. It is the repository. Even though it may have been years since you've stored them there, a psychic who is truly open can "feel" these "feelings" here and now. That's because—all together now—

There's no such thing as time—

That's how a psychic can tell you about your "past."
"Tomorrow" also does not exist. All things are occurring right now. Every occurrence sends off a wave of
energy, prints an indelible picture on the cosmic photo-
graphic plate. The psychic sees, or feels, the picture of
"tomorrow" as if it is happening right now—_which it is._
That is how some psychics tell the "future."

How is this done, physiologically? Perhaps without actually knowing what he's doing, a psychic, through the act
of intense focusing, is sending out an actual submolecular
component of himself. His "thought," if you will, leaves
the body, zings out into space, and goes far enough, fast
enough, to be able to turn around and "see" from a distance the "now" that you have not yet experienced.

Submolecular time travel!

You could say that.

Submolecular time travel!

Ohhhh-_kay._ We've decided to turn this into a
vaudeville show.

No, no, I'll be good. I promise . . . really. Go on. I really do
want to hear this.

Okay. The submolecular part of the psychic, having
absorbed the energy of the image gained from focusing,
zings back to the psychic's body, bringing the energy
with it. The psychic "gets a picture"—sometimes with a
shiver—or "feels a feeling," and tries very hard not to do
any "processing" of the data, but simply—and instantly—describes it. The psychic has learned not to
question what he's "thinking" or suddenly "seeing" or
"feeling," but merely to allow it to "come through" as
untouched as possible.

Weeks later, if the event pictured or "felt" actually occurs, the psychic is called a clairvoyant—which, of course, is true!

If that's the case, how come some "predictions" are "wrong"; that is, they never "happen"?

Because the psychic has not "predicted the future," merely offered a glimpse of one of the "possible possibilities" observed in the Eternal Moment of Now. It is always the subject of the psychic reading who has made the choice. He could just as easily make another choice—a choice not in concert with the prediction.

The Eternal Moment contains all "possible possibilities." As I have explained now several times, everything has already happened, in a million different ways. All that's left is for you to make some perception choices.

It is all a question of perception. When you change your perception, you change your thought, and your thought creates your reality. Whatever outcome you could anticipate in any situation is already there for you. All you have to do is perceive it. Know it.

This is what is meant by "even before you ask, I will have answered." In truth, your prayers are "answered" before the prayer is offered.

Then how come we don't all get what we pray for?

This was covered in *Book 1*. You don't always get what you ask, but you always get what you create. Creation follows thought, which follows perception.

This is mind-boggling. Even though we've been over this before, this is still mind-boggling.

Isn't it, though? That's why it's good to keep going over it. Hearing it several times gives you a chance to wrap your mind around it. Then your mind gets "unboggled."

If everything is all happening now, what dictates which *part* of it all I'm experiencing in *my* moment of "now"?

Your choices—and your belief in your choices. That belief will be created by your thoughts on a particular subject, and those thoughts arise out of your perceptions—that is, "the way you look at it."

So the psychic sees the choice you are now making about "tomorrow," and sees that played out. But a true psychic will always tell you it doesn't have to be that way. You can "choose again," and change the outcome.

In effect, I'd be changing the experience I've already had!

Exactly! Now you're getting it. Now you're understanding how to live in the paradox.

But if it's "already happened," to whom has it "happened"? And if I change it, who is the "me" that experiences the change?

There is more than one of "you" moving down the time-line. This was all described in detail in *Book 2*. I'm going to suggest that you re-read that. Then combine what's there with what's here, for a richer understanding.

Okay. Fair enough. But I'd like to talk about this psychic stuff a while longer. A lot of people claim to be psychic. How can I tell the real from the fake?

Everyone *is* "psychic," so they're *all* "real." What you want to look for is their purpose. Are they seeking to help you, or to enrich themselves?

Psychics—so called "professional psychics"—who are seeking to enrich themselves often promise to do things with their psychic power—"return a lost lover," "bring wealth and fame," even help you lose weight!

They promise they can do all this—but only for a fee. They'll even do a "reading" on another—your boss,

118

your lover, a friend—and tell you all about them. They'll say, "Bring me something. A scarf, a picture, a sample of their handwriting."

And they *can* tell you about the other. Often, quite a bit. Because everyone leaves a trace, a "psychic fingerprint," an energy trail. And a true sensitive can feel this.

But a sincere intuitive will never offer to cause another to come back to you, get a person to change his mind, or *create any result whatsoever with her psychic "power."* A true psychic—one who has given her life to the development and use of this gift—knows that another's free will is never to be tampered with, and that another's thoughts are never to be invaded, and that another's psychic space is never to be violated.

I thought You said there is no "right" and "wrong." What are all these "nevers" all of a sudden?

Every time I lay down an "always" or a "never," it is within the context of what I know you are seeking to accomplish; what it is you are trying to do.

I know that you are all seeking to evolve, to grow spiritually, to return to the Oneness. You are seeking to experience yourself as the grandest version of the greatest vision you ever had about Who You Are. You are seeking this individually, and as a race.

Now there are no "rights" and "wrongs," no "do's" and "don'ts" in My world—as I have said many times—and you do not burn in the everlasting fires of hell if you make a "bad" choice, because neither "bad" nor "hell" exists—unless, of course, you think that it does.

Still there are natural laws that have been built into the physical universe—and one of those is the law of cause and effect.

One of the most important laws of cause and effect is this:

All caused effect is ultimately experienced by the Self.

119

What does that mean?

Whatever you cause another to experience, you will one day experience.

Members of your New Age community have a more colorful way of putting it.

"What goes around, comes around."

Right. Others know this as the Jesus Injunction: *Do unto others as you would have it done unto you.*

Jesus was teaching the law of cause and effect. It is what might be called the Prime Law. Somewhat like the Prime Directive given to Kirk, Picard, and Janeway.

Hey, God is a *Trekkie!*

Are you kidding? I wrote half the episodes.

Better not let Gene hear You say that.

Come on...Gene *told* Me to say that.

You're in touch with Gene Roddenberry?

And Carl Sagan, and Bob Heinlein, and the *whole gang* up here.

You know, we shouldn't kid around like this. It takes away from the believability of the whole dialogue.

I see. A conversation with God has to be serious.

Well, at least believable.

It's not believable that I've got Gene, Carl, and Bob right here? I'll have to tell them that. Well, back to how you can tell a true psychic from a "fake" one. A true psychic knows and lives the Prime Directive. That's why, if you ask her to bring back a "long-lost love," or read the aura of another person whose handkerchief or letter you have, a true psychic will tell you:

"I'm sorry, but I won't do that. I will never interfere with, intervene in, or look in on, the path walked by another.

"I will not attempt to affect, direct, or impact their choices in any way.

"And I will not divulge to you information about any individual that is personal or private."

If a person offers to perform one of these "services" for you, that person is what you would call a shyster, using your own human weaknesses and vulnerabilities to extract money from you.

But what about psychics who help people locate a missing loved one—a child who was abducted, a teenager who ran away and has too much pride to call home, even though they desperately want to? Or how about the classic case of locating a person—dead or alive—for the police?

Of course, these questions all answer themselves. What the true psychic always avoids is imposing his will upon another. She is there only to serve.

Is it okay to ask a psychic to contact the dead? Should we attempt to reach out to those who have "gone before"?

Why would you want to?

To see if they have something they want to say to us; to tell us.

If somebody from "the other side" has something they want you to know, they'll find a way to cause you to know it, don't worry.

The aunt, the uncle, the brother, the sister, the father, the mother, the spouse, and lover who have "gone before" are continuing their own journey, experiencing complete joy, moving toward total understanding.

If part of what they want to do is to come back to you—to see how you are, to bring you an awareness that they're all right, whatever—trust that they'll do that.

Then, watch for the "sign" and catch it. Don't dismiss it as just your imagination, "wishful thinking," or coincidence. Watch for the message, and receive it.

I know of a lady who was nursing her dying husband, and she begged him: If he had to go, please come back to her and let her know that he was all right. He promised he would, and died two days later. Not a week went by when the lady was awakened one night by the feeling that someone had just sat down on the bed beside her. When she opened her eyes, she could have sworn she saw her husband, sitting at the foot of the bed, smiling at her. But when she blinked and looked again, he was gone. She told me the story later, saying then that she must have been hallucinating.

Yes, that's very common. You receive signs—irrefutable, obvious signs—and you ignore them. Or dismiss them as your own mind playing tricks on you.

You have the same choice now, with this book.

Why do we do that? Why do we ask for something—like the wisdom contained in these three books—then refuse to believe it when we receive it?

Because you doubt the greater glory of God. Like Thomas, you have to see, feel, touch, before you will believe. Yet that which you wish to know cannot be seen, felt, or touched. It is of another realm. And you are not open to that; you are not ready. Yet do not fret. When the student is ready, the teacher will appear.

So are You saying, then—to get back to the original line of questioning—that we should _not_ go to a psychic or a séance seeking to contact those on the other side?

I'm not saying that you should or shouldn't do anything. I'm just not sure what the point would be.

Well, supposing you had something *you* wanted to say to the other, rather than something you wanted to hear from *them?*

Do you imagine that you could say it and they not hear it? The slightest thought having to do with a being existing on what you call "the other side" brings that being's consciousness flying to you.

You cannot have a thought or an idea about a person who is what you call "deceased" without that person's Essence becoming completely aware of it. It is not necessary to use a medium to produce such communication. *Love is the best "medium" of communication.*

Ah, but how about *two-way* communication? Would a medium be helpful there? Or is such communication even possible? Is it all hogwash? Is it dangerous?

You are talking now about communication with spirits. Yes, such communication is possible. It is dangerous? Virtually everything is "dangerous" if you are afraid. What you fear, you create. Yet there is really nothing to be afraid of.

Loved ones are never far from you, never more than a thought away, and will always be there if you need them, ready with counsel or comfort or advice. If there is a high level of stress on your part about a loved one being "okay," they will send you a sign, a signal, a little "message" that will allow you to know everything's fine.

You won't even have to call on them, because souls who loved you in this life are drawn to you, pulled to you, fly to you, the moment they sense the slightest trouble or disturbance in your auric field.

One of their first opportunities, as they learn about the possibilities of their new existence, is to provide aid and comfort to those they love. And you will feel their comforting presence if you are really open to them.

So the stories we hear of people "who could have sworn" that a deceased loved one was in the room could be true.

Most assuredly. One might smell the loved one's perfume or cologne, or get a whiff of the cigar they smoked, or faintly hear a song they used to hum. Or, out of nowhere, some personal possession of theirs may suddenly appear. A handkerchief, or a wallet, or some cufflink or piece of jewelry just "shows up" for "no reason." It's "found" in a chair cushion, or under a stack of old magazines. There it is. A picture, a photograph, of a special moment—just when you were missing that person and thinking about them and feeling sad about their death. These things don't "just happen." These kinds of things don't "just appear" at "just the right moment" by chance. I tell you this: *There are no coincidences in the universe.*

This is very common. Very common.

Now, back to your question: Do you need a so-called "medium" or "channel" to communicate with beings out of the body? No. Is it sometimes helpful? Sometimes. So much depends, again, on the psychic or medium—and on their motivation.

If someone refuses to work in this way with you—or to do any kind of "channeling" or "go-between" work—without high compensation; run, don't walk, the other way. That person may be in it only for the money. Don't be surprised if you get "hooked" into returning time and time again for weeks or months, or even years, as they play on your need or desire for contact with the "spirit world."

A person who is only there—as the spirit is there—to help, asks nothing for himself except what is needed to continue to do the work they seek to do.

If a psychic or medium is coming from that place when she agrees to help you, make sure you offer all the help in return that you can. Don't take advantage of such extraordinary generosity of the spirit by giving little, or not at all, when you know you could do more.

Look to see who is truly serving the world, truly seeking to share wisdom and knowledge, insight and understanding, caring and compassion. Provide for those people, and provide grandly. Pay them the highest honor. Give them the largest amount. For these are the Bringers of the Light.

7

We've covered a lot here. Boy, we've really covered a lot. Can we make another shift? Are You ready to go on?

Are you?

Yes, I'm rolling now. I've finally gotten on a roll. And I want to ask every question I've been waiting three years to ask.

I'm okay with that. Go.

Coolness. So I would like now to talk about another of the esoteric mysteries. Will You speak to me about reincarnation?

Sure.

Many religions say that reincarnation is a false doctrine; that we get only one life here; one chance.

I know. That is not accurate.

How can they be so wrong about something so important? How can they not know the truth about something so basic?

You must understand that humans have many fear-based religions whose teachings surround a doctrine of a God who is to be worshipped and feared.

It was through fear that your entire Earth society reformed itself from the matriarchy into the patriarchy. It was through fear that the early priests got people to "mend their wicked ways" and "heed the word of the Lord." It was through fear that churches gained, and controlled, their membership.

One church even insisted that God would punish you if you did not go to church every Sunday. Not going to church was declared a sin.

And not just any church. One had to attend one particular church. If you went to a church of a different denomination, that, too, was a sin. This was an attempt at control, pure and simple, using fear. The amazing thing is, it worked. Hell, it still works.

Say, You're God. Don't swear.

Who was swearing? I was making a statement of fact. I said, "Hell—it *still works.*"

People will always believe in hell, and in a God who would send them there, as long as they believe that God is like man—ruthless, self-serving, unforgiving, and vengeful.

In days past, most people could not imagine a God who might rise above all of that. So they accepted the teaching of many churches to "fear the terrible vengeance of the Lord."

It was as if people couldn't trust themselves to be good, to act appropriately, on their own, for their own built-in reasons. So they had to create a religion that taught the doctrine of an angry, retributive God in order to keep themselves in line.

Now the idea of reincarnation threw a monkey wrench into all of that.

How so? What made that doctrine so threatening?

The church was proclaiming that you'd better be nice, or *else*—and along came the reincarnationists, saying: "You'll have another chance after this, and another chance after that. And still more chances. So don't worry. Do the best you can. Don't become so paralyzed with fear that you can't budge. Promise yourself to do better, and get on with it."

Naturally, the early church couldn't hear of such a thing. So it did two things. First, it denounced the doctrine of reincarnation as heretical. Then it created the sacrament of confession. Confession could do for the churchgoer what reincarnation promised. That is, *give him another chance.*

So then we had a setup where God would punish you for your sins, unless you *confessed them.* In that case you could feel safe, knowing that God had heard your confession and forgiven you.

Yes. But there was a catch. This absolution *could not come directly from God.* It had to flow through the church, whose priests pronounced "penances" which had to be performed. These were usually prayers which were required of the sinner. So now you had two reasons to keep up your membership.

The church found confession to be such a good drawing card that soon it declared it to be a sin *not to go to confession.* Everybody had to do it at least once a year. If they didn't, God would have *another* reason to be angry.

More and more rules—many of them arbitrary and capricious—began to be promulgated by the church, each rule having the power of God's eternal condemnation behind it, unless, of course, failure was *confessed.* Then the person was forgiven by God, and condemnation avoided.

But now there was another problem. People figured out that this must mean they could do anything, as long as they confessed it. The church was in a quandary. Fear had left the hearts of the people. Church attendance and membership dropped. People came to "confess" once a year, said their penances, were absolved of their sins, and went on with their lives.

There was no question about it. A way had to be found to strike fear into the heart again.

So purgatory was invented.

Purgatory?

Purgatory. This was described as a place something like hell, but not eternal. This new doctrine declared that God would make you suffer for your sins *even if you confessed them.*

Under the doctrine, a certain amount of suffering was decreed by God for each nonperfect soul, based on the number and type of sins committed. There were "mortal" sins and "venial" sins. Mortal sins would send you right to hell if not confessed before death.

Once more, church attendance shot up. Collections were up, too, and especially contributions—for the doctrine of purgatory also included a way one could *buy one's way out of the suffering.*

I'm sorry—?

According to the church's teaching, one could receive a special indulgence—but again, not directly from God—only from an official of the church. These special indulgences freed one from the suffering in purgatory which they had "earned" with their sins—or at least part of it.

Something like "time off for good behavior?"

Yes. But, of course, these reprieves were granted to very few. Generally, those who made a conspicuous contribution to the church.

For a really huge sum, one could obtain a *plenary* indulgence. This meant *no time in purgatory at all.* It was a nonstop ticket straight to heaven.

This special favor from God was available for even fewer. Royalty, perhaps. And the super rich. The amount of money, jewels, and land given to the church in exchange for these plenary indulgences was enormous. But the exclusivity of all this brought great frustration and resentment to the masses—no pun intended.

The poorest peasant hadn't a hope of gaining a bishop's indulgence—and so the rank and file lost faith in the system, with attendance threatening to drop once again.

Now what did they do?

They brought in the novena candles.

People could come to the church and light a novena candle for the "poor souls in purgatory," and by saying a novena (a series of prayers in a particular order that took some time to complete), they could knock years off the "sentence" of the dearly departed, extricating them from purgatory sooner than God would otherwise have allowed.

They couldn't do anything for themselves, but at least they could pray for mercy for the departed. Of course, it would be helpful if a coin or two were dropped through the slot for each candle lit.

A lot of little candles were flickering behind a lot of red glass, and a lot of pesos and pennies were being dropped into a lot of tin boxes, in an attempt to get Me to "ease up" on the suffering being inflicted on the souls in purgatory.

Whew! This is *unbelievable.* And You mean people could not see right through all that? People did not see it as the desperate attempt of a desperate church to keep its members desperate to do anything to protect themselves from this *desperado* they called God? You mean people actually bought this stuff?

Quite literally.

No wonder the church declared reincarnation to be an untruth.

Yes. Yet when I created you, I did not create you so that you could live one lifetime—an infinitesimal period, really, given the age of the universe—make the mistakes you were inevitably going to make, then hope for the best at the end. I've tried to imagine setting it up that way, but I can never figure out what My purpose would be.

You could never figure it out either. That's why you've had to keep saying things like, "The Lord works in mysterious ways, His wonders to perform." But I don't work in mysterious ways. Everything I do has a reason, and it's perfectly clear. I've explained why I created you, and the purpose of your life, many times now during this trilogy.

Reincarnation fits perfectly into that purpose, which is for Me to create and experience Who I Am through you, lifetime after lifetime, and through the millions of other creatures of consciousness I have placed in the universe.

Then there IS life on other—

Of course there is. Do you really believe that you are alone in this gigantic universe? But that's another topic we can get to later . . . .

. . . Promise?

Promise.

So, your purpose as a soul is to experience yourself as All Of It. We are evolving. We are . . . becoming.

Becoming what? We do not know! We cannot know until We get there! But for Us, the journey is the joy. And as soon as We "get there," as soon as We create the next highest idea of Who We Are, We'll create a grander thought, a higher idea, and *continue the joy forever.*

Are you with Me here?

Yes. By this time I almost *could* repeat this verbatim.

Good.

So . . . the point and purpose of your life is to decide and to be Who You Really Are. You're doing that every day. With every action, with every thought, with every word. That's what you're doing.

Now, to the degree that you're pleased with that—pleased with Who You Are in your experience—to that degree you'll stick, more or less, with the creation, making only minor adjustments here and there to get it closer and closer to perfect.

Paramahansa Yogananda is an example of a person who was very close to "perfect" as an out-picturing of what he thought of himself. He had a very clear idea about himself, and about his relationship to Me, and he used his life to "out-picture" that. He wanted to experience his idea about himself in his own reality; to know himself as that, experientially.

Babe Ruth did the same thing. He had a very clear idea about himself, and his relationship to Me, and he used his life to out-picture that; to know himself in his own experience.

Not many people live that level. Now granted, the Master and the Babe had two entirely different ideas about themselves, yet they both played them out magnificently.

They also both had different ideas about Me, that's for sure, and were coming from different levels of consciousness about Who I Am, and about their true relationship to Me. And those levels of consciousness were reflected in their thoughts, words, and actions.

One was in a place of peace and serenity most of his life, and brought deep peace and serenity to others. The other was in a place of anxiousness, turmoil, and occasional anger (particularly when he couldn't get his way), and brought turmoil to the lives of those around him.

Both were good-hearted, however—there was never a softer touch than the Babe—and the difference between the two is that one had virtually nothing in terms of physical acquisitions, but never wanted more

132

than what he got, while the other "had everything," and never got what he really wanted.

If that were the end of it for George Herman, I suppose we could all feel a little sad about that, but the soul that embodied itself as Babe Ruth is far from finished with this process called evolution. It has had an opportunity to review the experiences it produced for itself, as well as the experiences it produced for others, and now gets to decide what next it would like to experience as it seeks to create and re-create itself in grander and grander versions.

We'll drop our narrative regarding these two souls here, because both have already made their next choice regarding what they want to now experience—and, in fact, both are now experiencing that.

You mean both have already reincarnated into other bodies?

It would be a mistake to assume that reincarnating—returning to another physical body—was the only option open to them.

What *are* the other options?

In truth, whatever they want them to be.

I've already explained here what occurs after what you call your death.

Some souls feel that there is a lot more they would like to know, and so they find themselves going to a "school," whereas other souls—what you call "old souls"—teach them. And what do they teach them? *That they have nothing to learn.* That they *never* had anything to learn. That all they ever had to do was remember. Remember Who and What They Really Are.

They are "taught" that the experience of Who They Are is gained in the acting out of it; in *being it.* They are reminded of this by having it gently shown to them.

Other souls have already remembered this by the time they get to—or soon after they get to—the "other side." (I'm using language now with which you are familiar, speaking in your vernacular, to keep, as much as possible, the words out of the way.) These souls may then seek the immediate joy of experiencing themselves as whatever they wish to "be." They may select from the million, kajillion aspects of Me, and choose to experience that, right then and there. Some may opt to return to physical form to do that.

Any physical form?

Any.

Then it's *true* that souls could return as animals—that God could be a cow? And that cows really are sacred? Holy cow!

(Ahem.)

Sorry.

You've had a whole lifetime to do stand-up comedy. And, by the way, looking at your life, you've done a pretty good job of it.

Cha-*boom*. That was a rim shot. If I had a cymbal here, I'd give you a cymbal crash.

Thank you, thank you.
But seriously, folks...
The answer to the question you are basically asking—can a soul return as an animal—is yes, of course. The real question is, would it? The answer is, probably not.

Do animals have souls?

Anyone who has ever stared into the eyes of an animal already knows the answer to that.

Then how do I know it is _not_ my grandmother, come back as my cat?

The Process we are discussing here is evolution. Self-creation and evolution. And evolution proceeds one way. Upward. Ever upward.

The soul's greatest desire is to experience higher and higher aspects of itself. And so it seeks to move upward, not downward, on the evolutionary scale, until it experiences what has been called nirvana—total Oneness with the All. That is, with Me.

But if the soul desires higher and higher experiences of itself, why would it even bother returning as a human being? Surely that can't be a step "upward."

If the soul returns to human form, it is always in an effort to further experience, and thus, further evolve. There are many levels of evolution observable and demonstrated in humans. One could come back for many lifetimes—many hundreds of lifetimes—and continue to evolve upward. Yet upward movement, the grandest desire of the soul, is not achieved with return to a lower life form. Thus, such a return does not occur. Not until the soul reaches ultimate reunion with All That Is.

That must mean there are "new souls" coming into the system every day, taking lower life forms.

No. Every soul that was ever created was created At Once. We are all here Now. But, as I have explained before, when a soul (a part of Me) reaches ultimate realization, it has the option to "start over," to literally "forget everything," so that it can remember all over again, and re-create itself anew once more. In this way, God continues to re-experience Itself.

Souls may also choose to "recycle" through a particular life form at a particular level as often as they like.

Without reincarnation—without the ability to return to a physical form—the soul would have to accomplish everything it seeks to accomplish within one lifetime, which is one billion times shorter than the blink of an eye on the cosmic clock.

So, yes, of course, reincarnation is a fact. It's real, it's purposeful, and it's perfect.

Okay, but there's one thing I'm confused about. You said there is nothing such as time; that all things are happening right now. Is that correct?

It is.

And then You implied—and in *Book 2* You went into depth on this—that we exist "all the time" on different levels, or at various points, in the Space-Time Continuum.

That's true.

Okay, but now here's where it gets crazy. If one of the "me's" on the Space-Time Continuum "dies," then *comes back* here as *another person* . . . then . . . then, who am I? I would have to be existing as *two people at once*. And if I kept on doing this through all eternity, which You say I do, then I am being a *hundred* people at once! A thousand. A *million*. A million versions of a million people at a million points on the Space-Time Continuum.

Yes.

I don't understand that. My mind can't grasp that.

Actually, you've done well. It's a very advanced concept, and you've done pretty well with it.

But . . . but . . . if that's true, then "I"—the part of "me" that is immortal—must be evolving in a billion different ways in a billion different forms at a billion different points on the Cosmic Wheel in the eternal moment of now.

Right again. That's exactly what I'm doing.

No, no. I said that's what *I* must be doing.

Right again. That's what I just said.

No, no, I said—

I know what you said. You said just what I said you said. The confusion here is that you still think there's more than one of Us here.

There's not?

There was never more than one of Us here. Ever. Are you just finding that out?

You mean I've just been talking to *myself* here?

Something like that.

You mean You're *not God?*

That's not what I said.

You mean You *are* God?

That's what I said.

But if You're God, and You're me, and I'm You—then . . . then . . . *I'm* God!

Thou art God, yes. That is correct. You grok it in fullness.

But I'm not only God—I'm also everyone *else.*

Yes.

But—does that mean that no one, and nothing else, exists but me?

Have I not said, I and My Father are One?

Yes, but . . .

And have I not said, We are all One?

Yes. But I didn't know You meant that *literally*. I thought You meant that figuratively. I thought it was more of a philosophical statement, not a statement of *fact*.

It's a statement of fact. We are all One. That is what is meant by "whatsoever ye do unto the least of these . . . ye do unto me." Do you understand now?

Yes.

Ah, at last. At long last.

But—You'll forgive me for arguing this, but . . . when I'm with another—my spouse for instance, or my children—it feels that I am *separate* from them; that they are *other* than "me."

Consciousness is a marvelous thing. It can be divided into a thousand pieces. A million. A million times a million.
I have divided Myself into an infinite number of "pieces"—so that each "piece" of Me could look back on Itself and behold the wonder of Who and What I Am.

But why do I have to go through this period of forgetfulness; of disbelief? I'm *still* not totally believing! I'm *still* hanging out in forgetfulness.

Don't be so hard on your Self. That's part of The Process. It's okay that it's happening this way.

Then why are You telling me all this now?

Because you were starting not to have fun. Life was beginning not to be a joy anymore. You were starting to get so caught up in The Process that you forgot it *was* just a process.

And so, you called out to Me. You asked Me to come to you; to help you understand; to show you the divine truth; to reveal to you the greatest secret. The secret you've kept from yourself. The secret of Who You Are.

Now I have done so. Now, once again, you have been caused to remember. Will it matter? Will it change how you act tomorrow? Will it cause you to see things differently tonight?

Will you now heal the hurts of the wounded, quell the anxieties of the fearful, meet the needs of the impoverished, celebrate the magnificence of the accomplished, and see the vision of Me everywhere?

Will this latest remembrance of truth change your life, and allow you to change the lives of others?

Or will you return to forgetfulness; fall back into selfishness; revisit, and reside again in, the smallness of who you imagined yourself to be before this awakening?

Which will it be?

8

Life really does go on forever and ever, doesn't it?

It most certainly does.

There is no end to it.

No end.

Reincarnation *is* a fact.

It is. You may return to mortal form—that is, a physical form which can "die"—whenever and however you wish.

Do we decide when we want to come back?

"If" and "when"—yes.

Do we also decide when we want to leave? Do we choose when we want to die?

No experience is visited upon any soul against the soul's will. That is, by definition, not possible, since the soul is creating every experience.

The soul wants nothing. The soul has everything. All wisdom, all knowing, all power, all glory. The soul is the part of You which never sleeps; never forgets.

Does the soul desire that the body dies? No. It is the soul's desire that you never die. Yet the soul will leave the body—change its bodily form, leaving most of the material body behind—at the drop of a hat when it sees no purpose in remaining in that form.

If it is the soul's desire that we never die, why *do* we?

You do not. You merely change form.

If it is the soul's desire that we never do *that*, why *do* we?

That is not the soul's desire!
You are a "shape-shifter"!
When there is no further usefulness in staying in a particular form, the soul changes form—willfully, voluntarily, joyfully—and moves on, on the Cosmic Wheel.

Joyfully?

With great joy.

No soul dies regretfully?

No soul dies—ever.

I mean, no soul has regrets that the current physical form is changing; is about to "die"?

The body never "dies," but merely changes form with the soul. Yet I understand your meaning, so for now I use the vocabulary you have established.
If you have a clear understanding of what you wish to create with regard to what you have chosen to call the afterlife, or if you have a clear set of beliefs that support an after-death experience of reuniting with God, then, no, the soul never, ever has regrets over what you call death.
Death in that instance is a glorious moment; a wonderful experience. Now the soul can return to its natural form; its normal state. There is an incredible lightness; a sense of total freedom; a limitlessness. And an awareness of Oneness that is at once blissful and sublime.
It is not possible for the soul to regret such a shift.

You're saying, then, that death is a *happy* experience?

For the soul that wishes it to be, yes, always.

Well, if the soul wants out of the body so bad, why doesn't it just leave it? Why is it hanging around?

I did not say the soul "wants out of the body," I said the soul is joyful when it is out. Those are two different things.

You can be happy doing one thing, and happy then doing another. The fact that you are joyful doing the second does not mean you were unhappy doing the first.

The soul is not unhappy being with the body. Quite to the contrary, the soul is pleased to be you in your present form. That does not preclude the possibility that the soul might be equally pleased to be disconnected from it.

There is obviously much about death I do not understand.

Yes, and that is because you do not like to think about it. Yet you must contemplate death and loss the instant you perceive any moment of life, or you will not have perceived life at all, but know only the half of it.

Each moment ends the instant it begins. If you do not see this, you will not see what is exquisite in it, and you will call the moment ordinary.

Each interaction "begins to end" the instant it "begins to begin." Only when this is truly contemplated and deeply understood does the full treasure of every moment—and of life itself—open to you.

Life cannot give itself to you if you do not understand death. You must do more than understand it. *You must love it, even as you love life.*

Your time with each person would be glorified if you thought it was your *last* time with that person. Your experience of each moment would be enhanced beyond

142

measure if you thought it was the last such moment. Your refusal to contemplate your own death leads to your refusal to contemplate your own life.

You do not see it for what it is. You miss the *moment*, and all it holds for you. You look right past it instead of right through it.

When you look deeply at something, you see right through it. To contemplate a thing deeply is to see right through it. Then the illusion ceases to exist. Then you see a thing for what it really is. Only then can you truly enjoy it—that is, *place joy into it*. (To "en-joy" is to render something joyful.)

Even the illusion you can then enjoy. For you will *know* it is an illusion, and that is half the enjoyment! It is the fact that you think it is real that causes you all the pain.

Nothing is painful which you understand is not real. Let Me repeat that.

Nothing is painful which you understand is not real.

It is like a movie, a drama, played out on the stage of your mind. You are creating the situation and the characters. You are writing the lines.

Nothing is painful the moment you understand that nothing is real.

This is as true of death as it is of life.

When you understand that death, too, is an illusion, then you *can* say, "O death, where is thy sting?"

You can even *enjoy* death! You can even enjoy someone *else's* death.

Does that seem strange? Does that seem a strange thing to say?

Only if you do not understand death—and life.

Death is never an end, but always a beginning. A death is a door opening, not a door closing.

When you understand that life is eternal, you understand that death is your illusion, keeping you very concerned with, and therefore helping you believe that you *are*, your body. Yet you are *not* your body, and so the destruction of your body is of no concern to you.

Death should teach you that what is real is life. And life teaches you that what is unavoidable is not death, but impermanence.

Impermanence is the only truth.

Nothing is permanent. All is changing. In every instant. In every moment.

Were anything permanent, it could not *be*. For even the very concept of permanence depends upon impermanence to have any meaning. Therefore, *even permanence is impermanent*. Look at this deeply. Contemplate this truth. Comprehend it, and you comprehend God.

This is the Dharma, and this is the Buddha. This is the Buddha Dharma. This is the teaching and the teacher. This is the lesson and the master. This is the object and the observer, rolled into one.

They never have been *other* than One. It is you who have unrolled them, so that your life may unroll before you.

Yet as you watch your own life roll out before you, do not yourself become unraveled. Keep your Self together! See the illusion! Enjoy it! But do not *become* it!

You are *not* the illusion, but the *creator of it*.

You are in this world, but not of it.

So use your illusion of death. *Use* it! Allow it to be the key that opens you to more of life.

See the flower as dying and you will see the flower sadly. Yet see the flower as part of a whole tree that is changing, and will soon bear fruit, and you see the flower's true beauty. When you understand that the blossoming and the falling away of the flower is a sign that the tree is ready to bear fruit, then you understand life.

Look at this carefully and you will see that life is its own metaphor.

Always remember, you are not the flower, nor are you even the fruit. You are the tree. And your roots are deep, embedded in Me. I am the soil from which you have sprung, and both your blossoms and your fruit will

144

return to Me, creating more rich soil. Thus, life begets life, and cannot know death, ever.

That is so beautiful. That is so, so beautiful. Thank You. Will You speak to me now of something that is troubling me ? I need to talk about suicide. Why is there such a taboo against the ending of one's life?

Indeed, why is there?

You mean it's not wrong to kill yourself?

The question cannot be answered to your satisfaction, because the question itself contains two false concepts; it is based on two false assumptions; it contains two errors.

The first false assumption is that there is such a thing as "right" and "wrong." The second false assumption is that killing is possible. Your question itself, therefore, disintegrates the moment it is dissected.

"Right" and "wrong" are philosophical polarities in a human value system which have nothing to do with ultimate reality—a point which I have made repeatedly throughout this dialogue. They are, furthermore, not even constant constructs within your own system, but rather, values which keep shifting from time to time.

You are doing the shifting, changing your mind about these values as it suits you (which rightly you should, as evolving beings), yet insisting at each step along the way that you haven't done this, and that it is your *unchanging* values which form the core of your society's integrity. You have thus built your society on a paradox. You keep changing your values, all the while proclaiming that it is unchanging values which you . . . well, *value!*

The answer to the problems presented by this paradox is not to throw cold water on the sand in an attempt to make it concrete, but to celebrate the shifting of the sand. Celebrate its beauty while it holds itself in the shape of your castle, but then also celebrate the new form and shape it takes as the tide comes in.

Celebrate the shifting sands as they form the new mountains you would climb, and atop which—and with which—you will build your new castles. Yet understand that these mountains and these castles are monuments to _change_, not to permanence.

Glorify what you are today, yet do not condemn what you were yesterday, nor preclude what you could become tomorrow.

Understand that "right" and "wrong" are figments of your imagination, and that "okay" and "not okay" are merely announcements of your latest preferences and imaginings.

For example, on the question of ending one's life, it is the current imagining of the majority of people on your planet that it is "not okay" to do that.

Similarly, many of you still insist that it is not okay to assist another who wishes to end his or her life.

In both cases you say this should be "against the law." You have come to this conclusion, presumably, because the ending of the life occurs relatively quickly. Actions which end a life over a somewhat longer period of time are not against the law, even though they achieve the same result.

Thus, if a person in your society kills himself with a gun, his family members lose insurance benefits. If he does so with cigarettes, they do not.

If a doctor assists you in your suicide, it is called manslaughter, while if a tobacco company does, it is called commerce.

With you, it seems to be merely a question of time. The legality of self-destruction—the "rightness" or "wrongness" of it—seems to have much to do with _how quickly_ the deed is done, as well as who is doing it. The faster the death, the more "wrong" it seems to be. The slower the death, the more it slips into "okayness."

Interestingly, this is the exact opposite of what a truly humane society would conclude. By any reasonable definition of what you would call "humane," the shorter the death, the better. Yet your society punishes those who would seek to do the humane thing, and rewards those who would do the insane.

It is insane to think that endless suffering is what God requires, and that a quick, humane end to the suffering is "wrong."

"Punish the humane, reward the insane."

This is a motto which only a society of beings with limited understanding could embrace.

So you poison your system by inhaling carcinogens, you poison your system by eating food treated with chemicals that over the long run kill you, and you poison your system by breathing air which you have continually polluted. You poison your system in a hundred different ways over a thousand different moments, and you do this *knowing these substances are no good for you*. But because it takes a longer time for them to kill you, *you commit suicide with impunity*.

If you poison yourself with something that works faster, you are said to have done something against moral law.

Now I tell you this: *It is no more immoral to kill yourself quickly than it is to kill yourself slowly.*

So a person who ends his own life is not punished by God?

I do not punish. I love.

What of the often-heard statement that those who think they are going to "escape" their predicament, or end their condition, with suicide only find that they are facing the same predicament or condition in the afterlife, and therefore escaped and ended nothing?

Your experience in what you call the afterlife is a reflection of your consciousness at the time you enter it. Yet you are always a being of free will, and may alter your experience whenever you choose.

147

So loved ones who have ended their physical life are okay?

Yes. They are very okay.

There is a wonderful book on this subject called _Stephen Lives,_ by Anne Puryear. It is about her son, who ended his life when he was a teenager. So many people have found it helpful.

Anne Puryear is a wonderful messenger. As is her son.

So You can recommend this book?

It is an important book. It says more on this subject than we are saying here, and those who have deep hurts or lingering issues surrounding the experience of a loved one ending their life will be opened to healing through this book.

It is sad that we even have such deep hurts or issues, but much of that, I think, is a result of what our society has "laid on us" about suicide.

In your society, you often do not see the contradictions of your own moral constructions. The contradiction between doing things that you know full well are going to shorten your life, but doing them slowly, and doing things that will shorten your life quickly is one of the most glaring in the human experience.

Yet it seems so obvious when You spell them out like this. Why can't we see such obvious truths on our own?

Because if you saw these truths, you would have to _do something about them._ This you do not wish to do. So you have no choice but to look right at something and not see it.

But why would we not want to do something about these truths if we saw them?

Because you believe that in order to do something about them, you would have to end your pleasures. And ending pleasures is something you have no desire to do.

Most of the things which cause your slow deaths are things which bring you pleasure, or result from those things. And most of the things which bring you pleasure are things which satisfy the body. Indeed, this is what marks yours as a primitive society. *Your lives are structured largely around seeking and experiencing pleasures of the body.*

Of course, all beings everywhere seek to experience pleasures. There is nothing primitive in that. In fact, it is the natural order of things. What differentiates societies, and beings within societies, is what they *define as pleasurable*. If a society is structured largely around pleasures of the *body*, it is operating at a different level from a society structured around pleasures of the soul.

And understand, too, that this does not mean that your Puritans were right, and that all pleasures of the body should be denied. It means that in elevated societies, pleasures of the physical body do not make up the largest number of pleasures which are enjoyed. They are not the prime focus.

The more elevated a society or being, the more elevated are its pleasures.

Wait a minute! That sounds like such a value judgment. I thought You—God—didn't make value judgments.

Is it a value judgment to say that Mt. Everest is higher than Mt. McKinley?

Is it a value judgment to say that Aunt Sarah is older than her nephew Tommy?

Are these value judgments or observations?

I have not said it is "better" to be elevated in one's consciousness. In fact, it is not. Any more than it is "better" to be in fourth grade than in first.

149

I am simply observing what fourth grade is.

And we are not in fourth grade in this planet. We are in first. Is that it?

My child, you are not yet even in kindergarten. You are in nursery school.

How can I not hear that as an insult? Why does it sound to me as if You're putting the human race down?

Because you are deeply ego invested in being something you are not—and in not being what you are.

Most people hear insults when only an observation has been made, if what is being observed is something they don't want to own.

Yet until you hold a thing, you cannot let it go. And you cannot disown that which you have never owned.

You cannot change that which you do not accept.

Precisely.

Enlightenment begins with acceptance, without judgment of "what is."

This is known as moving into the Isness. It is in the Isness where freedom will be found.

What you resist, persists. What you look at disappears. That is, it ceases to have its illusory form. You see it for what it Is. And what Is can always be changed. It is only what Is Not that cannot be changed. Therefore, to change the Isness, move into it. Do not resist it. Do not deny it.

What you deny you declare. What you declare you create.

Denial of something is re-creation of it, for the very act of denying something places it there.

Acceptance of something places you in control of it. That which you deny you cannot control, for you have said it is not there. Therefore what you deny controls you.

The majority of your race does not want to accept that you have not yet evolved to kindergarten. It does not want to accept that the human race is still in nursery school. Yet this lack of acceptance is exactly what keeps it there.

You are so deeply ego invested in being what you are not (highly evolved) that you are not being what you are (evolving). You are thus working against yourself, fighting yourself. And hence, evolving very slowly.

The fast track of evolution begins with admitting and accepting what is, not what is not.

And I will know I have accepted "what is" when I no longer feel insulted as I hear it described.

Exactly. Are you insulted if I say you have blue eyes?

So now I tell you this: The more elevated a society or being, the more elevated are its pleasures.

What you call "pleasure" is what declares your level of evolution.

Help me with this term "elevated." What do You mean by that?

Your being is the universe in microcosm. You, and your whole physical body, are composed of raw energy, clustered around seven centers, or chakras. Study the chakra centers and what they mean. There are hundreds of books written about this. This is wisdom I have given the human race before.

What is pleasurable, or stimulates, your lower chakras is not the same as what is pleasurable to your higher chakras.

The higher you raise the energy of life through your physical being, the more elevated will be your consciousness.

Well, here we go again. That seems to argue for celibacy. That seems to be the whole argument against expression of sexual passion. People who are "elevated" in their consciousness don't "come from" their root chakra—their first, or lowest, chakra—in their interactions with other humans.

That is true.

But I thought You've said throughout this dialogue that human sexuality was to be *celebrated,* not repressed.

That is correct.

Well, help me out here, because we seem to have a contradiction.

The world is full of contradictions, My son. Lack of contradictions is not a necessary ingredient in truth. Sometimes greater truth lies *within* the contradiction. What we have here is Divine Dichotomy.

Then help me understand the dichotomy. Because all my life I've heard about how desirable it was, how "elevated" it was, to "raise the kundalini energy" out of the root chakra. This has been the chief justification for mystics living lives of sexless ecstasy.

I realize we've gotten way off the subject of death here; and I apologize for dragging us into this unrelated territory—

What are you apologizing for? A conversation goes where a conversation goes. The "topic" we are on in this whole dialogue is what it means to be fully human, and what life is about in this universe. That is the only topic, and this falls within that.

Wanting to know about death is wanting to know about life—a point I made earlier. And if our exchanges lead to an expansion of our inquiry to include the very act which creates life, and celebrates it magnificently, so be it.

Now let's get clear again about one thing. It is not a requirement of the "highly evolved" that all sexual expression be muted, and all sexual energy be elevated. If that were true, then there would be no "highly evolved" beings anywhere, because all evolution would have stopped.

A rather obvious point.

Yes. And so anyone who says that the very holiest people never have sex, and that this is a sign of their holiness, does not understand how life was meant to work.

Let Me put this in very clear terms. If you want a yardstick with which to judge whether a thing is good for the human race or not, ask yourself a simple question:

What would happen if everyone did it?

This is a very easy measure, and a very accurate one. If everyone did a thing, and the result was of ultimate benefit to the human race, then that is "evolved." If everyone did it and it brought disaster to the human race, then that is not a very "elevated" thing to recommend. Do you agree?

Of course.

Then you've just agreed that no real master will ever say that sexual celibacy is the path to mastery. Yet it is this idea that sexual abstinence is somehow the "higher way," and that sexual expression is a "lower desire," that has shamed the sexual experience, and caused all manner of guilt and dysfunction to develop around it.

Yet if the reasoning against sexual abstinence is that it would prohibit procreation, couldn't it be argued that once sex has served this function, there is no more need for it?

One does not engage in sex because one realizes one's responsibility to the human race to procreate. One engages in sex because it is *the natural thing to do*. It is built into the genes. You obey a biological imperative.

Precisely! It is a *genetic signal* that drives to the question of species survival. But once the survival of the species is assured, isn't it the "elevated" thing to do to "ignore the signal"?

You misinterpret the signal. The biological imperative is not to guarantee the survival of the species, but to *experience the Oneness* which is the true nature of your being. Creating new life is what happens when Oneness is achieved, but it is not the reason Oneness is sought.

If procreation were the only reason for sexual expression—if it were nothing more than a "delivery system"—you would no longer need to engage in it with one another. You can unite the chemical elements of life in a petri dish.

Yet this would not satisfy the most basic urges of the soul, which it turns out, are much larger than mere procreation, but have to do with re-creation of Who and What You Really Are.

The biological imperative is not to *create* more life, but to *experience* more life—and to experience that life as it really is: *a manifestation of Oneness.*

That is why You will never stop people from having sex, even though they have long ago stopped having children.

Of course.

Yet some say that sex *should* stop when people stop having children, and that those couples who continue with this activity are just caving in to base physical urges.

Yes.

And that this is not "elevated," but merely animalistic behavior, beneath the more noble nature of man.

This gets us back to the subject of chakras, or energy centers.

154

I said earlier that "the higher you raise the energy of life through your physical being, the more elevated will be your consciousness."

Yes! And that seems to say "no sex."

No, it does not. Not when you understand it.

Let Me go back to your previous comment and make something clear: There is nothing ignoble, or unholy, about having sex. You have got to get that idea out of your mind, and out of your culture.

There is nothing base, or gross, or "less than dignified" (much less *sanctified*), about a passionate, desire-filled sexual experience. Physical urges are not manifestations of "animalistic behavior." Those physical urges were *built into the system—by Me.*

Who do you suppose created it that way?

Yet physical urges are but *one ingredient* in a complex mixture of responses that you all have to each other. Remember, you are a three-part being, with seven chakra centers. When you respond to one another from all three parts, and all seven centers, at the same time, then you have the peak experience you are looking for—that you have been created for!

And there is nothing unholy about any of these energies—yet if you choose just one of them, that is "unwhole-y." *It is not being whole!*

When you are not being whole, you are being less than yourself. *That* is what is meant by "unholy."

Wow! I get it. I *get* it!

The admonition against sex for those who choose to be "elevated" was never an admonition from Me. It was an invitation. An invitation is not an admonition, yet you have made it so.

And the invitation was not to stop having sex, but to stop being *un-whole*.

155

Whatever you are doing—having sex or having breakfast, going to work or walking the beach, jumping rope or reading a good book—*whatever* you are doing, do it as a whole being; as the whole being *you are.*

If you are having sex from only your lower chakra center, you are operating from the root chakra alone, and missing by far the most glorious part of the experience. Yet if you are being loving with another person and coming from all *seven* energy centers while you are being that, now you are having a peak experience. How can this not be holy?

It can't. I'm unable to imagine such an experience not being holy.

And so the invitation to raise the life energy through your physical being to the top chakra was never meant to be a suggestion or a demand that you *disconnect from the bottom.*

If you have raised the energy to your heart chakra, or even to your crown chakra, that doesn't mean it cannot be in your root chakra as well.

Indeed, if it is not, you are disconnected.

When you have raised the life energy to your higher centers, you may or may not choose to have what you would call a sexual experience with another. But if you do not, it will not be because to do so would be to violate some cosmic law on holiness. Nor will it make you somehow more "elevated." And if you do choose to be sexual with another, it will not "lower" you to a root-chakra-only level—unless you do the opposite of disconnecting at the bottom, and *disconnect from the top.*

So here is the invitation—not an admonition, but an invitation:

Raise your energy, your life force, to the highest level possible in every moment, and you will be elevated. This has nothing to do with having sex or not having sex. It has to do with raising your consciousness no matter *what* you are doing.

I get it! I understand. Although I don't know *how* to raise my consciousness. I don't think I know *how* to raise the life energy through my chakra centers. And I'm not sure most people even know what these centers are.

Anyone who earnestly wishes to know more about the "physiology of spirituality" can find out easily enough. I have sourced this information before, in very clear terms.

You mean in other books, through other writers.

Yes. Read the writings of Deepak Chopra. He is one of the clearest enunciators right now on your planet. He understands the mystery of spirituality, and the *science* of it.

And there are other wonderful messengers as well. Their books describe not only how to raise your life force up through your body, but also how to *leave* your physical body.

You can remember through these additional readings how joyous it is letting the body go. Then you will understand how it could be that you might never again fear death. You will understand the dichotomy: how it is a joy to be with the body, and a joy to be free of it.

157

9

Life must be kind of like school. I can remember being excited every fall about the first day of school—and, at the end of the year, thrilled to be getting out.

Precisely! Exactly! You've hit it. That's it exactly. Only life is not a school.

Yes, I remember. You explained all that in *Book 1*. Until then, I thought that life *was* a "school," and that we had come here to "learn our lessons." You helped me tremendously in *Book 1* to see that this was a false doctrine.

I'm glad. That's what we're trying to do here with this trilogy—bring you to clarity. And now you're clear about why and how the soul can be overjoyed after "death" without necessarily *ever* regretting "life."

But you asked a larger question before, and we should revisit it.

I'm sorry?

You said, "If the soul is so unhappy in the body, why doesn't it just leave?"

Oh, yes.

Well, it *does*. And I don't mean only at "death," as I've just explained. But it does not leave because it is unhappy. Rather, it leaves because it wishes to regenerate, rejuvenate.

Does it do this often?

Every day.

The soul leaves the body *every day?* When?

When the soul yearns for its larger experience. It finds this experience rejuvenating.

It just *leaves?*

Yes. The soul leaves your body all the time. Continually. Throughout your life. This is why We invented sleep.

The soul leaves the body during sleep?

Of course. That is *what sleep is.*

Periodically throughout your life the soul seeks rejuvenation, refueling, if you will, so that it can continue lumbering along in this carrier you call your body.

You think it is easy for your soul to inhabit your body? It is not! It may be *simple*, but it is not *easy!* It is a joy, but it is not *easy*. It is the most difficult thing your soul has ever done!

The soul, which knows a lightness and a freedom which you can't imagine, yearns for that state of being again, just as a child who loves school can yearn for summer vacation. Just as an adult who yearns for company can also, while having company, yearn to be alone. The soul seeks a true state of being. The soul is lightness and freedom. It is also peace and joy. It is also limitlessness and painlessness; perfect wisdom and perfect love.

It is all these things, and more. Yet it experiences precious few of these things while it is with the body. And so it made an arrangement with itself. It told itself it would stay with the body as long as it needs to in order to create and experience itself as it now chooses—but only if it could *leave* the body whenever it wished!

It does this daily, through the experience you call sleep.

"Sleep" is the experience of the soul leaving the body?

Yes.

I thought we fell asleep because the body needed rest.

You are mistaken. It is the other way around. The *soul* seeks the rest, and so, *causes* the body to "fall asleep."

The soul literally drops the body (sometimes right where it is standing) when it is tired of the limits, tired of the heaviness and lack of freedom of being with the body.

It will just leave the body when it seeks "refueling"; when it becomes weary of all the nontruth and false reality and imagined dangers, and when it seeks, once again, reconnection, reassurance, restfulness, and re-awakening for the mind.

When the soul first embraces a body, it finds the experience extremely difficult. It is very tiring, particularly for a newly arriving soul. That is why babies sleep a lot.

When the soul gets over the initial shock of being attached to a body once more, it begins to increase its tolerance for that. It stays with it more.

At the same time, the part of you called your mind moves into forgetfulness—just as it was designed to do. Even the soul's flights out of the body, taken now on a less-frequent, but still usually daily, basis do not always bring the mind back to remembrance.

Indeed, during these times the soul may be free, but the mind may be confused. Thus, the whole being may ask: "Where am I? What am I creating here?" These searchings may lead to fitful journeys; even frightening ones. You call these trips "nightmares."

Sometimes just the opposite will occur. The soul will arrive at a place of great remembering. Now the mind will have an awakening. This will fill it with peace and joy—which you will experience in your body when you return to it.

The more your whole being experiences the reassurance of these rejuvenations—and the more it remembers what it is doing, and trying to do, with the body—the less your soul will choose to stay away from the body, for now it knows that *it came to the body for a reason, and with a purpose.* Its desire is to get on with that, and to make best use of all the time with the body that it has.

The person of great wisdom needs little sleep.

Are You saying you can tell how evolved a person is by how much sleep that person needs?

Almost, yes. You could almost say that. Sometimes a soul chooses to leave the body just for the sheer joy of it, though. It may not be seeking reawakening for the mind or rejuvenation for the body. It may simply be choosing to re-create the sheer ecstasy of knowing the Oneness. So it would not always be valid to say that the more sleep a person gets, the less evolved that person is.

Still, it is not a coincidence that as beings become more and more aware of what they are doing with their bodies—and that they are *not* their bodies, but that which is *with* their bodies—they become willing and able to spend more and more time with their bodies, and thus *appear to "need less sleep."*

Now some beings even choose to experience both the forgetfulness of being with the body, and the oneness of the soul, at once. These beings can train a *part* of themselves to not identify with the body while they are still with the body, thus experiencing the ecstasy of knowing Who They Really Are, without having to lose human wakefulness in order to do it.

How do they do this? How can I do this?

It is a question of awareness, of reaching a state of total awareness, as I said before. You cannot *do* totally aware, you can only *be* totally aware.

161

How? *How?* There must be *some* tools You can give me.

Daily meditation is one of the best tools with which to create this experience. With it, you can raise your life energy to the highest chakra . . . and even *leave your body while you are "awake."*

In meditation you place yourself in a state of readiness to experience total awareness while your body is in a wakened state. This state of readiness is called *true wakefulness.* You do not have to be sitting in meditation to experience this. Meditation is simply a device, a "tool," as you put it. But you do not *have* to do sitting meditation in order to experience this.

You should also know that sitting meditation is not the only kind of meditation there is. There is also stopping meditation. Walking meditation. Doing meditation. Sexual meditation.

This is the state of *true wakefulness.*

When you stop in this state, simply stop in your tracks, stop going where you are going, stop doing what you are doing, just *stop* for a moment, and just "be" right where you are, you become *right*, exactly where you *are*. Stopping, even just for a moment, can be blessed. You look around, slowly, and you notice things you did not notice while you were passing them by. The deep smell of the earth just after it rains. That curl of hair over the left ear of your beloved. How truly good it feels to see a child at play.

You don't have to leave your body to experience this. This is the state of true wakefulness.

When you walk in this state, you breathe in every flower, you fly with every bird, you feel every crunch beneath your feet. You find beauty and wisdom. For wisdom is found wherever beauty is formed. And beauty is formed everywhere, out of all the stuff of life. You do not have to seek it. It will come to you.

And you don't have to leave your body to experience this. This is the state of true wakefulness.

When you "do" in this state, you turn whatever you

are doing into a meditation, and thus, into a gift, an offering, from you to your soul, and from your soul to The All. Washing dishes, you enjoy the warmth of the water caressing your hands, and marvel at the wonder of both water, and warmth. Working at your computer, you see the words appear on the screen in front of you in response to the command of your fingers, and exhilarate over the power of the mind and body, when it is harnessed to do your bidding. Preparing dinner, you feel the love of the universe which brought you this nourishment, and as your return gift, pour into the making of this meal all the love of your being. It does not matter how extravagant or how simple the meal is. Soup can be loved into deliciousness.

You don't have to leave your body to experience this. This is the state of true wakefulness.

When you experience sexual energy exchange in this state, you know the highest truth of Who You Are. The heart of your lover becomes your home. The body of your lover becomes your own. Your soul no longer imagines itself separate from anything.

You don't have to leave your body to experience this. This is the state of true wakefulness.

When you are in readiness, you are in wakefulness. A smile can take you there. A simple smile. Just stop everything for one moment, and smile. At nothing. Just because it feels good. Just because your heart knows a secret. And because your soul knows what the secret is. Smile at that. Smile a lot. It will cure whatever ails you.

You are asking me for tools, and I am giving them to you.

Breathe. That is another tool. Breathe long and deep. Breathe slowly and gently. Breathe in the soft, sweet nothingness of life, so full of energy, so full of love. It is God's love you are breathing. Breathe deeply, and you can feel it. Breathe very, very deeply, and the love will make you cry.

For joy.

For you have met your God, and your God has introduced you to your soul.

163

Once this experience has taken place, life is never the same. People talk of having "been to the mountain top," or having slipped into sublime ecstasy. Their be-ingness is changed forever.

Thank You. I understand. It is the simple things. The simple acts, and the purest.

Yes. But know this. Some people meditate for years and never experience this. It has to do with how open one is, how willing. And also, how able to move away from any expectation.

Should I meditate every day?

As in all things, there are no "shoulds" or "shouldn'ts" here. It is not a question of what you should do, but what you choose to do.

Some souls seek to walk in awareness. Some recognize that in this life most people are sleepwalking; unconscious. They are going through life without consciousness. Yet souls who walk in awareness choose a different path. They choose another way.

They seek to experience all the peace and joy, limitlessness and freedom, wisdom and love that Oneness brings, not just when they have dropped the body and it has "fallen" (asleep), but when they have risen the body up.

It is said of a soul which creates such an experience, "His is risen."

Others, in the so-called "New Age," term this a process of "consciousness raising."

It doesn't matter what terms you use (words are the least reliable form of communication), it all comes down to living in awareness. And then, it becomes total awareness.

And what is it of which you eventually become totally aware? You eventually become totally aware of Who You Are.

Daily meditation is one way you may achieve this. Yet it requires commitment, dedication—a decision to seek inner experience, not outer reward.

And remember, the silences hold the secrets. And so the sweetest sound is the sound of silence. This is the song of the soul.

If you believe the noises of the world rather than the silences of your soul, you will be lost.

So daily meditation *is* a good idea.

A good idea? Yes. Yet know again what I have just said here. The song of the soul may be sung many ways. The sweet sound of silence may be heard many times.

Some hear the silence in prayer. Some sing the song in their work. Some seek the secrets in quiet contemplation, others in less contemplative surroundings.

When mastery is reached—or even intermittently experienced—the noises of the world can be muffled, the distractions quieted, even in the midst of them. All of life becomes a meditation.

All of life *is* a meditation, in which you are contemplating the Divine. This is called true wakefulness, or mindfulness.

Experienced in this way, everything in life is blessed. There is struggle and pain and worry no more. There is only experience, which you may choose to label in any way you wish. You may choose to label all of it perfection.

So use your *life* as a meditation, and all the events in it. Walk in wakefulness, not as one asleep. Move with mindfulness, not mindlessly, and do not tarry in doubt and fear, neither in guilt nor self-recrimination, yet reside in permanent splendor in the assurance that you are grandly loved. You are always One with Me. You are forever welcome. Welcome home.

For your home is in My heart, and Mine in yours. I invite you to see this in life as you will surely see it in death. Then you will know that there is no death, and that what you have called life and death are both part of the same unending experience.

We are all that is, all that ever was, and all that ever will be, world without end.

Amen.

10

I love You, do You know that?

Yes. And I love you. Do *you* know *that?*

I'm starting to. I'm really starting to.

Good.

11

Will You tell me some things about the soul, please?

Sure. I will try to explain, within your limited realm of understanding. But do not allow yourself to become frustrated if certain things don't "make sense" to you. Try to remember that you're bringing this information through a unique filter—a filter which has been designed by you to shield you from too much remembering.

Remind me again why I did that.

The game would be over if you remembered everything. You came here for a particular reason, and your Divine Purpose would be thwarted if you understood how everything is put together. Some things will always remain a mystery at this level of consciousness, and it is right that they should.

So do not try to solve all the mysteries. Not at one time, anyway. Give the universe a chance. It will unfold itself in due course.

Enjoy the experience of becoming.

Make haste slowly.

Exactly.

My father used to say that.

Your father was a wise and wonderful man.

Not many people would describe him that way.

Not many people knew him.

My mother did.

Yes, she did.

And she loved him.

Yes, she did.

And she forgave him.

Yes, she did.

For all of his behaviors that were hurtful.

Yes. She understood, and loved, and forgave, and in this she was, and is, a wonderful model, a blessed teacher.

Yes. So . . . will You tell me about the soul?

I will. What do you want to know?

Let's start with the first, and obvious, question: I already know the answer, but it gives us a starting point. Is there such a thing as the human soul?

Yes. It is the third aspect of your being. You are a three-part being, made up of body, mind, and spirit.

I know where my body is; I can see that. And I think I know where my mind is—it's in the part of my body called my head. But I'm not sure I have any idea where—

Wait a minute. Hold it. You're wrong about something. Your mind is not in your head.

It's not?

169

No. Your *brain* is in your skull. Your mind is not.

Where is it, then?

In every cell of your body.

Whoa . . .

What you call the mind is really an energy. It is . . . thought. And thought is an energy, not an object.

Your brain is an object. It is a physical, biochemical mechanism—the largest, most sophisticated, but not the only—mechanism in the human body, with which the body translates, or converts, the energy which is your thought into physical impulses. Your brain is a transformer. So is your whole body. You have little transformers in every cell. Biochemists have often remarked at how individual cells—blood cells, for instance—seem to have their own intelligence. They do, in fact.

That goes not just for cells, but for larger parts of the body. Every man on the planet knows about a particular body part that often seems to have a mind of its own . . .

Yes, and every woman knows how absurd men become when that is the body part they allow to influence their choices and decisions.

Some women use that knowledge to control men.

Undeniable. And some men control women through choices and decisions made from that place.

Undeniable.

Want to know how to stop the circus?

Absolutely!

This is what was meant earlier by all that talk about raising the energy of life to include all seven chakra centers.

When your choices and decisions come from a place larger than the limited locale you have described, it is impossible for women to control you, and you would never seek to control them.

The only reason that women would ever resort to such means of manipulation and control is that there seems to be no other means of control—at least none nearly as effective—and without some means of control, men often become—well—uncontrollable.

Yet if men would demonstrate more of their higher nature, and if women would appeal more to that part of men, the so-called "battle of the sexes" would be over. As would most other battles of any kind on your planet.

As I have said earlier, this does not mean men and women should give up sex, or that sex is part of a human being's lower nature. It means that sexual energy alone, when not raised to higher chakras and combined with the other energies that make one a whole person, produces choices and outcomes that do not *reflect* the whole person. These are often less than magnificent.

The Whole of You is magnificence itself, yet anything less than the Whole of You is less than magnificent. So if you want to guarantee that you'll produce a less-than-magnificent choice or outcome, make a decision from your root chakra center only. Then watch the results.

They are as predictable as can be.

Hmmm. I think I knew that.

Of course, you did. The largest question facing the human race is not when will you learn, but when will you *act on what you've already learned?*

So the mind is in every cell . . .

171

Yes. And there are more cells in your brain than anywhere else, so it seems as though your mind is there. Yet that is just the main processing center, not the only one.

Good. I'm clear. So where is the soul?

Where do you think it is?

Behind the Third Eye?

No.

In the middle of my chest, to the right of my heart, just beneath the breastbone?

No.

Okay, I give up.

It is everywhere.

Everywhere?

Everywhere.

Like the mind.

Whoops. Wait a minute. The mind is not everywhere.

It's not? I thought You just said it was in every cell of the body.

That is not "everywhere." There are spaces between the cells. In fact, your body is 99 percent space.

This is where the soul is?

The soul is *everywhere* in, through, and around you. It is that which *contains* you.

172

Wait a minute! Now *You* wait a minute! I was always taught that the body is the container of my soul. Whatever happened to "Your body is the temple of your being"?

A figure of speech.

It is useful in helping people to understand that they are more than their bodies; that there is something larger that they are. There is. Literally. The soul is *larger than the body*. It is not carried within the body, but carries the body within *it*.

I'm hearing You, but still having a hard time picturing this.

Have you ever heard of an "aura"?

Yes. *Yes*. Is *this* the soul?

It is as close as we can come in your language, in your understanding, to giving you a picture of an enormous and complex reality. The soul is that which holds you together—just as *the Soul of God is that which contains the universe, and holds it together.*

Wow. This is a complete reversal of everything I've ever thought.

Hang on, My son. The reversals have just begun.

But if the soul is, in a sense, the "air in and around us," and if everyone else's soul is the same, where does one soul *end*, and another begin?

Uh-oh, don't tell me, don't tell me . . .

You see? You already know the answer!

There *is* no place where another soul "ends" and ours "begins"! Just like there is no place where the air in the living room "stops" and the air in the dining room "starts." It's all *the same air*. It's all *the same soul!*

173

You've just discovered the secret of the universe.

And if *You* are that which contains the *universe*, just as we are that which contains our bodies, then there is no place where *You* "end" and *we* "begin"!

(Ahem)

You can clear Your throat all You want. For me this is a miraculous revelation! I mean, I knew I always understood this—but now I *understand* it!

That's great. Isn't that great?

You see, my problem with understanding in the past had to do with the fact that the body is a discreet container, making it possible to differentiate between "this" body and "that" body, and since I always thought the soul was housed in the body, I therefore differentiated between "this" soul and "that" soul.

Quite naturally, yes.

But if the soul is everywhere inside *and outside* the body—in its "aura," as You put it—then when does one aura "end" and another "begin"? And now I'm able to see, for the first time, really, in *physical terms,* how it is possible that one soul does *not* "end" and another "begin," and that it is *physically true* that We Are All One!

Yippee! That's all I can say. Yippee.

I always thought this was a *meta*physical truth. Now I see that it's a *physical* truth! Holy smoke, religion has just become science!

Don't say I didn't tell you so.

But hold on here. If there is no place where one soul ends and another begins, does that mean there is no such thing as an individual soul?

Well, yes and no.

An answer truly befitting God.

Thank you.

But, frankly, I was hoping for more clarity.

Give Me a break here. We're moving so fast, your hand is hurting from writing.

You mean, furiously scribbling.

Yes. So let's just catch our breath here. Everybody relax. I'm going to explain it all to you.

Okay. Go ahead. I'm ready.

You remember how I've talked to you many times now about what I've called Divine Dichotomy?

Yes.

Well, this is one of them. In fact, it's the biggest one.

I see.

It's important to learn about Divine Dichotomy and understand it thoroughly if you are to live in our universe with grace.

Divine Dichotomy holds that it is possible for two apparently contradictory truths to exist simultaneously in the same space.

Now on your planet people find this difficult to accept. They like to have order, and anything that does not fit into their picture is automatically rejected. For this reason, when two realities begin to assert themselves and they seem to contradict one another, the immediate assumption is that one of them must be wrong,

175

false, untrue. It takes a great deal of maturity to see, and accept, that, in fact, they might both be true.

Yet in the realm of the absolute—as opposed to the realm of the relative, in which you live—it is very clear that the one truth which is All There Is sometimes produces an effect which, viewed in relative terms, looks like a contradiction.

This is called a Divine Dichotomy, and it is a very real part of the human experience. And as I've said, it's virtually impossible to live gracefully without accepting this. One is always grumbling, angry, thrashing about, vainly seeking "justice," or earnestly trying to reconcile opposing forces which were never meant to be reconciled, but which, *by the very nature of the tension between them,* produce exactly the desired effect.

The realm of the relative is, in fact, held together by just such tensions. As an example, the tension between good and evil. In ultimate reality there is no such thing as good and evil. In the realm of the absolute, all there is is love. Yet in the realm of the relative you have created the experience of what you "call" evil, and you have done it for a very sound reason. You wanted to *experience* love, not just "know" that love is All There Is, and you cannot experience something when there is nothing else *but* that. And so, you created in your reality (and continue to do so every day) a polarity of good and evil, thus using one so that you might experience the other.

And here we have a Divine Dichotomy—two seemingly contradictory truths existing simultaneously in the same place. Specifically:

There is such a thing as good and evil.

All there is is love.

Thank You for explaining this to me. You've touched on this before, but thank You for helping me understand Divine Dichotomy even better.

You're welcome.

176

Now, as I said, the greatest Divine Dichotomy is the one we are looking at now.

There is only One Being, and hence, only One Soul. *And,* there are many souls in the One Being.

Here's how the dichotomy works: You've just had it explained to you that there is no separation between souls. The soul is the energy of life that exists within and around (as the *aura* of) all physical objects. In a sense, it is that which is "holding" all physical objects in place. The "Soul of God" holds in the universe, the "soul of man" holds in each individual human body.

The body is not a container, a "housing," for the soul; the soul is a container for the body.

That's right.

Yet there is no "dividing line" between souls—there is no place where "one soul" ends and "another" begins. And so, it is really one soul holding all bodies.

Correct.

Yet the one soul "feels like" a bunch of individual souls.

Indeed it does—indeed I do—by design.

Can You explain how it works?

Yes.

While there is no actual separation between souls, it is true that the stuff of which the One Soul is made manifests in physical reality at different speeds, producing different degrees of density.

Different speeds? When did speed come in?

All of life is a vibration. That which you call life (you could just as easily call it God) is pure energy. That energy is vibrating constantly, always. It is moving in *waves*. The waves vibrate at different speeds, producing differing degrees of density, or light. This, in turn, produces what you would call different "effects" in the physical world—actually, different physical objects. Yet while the objects are different and discreet, the energy which produces them is exactly the same.

Let Me go back to the example that you used of the air between your living room and dining room. It was a good use of imagery that just popped right out of you. An inspiration.

From guess where.

Yes, I gave it to you. Now you said that there was no specific place between those two physical locations where the "air of the living room" stopped and the "air of the dining room" began. And that is true. Yet there *is* a place where the "air of the living room" becomes *less dense*. That is, it dissipates, becomes "thinner." So, too, the "air of the dining room." The further from the dining room you go, the less you smell dinner!

Now the air in the *house* is the *same air*. There is no "separate air" in the dining room. Yet the air in the dining room sure *seems* like "other air." For one thing, it smells different!

So because the air has taken on different *characteristics*, it seems as though it is *different air*. But it is not. It is all the *same* air, *seeming* different. In the living room you smell the fireplace, in the dining room you smell dinner. You might even go into one room and say, "Whew, it's stuffy. *Let's get some air in here,*" as if there was no air at all. And yet, of course, there's plenty of air. What you are wanting to do is change its characteristics.

So you bring in some air from the outside. *Yet that is the same air, too.* There is only one air, moving in, around, and through *everything*.

178

This is cool. I totally "get" this. I love the way You explain the universe to me in ways I can totally "get."

Well, thank you. I'm trying here. So let Me go on.

Please.

Like the air in your house, the energy of life—what we'll call the "Soul of God"—takes on different characteristics as it surrounds different physical objects. Indeed, that energy coalesces in a particular way to *form* those objects.

As particles of energy join together to form physical matter, they become very concentrated. Mashed up. Pushed together. They begin to "look like," even "feel like," distinct units. That is, they begin to seem "separate," "different," from all the other energy. Yet this is all the same energy, *behaving differently*.

It is this very act of behaving differently which makes it possible for That Which Is All to manifest as That Which Is Many.

As I explain in *Book 1*, That Which Is could not experience Itself as *What* It is until It developed this *ability to differentiate*. So That Which Is All *separated* into That Which Is *This*, and That Which Is *That*. (I'm trying to make this very simple now.)

The "clumps of energy" which coalesced into discreet units that held in physical beings are what you have chosen to call "souls." The parts of Me that have become the lot of You are what We are talking about here. Thus, the Divine Dichotomy:

There is only One of us.

There are Many of us.

Whoa—this is great.

You're telling Me.

Shall I go on?

179

No, stop here. I'm bored.
Yes, go on!

Okay.

Now as energy coalesces, it becomes, as I said, very concentrated. But the further one moves from the point of this concentration, the more dissipated the energy becomes. The "air becomes thinner." The aura fades. The energy never completely disappears, because it cannot. It is the stuff of which everything is made. It's All There Is. Yet it can become very, very thin, very subtle—almost "not there."

Then, in another place (read that, another part of Itself) it can again coalesce, once more "clumping together" to form what you call matter, and what "looks like" a discreet unit. Now the two units appear separate from each other, and in truth there is no separation at all.

This is, in very, very simple and elementary terms, the explanation behind the whole physical universe.

Wow. But can it be true? How do I know I haven't just made this all up?

Your scientists are already discovering that the building blocks of all of life are the same.

They brought back rocks from the moon and found the same stuff they find in trees. They take apart a tree and find the same stuff they find in you.

I tell you this: We are all the *same stuff.*

We are all the same energy, coalesced, compressed in different ways to create different forms and different matter.

Nothing "matters" in and of itself. That is, nothing can *become matter* all by itself. Jesus said, "Without the Father, I am nothing." The Father of all is pure thought. This is the energy of life. This is what you have chosen to call Absolute Love. This is the God and the Goddess, the Alpha and the Omega, the Beginning and the End. It is the All-in-All, the Unmoved Mover, the Prime Source. It is that which you have sought to understand from the beginning of time. The Great Mystery, the Endless Enigma, the eternal truth.

There is only One of Us, and so, it is THAT WHICH YOU ARE.

12

I am filled with awe and reverence at the reading of those words. Thank You for being here with me in this way. Thank You for being here with all of us. For millions have read the words in these dialogues, and millions more will yet do so. And we are breathlessly gifted by the coming of You to our hearts.

My dearest beings—I have always been in your hearts. I am only glad you can now actually *feel Me there.*
I have always been with you. I have never left you. I am you, and you are Me, and We shall never be separated, *ever,* because that is not *possible.*

Yet on some days I feel so terribly alone. At some moments I feel that I am fighting this battle by myself.

That's because you have left Me, My child. You have abandoned your awareness of Me. Yet where there is awareness of Me, you can never be alone.

How can I stay in my awareness?

Bring your awareness to others. Not by proselytizing, but by example. Be the source of the love which I Am in the lives of all others. For that which you give to others, you give to yourself. Because there is only One of Us.

Thank You. Yes, You have given me that clue before. Be the source. Whatever you want to experience in yourself, You have said, be the source of it in the lives of others.

Yes. This is the great secret. This is the sacred wisdom. *Do unto others as you would have it done unto you.*

All of your problems, all of your conflicts, all of your difficulties in creating a life on your planet of peace and joy are based in your failure to understand this simple instruction, and to follow it.

I get it. Once more You have said it so plainly, so clearly, that I get it. I will try never to "lose it" again.

You cannot "lose" that which you give away. Always remember that.

Thank You. May I ask You a few more questions now about the soul?

I have one more general comment to make about life as you're living it.

Please.

You just said that there are times when you feel as though you're fighting this battle by yourself.

Yes.

What battle?

It was a figure of speech.

I think not. I think it was a real indicator of how you (and many people) really think of life.

You have it in your head that it's a "battle"—that there is some kind of struggle going on here.

Well, it's seemed that way to me sometimes.

It is not that way inherently, and it doesn't have to seem that way, ever.

You'll forgive me, but that's hard for me to believe.

Which is exactly why it hasn't been your reality. For you will make real what you believe is real. Yet I tell you this: Your life was never meant to be a struggle, and doesn't have to be, now or ever.

I have given you the tools with which to create the grandest reality. You have simply chosen not to use them. Or, to be more accurate, you have *misused* them.

The tools I am referring to here are the three tools of creation. We have talked about them much in our ongoing dialogue. Do you know what they are?

Thought, word, and action.

Good. You've remembered. I once inspired Mildred Hinckley, a spiritual teacher of Mine, to say, "You were born with the creative power of the universe at the tip of your tongue."

That is a statement of astonishing implications. As is this truth, from another of My teachers:

"As thou has believed, so be it done unto you."

These two statements have to do with thought and word. Another of My teachers had this to say, about action:

"The beginning is God. The end is action. Action is God creating—or God experienced."

You said that, in *Book 1*.

Book 1 was brought through by you, My son, just as all great teachings have been inspired by Me, and brought through human forms. Those who allow such inspirations to move them, and who fearlessly share them publicly, are My greatest teachers.

I am not sure that I would put myself in that category.

The words you have been inspired to share have touched millions.

Millions, My son.

They have been translated into 24 languages. They have reached around the world.

By what measure would you grant the status of great teacher?

By the measure of one's actions, not one's words.

That is a very wise answer.

And my actions in this lifetime do not speak well of me, and certainly do not qualify me as a teacher.

You've just written off half the teachers who have ever lived.

What are You saying?

I'm saying what I said through Judith Schucman in *A Course in Miracles*: You teach what you have to learn.

Do you believe that you must be demonstrating perfection before you can teach how to reach it?

And while you have made your share of what you would call mistakes—

—more than my share—

—you have also shown great courage in bringing this conversation with Me forward.

Or great foolhardiness.

Why do you insist on putting yourself down like that? You *all* do it! Every one of you! You deny your own greatness as you deny the existence of Me *in* you.

Not me! I have *never* denied that!

What?

Well, not recently . . .

I tell you, before the cock crows, you will deny Me three times.

Every thought of your Self as smaller than you really are is a denial of Me.

Every word about your Self that puts you down is a denial of Me.

Every action flowing through your Self that plays out a role of "not-good-enough," or lack, or insufficiency of any kind, is a denial indeed. Not just in thought, not just in word, but in deed.

I really—

—Do not allow your life to represent *anything* but the grandest version of the greatest vision you *ever had* about Who You Are.

Now, what is the greatest vision you've ever had for your Self? Is it not that you would one day be a great teacher?

Well . . .

Isn't it?

Yes.

Then *so be it*. And so it *is*. Until you once again *deny it*.

I won't deny it again.

You won't?

No.

Prove it.

Prove it?

Prove it.

How?

Say, right now, "I am a great teacher."

Uh . . .

Go ahead, say it.

I am . . . you see, the problem is, all of this is going to be published. I am aware that everything I am writing on this legal pad is going to appear in print somewhere. People in Peoria are going to be reading this.

Peoria! Ha! Try *Beijing!*

Okay, China, too. That's my point. People have been asking me—bugging me—about *Book 3* since the month after *Book 2* came out! I've tried to explain why it's taken so long. I've tried to get them to understand what it's like having this dialogue when you know the *whole world* is watching, waiting. It's not like it was with *Book 1* and *Book 2*. Both of those were dialogues conducted in a void. I never even knew they *would* be books.

Yes, you did. In your heart of hearts you did.

Well, maybe I hoped they'd be. But now I *know*, and it's different writing on this legal pad.

Because now you know everyone will be reading every word you write.

Yes. And now You want me to say that I'm a great teacher. And it's difficult in front of all these people.

You want I should ask you to declare yourself in private? Is that how you think you empower yourself?

I asked you to declare Who You Are in *public* precisely because you are in public here. The whole *idea* was to get you to say it in public.

Public declaration is the highest form of visioning.

Live the grandest version of the greatest vision you ever had about Who You Are. Begin the living of it by declaring it.

Publicly.

The first step in making it so is *saying* it is so.

But what of modesty? What of decorum? Is it seemly to declare our grandest idea about ourselves to everyone we see?

Every great master has done so.

Yes, but not arrogantly.

How "arrogant" is "I am the life and the way"? Is that arrogant enough for you?

Now you said you would never deny Me again, yet you've spent the last ten minutes trying to justify doing so.

I'm not denying *You.* We are talking here about my greatest vision of *me.*

Your greatest vision of you *is* Me! *That is Who I Am!*

When you deny the greatest part of you, you deny Me. And I tell you, before the dawn tomorrow you will do this three times.

Unless I don't.

Unless you don't. That is right. And only you can decide. Only you can choose.

Now, do you know of any great teacher who was ever a great teacher *in private?* The Buddha, Jesus, Krishna—all were teachers in public, no?

Yes. But there are great teachers who are not widely known. My mother was one. You just said so earlier. It is not necessary to be widely known to be a great teacher.

Your mother was a harbinger. A messenger. A preparer of the way. She prepared *you* for the way, by *showing* you the way. Yet you, too, are a teacher.

And as good a teacher as you know your mother to be, she apparently did not teach you never to deny yourself. Yet this *you will teach others.*

Oh, I want to so badly! That is what I want to do!

Do not "want to." You may not have what you "want." You merely declare that you are in "want" of it, and that's where you will be left—you will be *left wanting.*

All right! Okay! I don't "want" to, I *choose* to!

That's better. That's much better. Now what do you choose?

I choose to teach others never to deny themselves.

Good, and what else do you choose to teach?

I choose to teach others never to deny You—God. Because to deny You is to deny themselves, and to deny themselves is to deny You.

Good. And do you choose to teach this haphazardly, almost "by chance"? Or do you choose to teach this grandly, as if on purpose?

I choose to teach it on purpose. Grandly. As my mother did. My mother *did* teach me never to deny my Self. She taught it to me every day. She was the greatest encourager I ever had. She taught me to have faith in myself, and in You. I should *be* such a teacher. I *choose* to be such a teacher of *all* the great wisdoms

189

my Mom taught me. She made her *whole life* a teaching, not just her words. *That's what makes a great teacher.*

You are right, your mother *was* a great teacher. And you were right in your larger truth. A person does *not* have to be widely known to be a great teacher.

I was "testing" you. I wanted to see where you'd go with this.

And did I "go" where I was "supposed to go"?

You went where all great teachers go. To your own wisdom. To your own truth. That is the place to which you must always go, for it is the place you must turn around and *come from* as you teach the world.

I know. This I know.

And what is your own *deepest truth* about Who You Are?

I am . . .
. . . a great teacher.
A great teacher of eternal truth.

There you have it. Calmly said, softly spoken. There you have it. You know the truth of it in your heart, and you have only spoken your heart.

You are not boasting, and no one will hear it as boasting. You are not bragging, and no one will hear it as bragging. You are not beating your chest, you are opening your heart, and there's a big difference.

Everyone knows Who They Are in their heart. They are a great ballerina, or a great lawyer, or a great actor, or a great first baseman. They are a great detective, or a great salesperson, or a great parent, or a great architect; a great poet or a great leader, a great builder or a great healer. And they are, each and every one, a *great person*.

Everyone knows Who They Are in their heart. If they open their heart, if they share with others their heart's desire, if they live their heartfelt truth, they fill their world with magnificence.

You *are* a great teacher. And where do you suppose that gift comes from?

You.

And so, when you declare yourself to be Who You Are, you are merely declaring who I Am. Always declare Me as Source, and no one will mind you declaring yourself as great.

Yet You've always urged me to declare *myself* as Source.

You *are* the Source—of everything *I Am*. The great teacher with whom you are most familiar in your life said, "I am the life and the way."

He also said, "All these things come to Me from the Father. Without the Father, I am nothing."

And he also said, "I and the Father are One."

Do you understand?

There is only One of us.

Exactly.

Which brings us back to the human soul. Can I now ask some more questions about the soul?

Go.

Okay. How many souls are there?

One.

Yes, in the largest sense. But how many "individuations" of the One That Is All are there?

Say, I like that word there. I like the way you've used that word. The One Energy that is All Energy _individuates_ Itself into many different parts. I like that.

I'm glad. So how many individuations did You create? How many souls are there?

I cannot answer that in terms you would understand.

Try me. Is it a constant number? A changing number? An infinite number? Have You created "new souls" since the "original batch"?

Yes, it is a constant number. Yes, it is a changing number. Yes, it is an infinite number. Yes, I have created new souls, and no, I have not.

I don't understand.

I know.

So help me.

Did you actually say that?

Say what?

"So help me, God?"

Ah, clever. Okay, I am going to understand this if it is the last thing I do, so help me, God.

I will. You are very determined, so I will help you—although I warn you that it is difficult to grasp or understand the infinite from a perspective that is finite. We will nevertheless give it a whirl.

Coolness!

Yes, coolness. Well, let's begin by noticing that your questions infer that a reality exists called time. In truth, there is no such reality. There is only one moment, and that is the eternal moment of Now.

All things that have ever happened, are happening Now, and ever will happen, are occurring in this moment. Nothing has happened "before," because there *is* no before. Nothing will happen "after," because there *is* no after. It is always and only Right Now.

In the Right Now of things, I am constantly changing. The number of ways in which I "individuate" (I like your word!) is therefore *always different*, and *always the same*. Given that there is only Now, the number of souls is always constant. But given that you like to think of Now in terms of now and *then*, it is always changing. We touched on this earlier when we spoke of reincarnation, and lower life forms, and how souls "come back."

Since I am always changing, the number of souls is infinite. Yet at any given "point in time" it appears to be finite.

And yes, there are "new souls" in the sense that they have allowed themselves, having reached ultimate awareness and unified with ultimate reality, to voluntarily "forget" everything and "start over"—they have decided to move to a new place on the Cosmic Wheel, and some have chosen to be "young souls" again. Yet all souls are part of the original batch, since all are being created (were created, will be created) in the Only Moment of Now.

So the number is finite and infinite, changing and unchanged, depending on how you look at it.

Because of this characteristic of ultimate reality, I am often called The Unmoved Mover. I am that which is Always Moving, and has Never Moved, is Always Changing and has Never Changed.

Okay. I get it. Nothing is absolute with You.

Except that everything is absolute.

193

Unless it's not.

Exactly. *Precisely.* You *do* "get it!" Bravo.

Well, the truth is, I think I have always understood this stuff.

Yes.

Except when I haven't.

That's right.

Unless it's not.

Exactly.

Who's on first.

No, What's on first. Who's on second.

Ta-da! So You're Abbott and I'm Costello, and it's all just a cosmic vaudeville show.

Except when it's not. There are moments and events you may want to take very seriously.

Unless I don't.

Unless you don't.

So, returning once again to the subject of souls . . .

Boy, that's a great book title there . . . *The Subject of Souls.*

Maybe we'll do that one.

Are you kidding? We already have.

Unless we haven't.

That's true.

Unless it's not.

You never know.

Except when you do.

You see? You *are* getting this. You're remembering now how it really is, and you're having fun with it! You're returning now to "living lightly." You're *lightening up*. This is what is meant by *enlightenment*.

Cool.

Very cool. Which means you're hot!

Yup. That's called "living within the contradiction." You've talked about it many times. Now, getting back to the subject of souls; what's the difference between an old soul and a young soul?

A body of energy (that is to say, a part of Me) can conceive of itself as "young" *or* "old," depending upon what it chooses after it reaches ultimate awareness.

When they return to the Cosmic Wheel, some souls choose to be old souls, and some choose to be "young."

Indeed, if the experience called "young" did not exist, neither could the experience called "old." So some souls have "volunteered" to be called "young," and some to be called "old," so that the One Soul, which is really All There Is, could know itself completely.

Similarly, some souls have chosen to be called "good," and some "bad," for exactly the same reason. And this is why no soul is ever punished. For why would the One Soul want to punish a Part of Itself for being a portion of the Whole?

This is all beautifully explained in the children's storybook *The Little Soul and The Sun,* which lays it out simply, for a child to understand.

You have a way of putting things so eloquently, of articulating terribly complex concepts so clearly, that even a child *can* understand.

Thank you.

So here comes another question about souls. Are there such things as "soul partners"?

Yes, but not the way you think of them.

What's different?

You have romanticized "soul partner" to mean the "other half of you." In truth, the human soul—the part of Me that "individuates"—is much larger than you have imagined.

In other words, what I call the soul is bigger than I think.

Much bigger. It is not the air in one room. It is the air in one entire house. And that house has many rooms. The "soul" is not limited to one identity. It is not the "air" in the dining room. Nor does the soul "split" into two individuals who are called soul partners. It is not the "air" in the living room-dining room combination. It is the "air" in the *whole mansion.*

And in My kingdom there are many mansions. And while it is the same air flowing around, in, and through every mansion, the air of the rooms in one mansion may feel "closer." You might walk into those rooms and say, "It feels 'close' in there."

So that you understand, then—there is only One Soul. Yet what you call the individuated soul is huge, hovering over, in, and through hundreds of physical forms.

At the same time?

There is no such thing as time. I can only answer this by saying, "Yes, and no." Some of the physical forms enveloped by your soul are "living now," in your understanding. Others individuated in forms that are now what you would call "dead." And some have enveloped forms that live in what you call the "future." It's all happening right now, of course, and yet, your contrivance called time serves as a tool, allowing you a greater sense of the realized experience.

So, these hundreds of physical bodies my soul has "enveloped"—that's an interesting word You've used—are all my "soul partners"?

That's closer to being accurate than the way you have been using the term, yes.

And some of my soul partners have lived before?

Yes. As you would describe it, yes.

Whoa. Hold it! I think I just *got* something here! Are these parts of me that have lived "before" what I would now describe as my "former lives"?

Good thinking! You are getting it! Yes! Some of these *are* the "other lives" you've lived "before." And some are not. And other parts of your soul are enveloping bodies that will be alive in what you call your future. And still others are embodied in different forms living on your planet right now.

When you run into one of these, you may feel an immediate sense of affinity. Sometimes you may even say, "We must have spent a 'past life' together." And you will be right. You *have* spent a "past life" *together*. Either as *the same physical form*, or as two forms in the same Space-Time Continuum.

197

This is fabulous! This explains everything!

Yes, it does.

Except one thing.

What's that?

How about when I just *know* that I've spent a "past life" with someone—I just *know* it; I feel it in my *bones*—and yet, when I mention this to them, they feel none of this at all? What's *that* about?

It's about your confusing the "past" with the "future."

Huh?

You *have* spent another life with them—it's just not a *past* life.

It's a "future life"?

Precisely. It's all happening in the Eternal Moment of Now, and you have an awareness of what, in a sense, has *not yet happened.*

Then why don't they "remember" the future, too?

These are very subtle vibrations, and some of you are more sensitive to them than others. Also, from person to person it is different. You may be more "sensitive" to your "past" or "future" experience with one person than another. This usually means you've spent that other time as the part of your very huge soul enveloping the *same* body, whereas when there is still that sensation of "having met before," but just not as strong of one, it may mean that you shared the same "time" together, but not the same body. Perhaps you were (or will be) husband and wife, brother and sister, parent and child, lover and beloved.

These are strong bonds, and it is natural that you would feel them when you "meet again" for the "first time" in "this" life.

If what You are saying is true, it would account for a phenomenon for which I have never before been able to account—the phenomenon of more than one person in this "lifetime" claiming to have memories of being Joan of Arc. Or Mozart. Or some other famous person from the "past." I have always thought this was proof for those who say that reincarnation is a false doctrine, for how could more than one person claim to have been the same person before? But now I see how this is possible! All that has happened is that several of the sentient beings now being enveloped by one soul are "remembering" (becoming members once again with) the part of their single soul which was (is *now*) Joan of Arc.

Good heavens, this blows the lid off all limitations, and makes all things possible. The minute I catch myself, in the future, saying "that's impossible," I'll know that all I'm doing is demonstrating that there's a great deal I don't know.

That is a good thing to remember. A very good thing to remember.

And, if we can have more than one "soul partner," that would explain how it is possible for us to experience those intense "soul partner feelings" with more than one person a lifetime—and even more than *one person at a time*!

Indeed.

Then it *is* possible to love more than one person at a time.

Of course.

No, no. I mean, with the kind of intense, personal love that we usually reserve for one person—or, at least, one person *at a time*!

Why would you ever want to "reserve" love? Why would you want to hold it "in reserve"?

199

Because it's not right to love more than one person "that way." It's a betrayal.

Who told you that?

Everybody. Everybody tells me that. My parents told me that. My religion told me that. My society tells me that. Everybody tells me that!

These are some of those "sins of the father" being passed onto the son.

Your own experience teaches you one thing—that loving everyone *full out* is the most joyful thing you can do. Yet your parents, teachers, ministers tell you something else—that you may only love one person at a time "that way." And we're not just talking about sex here. If you consider one person as special as another in *any* way, you are often made to feel that you have betrayed that other.

Right! Exactly! That's how we've got it set up!

Then you are not expressing true love, but some counterfeit variety.

To what extent will true love be allowed to express itself within the framework of the human experience? What limits shall we—indeed, some would say *must* we—place on that expression? If all social and sexual energies were to be unleashed without restriction, what would be the result? Is complete social and sexual freedom the abdication of all responsibility, or the absolute height of it?

Any attempt to restrict the natural expressions of love is a denial of the experience of freedom—and thus a denial of the soul itself. For the soul *is* freedom personified. God *is* freedom, by definition—for God is limitless and without restriction of *any* kind. The soul is God, miniaturized. Therefore, the soul rebels at any imposition of limitation, and dies a new death each time it accepts boundaries from without.

In this sense, birth itself is a death, and death a birth. For in birth, the soul finds itself constricted within the awful limitations of a body, and at death escapes those constrictions again. It does the same thing during sleep.

Back to freedom the soul flies—and rejoices once again with the expression and experience of its true nature.

Yet can its true nature be expressed and experienced while *with* the body?

That is the question you ask—and it drives to the very reason and purpose of life itself. For if life with the body is nothing more than a prison or a limitation, then what good can come of it, and what can be its function, much less its justification?

Yes, I suppose that is what I am asking. And I ask it on behalf of all beings everywhere who have felt the awful constrictions of the human experience. And I am not speaking now of physical limitations—

—I know you are not—

—but emotional and psychological ones.

Yes, I know. I understand. Yet your concerns all relate to the same larger question.

Yes, all right. Still, let me finish. All my life I have been deeply frustrated by the world's inability to let me love everyone in exactly the way I've wanted to.

When I was young, it was about not talking to strangers, not saying things inappropriately. I remember once, walking down a street with my father, we came across a poor man, begging for coins. I immediately felt sorry for the man and wanted to give him some of the pennies in my pocket. My father stopped me, and brushed me past. "Trash," he said. "That's just trash." That was my father's label for all those who did not live up to his definitions of what it meant to be humans of worth.

Later, I remember an experience of my older brother, who was no longer living with us, not being allowed into the house on Christmas Eve because of some argument he'd had with my father. I loved my brother and wanted him to be with us that night, but my father stopped him on the front porch and barred him from entering the home. My mother was devastated (it was her son from a previous marriage), and I was simply mystified. How could we not love or want my brother on Christmas Eve simply because of an argument?

What kind of disagreement could be so bad that it would be allowed to ruin Christmas, when even wars were suspended for a 24-hour truce? This, my little seven-year-old heart begged to know.

As I grew older, I learned that it was not just anger that stopped the love from flowing, but also fear. This was why we oughtn't talk to strangers—but not just when we were defenseless children. Also when we were adults. I learned that it was just not okay to openly and eagerly meet and greet strangers, and that there was a certain etiquette to be followed with people to whom you've just been introduced—none of which made sense to me. I wanted to know *everything* about that new person and I wanted them to know everything about *me!* But *no.* The rules said we had to wait.

And now, in my adult life, when sexuality enters into it, I've learned that the rules are even more rigid and limiting. And I *still don't get it.*

I find that I just want to love and be loved—that I just want to love everyone in whatever way feels natural to me, in whatever way feels good. Yet society has its rules and regulations about all this—and so rigid are they that *even if the other person who is involved* agrees to an experience, if *society* doesn't agree, those two lovers are called "wrong," and are thus doomed.

What *is* that? What is that all *about?*

Well, you've said it yourself. Fear.
It's all about fear.

Yes, but are these fears justified? Aren't these restrictions and constrictions only appropriate, given the behaviors of our race? A man meets a younger woman, falls in love (or "in lust") with her, and leaves his wife, for instance. I use only one example. So there she is, left with the kids and no employment skills at thirty-nine or forty-three—or, worse yet, left high and dry at sixty-four by a sixty-eight-year-old man who's become enamored of a woman younger than his daughter.

Is it your supposing that the man you describe has ceased to love his sixty-four-year-old wife?

Well, he sure acts like it.

No. It is not his wife he does not love, and seeks to escape. It is the limitations he feels placed on him.

Oh, nonsense. It's lust, pure and simple. It's an old geezer simply trying to recapture his youth, wanting to be with a younger woman, unable to curb his childish appetites and keep his promise to the partner who has remained with him through all the tough and lean years.

Of course. You've described it perfectly. Yet nothing you have said has changed a thing that I have said. In virtually every case, this man has not stopped loving his wife. It is the limitations his wife places on him, or those placed on him by the younger woman who will have nothing to do with him if he stays with his wife, that creates the rebellion.

The point I am trying to make is that the soul will *always* rebel at limitation. Of *any* kind. That is what has sparked *every* revolution in the history of humankind, not just the revolution which causes a man to leave his wife—or a wife to suddenly leave her husband. (Which, by the way, also happens.)

Surely You are not arguing for the complete abolition of behavioral limitations of any kind! That would be behavioral anarchy. Social chaos. Surely You are not advocating people having "affairs"—or, take my breath away, *open marriage!*

I do not advocate, or fail to advocate, *anything.* I am not "for" or "against" anything. The human race keeps

203

trying to make me a "for" or "against" kind of God, and I am not that.

I merely observe what is so. I simply watch *you* create your *own* systems of right and wrong, for and against, and I look to see whether your current ideas about that serve you, given what you say you choose and desire as a species, and as individuals.

Now, to the question of "open marriage."

I am not for or against "open marriage." Whether you are or not depends upon what you decide you want in, and out of, your marriage. And your decision about *that* creates Who You Are with regard to the experience you call "marriage." For it is as I have told you: Every act is an act of self-definition.

When making any decision, it is important to make sure the right question is being answered. The question with regard to so-called "open marriage," for instance, is not "shall we have an open marriage where sexual contact by both parties with persons outside the marriage is allowed?" The question is "Who Am I—and Who Are We—with regard to the experience called marriage?"

The answer to that question will be found in the answer to life's largest question: Who *Am* I—*period*—with regard to anything, in relationship to anything; Who Am I, and Who Do I Choose to Be?

As I have said repeatedly throughout this dialogue, the answer to that question is the answer to *every* question.

God, that frustrates me. Because the answer to that question is so broad and so general that it answers no other question at all.

Oh, really? Then what is your answer to that question?

According to these books—according to what You seem to be saying in this dialogue—I am "love." That is Who I Really Am.

Excellent! You *have* learned! That is correct. You are love. Love is all there is. So you are love, I am love, and there is nothing which is *not* love.

What about fear?

Fear is that which you are not. Fear is False Evidence Appearing Real. Fear is the opposite of love, which you have created in your reality so that you may know experientially That Which You Are.

This is what is true in the relative world of your existence: In the absence of that which you are not, that which you are . . . is *not.*

Yes, yes, we've been through this a number of times now in our dialogue. But it feels as though You have evaded my complaint. I said that the answer to the question of Who We Are (which is love) is so broad as to render it a nonanswer—it is no answer at all—to almost any other question. You say it is the answer to *every* question, and I say it is not the answer to *any*—much less to one as specific as "Should our marriage be an open marriage?"

If that is true for you, it is because you do not know what love is.

Does anybody? The human race has been trying to figure that one out since the beginning of time.

Which does not exist.

Which does not exist, yes, yes, I know. It's a figure of speech.

Let me see if I can find, using your "figures of speech," some words and some ways to explain what love is.

Super. That'd be great.

205

The first word that comes to mind is unlimited. That which is love is unlimited.

Well, we're right where we were when we opened this subject. We're going around in circles.

Circles are good. Don't berate them. Keep circling; keep circling around the question. Circling is okay. Repeating is okay. Revisiting, restating is okay.

I sometimes get impatient.

Sometimes? That's pretty funny.

Okay, okay, go on with what You were saying.

Love is that which is unlimited. There is no beginning and no end to it. No before and no after. Love always was, always is, and always will be.

So love is also always. It's the always reality.

Now we get back to another word we used before—freedom. For if love is unlimited, and always, then love is . . . free. Love is that which is perfectly free.

Now in the human reality, you will find that you always seek to love, and to be loved. You will find that you will always yearn for that love to be unlimited. And you will find that you will always wish you could be free to express it.

You will seek freedom, unlimitedness, and eternality in every experience of love. You may not always get it, but that is what you will seek. You will seek this because this is what love *is,* and at some deep place you *know* that, because you *are* love, and through the expression of love you are seeking to know and to experience Who and What You Are.

You are life expressing life, love expressing love, God expressing God.

All these words are therefore synonymous. Think of them as the same thing:

God
Life
Love
Unlimited
Eternal
Free

Anything which is not one of these things is *not any of these things.*

You are all of those things, and you will seek to *experience* yourself as *all of these things* sooner or later.

What does that mean, "sooner or later"?

It depends on when you get over your fear. As I've said, fear is False Evidence Appearing Real. It is that which you are not.

You will seek to experience That Which You Are when you are through experiencing that which you are not.

Who wants to experience fear?

Nobody wants to; you are taught to.

A child experiences no fear. He thinks he can do anything. Nor does a child experience lack of freedom. She thinks she can love anyone. Nor does a child experience lack of life. Children believe they will live forever—and people who act like children think nothing can hurt them. Nor does a child know any ungodly things—until that child is taught ungodly things by grownups.

And so, children run around naked and hug everyone, thinking nothing of it. If adults could only do the same thing.

Well, children do so with the beauty of innocence. Adults cannot get back to that innocence, because when adults "get naked" there is always that sex thing.

207

Yes. And, of course, God forbid that "that sex thing" be innocent and freely experienced.

Actually, God *did* forbid it. Adam and Eve were perfectly happy running around naked in the Garden of Eden until Eve ate of the fruit of the tree—the Knowledge of Good and Evil. Then You condemned us to our present state, for we are all guilty of that original sin.

I did no such thing.

I know. But I had to give organized religion a shot here.

Try to avoid that if you can.

Yes, I should. Organized religionists have very little sense of humor.

There you go again.

Sorry.

I was *saying* . . . you will strive as a species to experience a love that is unlimited, eternal, and free. The institution of marriage has been your attempt at creating eternality. With it, you agreed to become partners for life. But this did little to produce a love which was "unlimited" and "free."

Why not? If the marriage is freely chosen, isn't it an expression of freedom? And to say that you are going to demonstrate your love sexually with no one else but your spouse is not a limitation, it's a choice. And a choice is not a limitation, it is the *exercise of freedom*.

So long as that continues to *be* the choice, yes.

Well, it *has* to be. That was the *promise*.

Yes—and that's where the trouble begins.

Help me here.

Look, there may come a time when you want to experience a high degree of specialness in a relationship. Not that one *person* is more special to you than another, but that the *way* you choose to demonstrate with one person the depth of love you have for all people—and for life itself—is unique to that person alone.

Indeed, the way you now demonstrate love to each person you *do* love is unique. You demonstrate your love to no two people in exactly the same way. Because you are a creature and a creator of originality, everything you create is original. It is not possible for any thought, word, or action to be duplicative. You *cannot* duplicate, you can only *originate*.

Do you know *why* no two snowflakes are alike? Because it is *impossible* for them to be. "Creation" is not "duplication," and the Creator can only create.

That is why no two snowflakes are alike, no two *people* are alike, no two thoughts are alike, no two relationships are alike, and no two of *anything* are alike.

The universe—and every thing in it—exists in singular form, and there truly is *nothing else like it.*

This is the Divine Dichotomy again. Everything is singular, yet everything is One.

Exactly. Each finger on your hand is different, yet it is all the same hand. The air in your house is the air that is everywhere, yet the air from room to room is *not* the same, but feels markedly different.

It is the same with people. All people are One, yet no two people are alike. You could not, therefore, love two people in the same way even if you tried—and you would never *want* to, because *love is a unique response to that which is unique.*

So when you demonstrate your love for one person, you are doing so in a way in which you cannot do so

209

with another. Your thoughts, words, and actions—your responses—are literally impossible to duplicate—one of a kind . . . just as is the person for whom you have these feelings.

If the time has come when you have desired this special demonstration with one person alone, then choose it, as you say. Announce it, and declare it. Yet make your declaration an announcement moment-to-moment of your *freedom,* not your ongoing *obligation.* For true love is always free, and obligation cannot exist in the space of love.

If you see your decision to express your love in a particular way with only one particular other as a sacred *promise,* never to be broken, the day may come when you will experience that promise as an obligation—and you will resent it. Yet if you see this decision not as a promise, made only once, but as a free choice, made over and over, that day of resentment will never come.

Remember this: There is only one sacred promise—and that is to *tell and live your truth.* All other promises are forfeitures of freedom, and that can never be sacred. For freedom is Who You Are. If you forfeit freedom, you forfeit your Self. And that is not a sacrament, that is a blasphemy.

13

Whew! Those are tough words. Are You saying we should never make promises—that we should never promise anything to anyone?

As most of you are now living your life, there is a lie built into every promise. The lie is that you can know now how you will feel about a thing, and what you will want to do about that thing, on any given tomorrow. You cannot know this if you are living your life as a reactive being—which most of you are. Only if you are living life as a creative being can your promise not contain a lie.

Creative beings *can* know how they are going to feel about a thing at any time in the future, because creative beings *create* their feelings, rather than experiencing them.

Until you can *create* your future, you cannot *predict* your future. Until you can *predict* your future, you cannot promise anything truthfully about it.

Yet even one who both creates and predicts her future has the authority and the right to change. Change is a fundamental right of all creatures. Indeed, it is more than a "right," for a "right" is that which is *given.* "Change" is that which Is.

Change is.

That which is change, you are.

You cannot be *given* this. You *are* this.

Now, since you *are* "change"—and since change is *the only thing constant about you*—you cannot truthfully promise to *always be the same.*

Do You mean there are no constants in the universe? Are You saying that there is nothing which remains constant in all of creativity?

211

The process you call life is a process of re-creation. All of life is constantly re-creating itself anew in each moment of now. In this process identicality is impossible, since if a thing is identical, it has not changed at all. Yet while identicality is impossible, similarity is not. Similarity is the result of the process of change producing a remarkably similar version of what went before.

When creativity reaches a high level of similarity, you call that identicality. And from the gross perspective of your limited viewpoint, it is.

Therefore, in human terms, there appears to be great constancy in the universe. That is, things seem to look alike, and act alike, and *react* alike. You see consistency here.

This is good, for it provides a framework within which you may consider, and experience, your existence in the physical.

Yet I tell you this. Viewed from the perspective of all life—that which is physical and that which is nonphysical—the appearance of constancy disappears. Things are experienced as they *really are*: constantly changing.

You are saying that sometimes the changes are so delicate, so subtle, that from our less discerning viewpoint they *appear* the same—sometimes exactly the same—when, in fact, they are not.

Precisely.

There are "no such things as identical twins."

Exactly. You have captured it perfectly.

Yet we *can* re-create ourselves anew in a form sufficiently similar to produce the *effect* of constancy.

Yes.

And we can do this in human relationships, in terms of Who We Are, and how we behave.

212

Yes—although most of you find this very difficult.

Because true constancy (as opposed to the appearance of constancy) violates the natural law, as we have just learned, and it takes a great master to even create the *appearance* of identicality.

A master overcomes every natural tendency (remember, the natural tendency is toward change) to show up as identicality. In truth, he cannot show up identically from moment to moment. But she *can* show up as sufficiently *similar* to create the *appearance* of being identical.

Yet people who are *not* "masters" show up "identically" all the time. I know people whose behaviors and appearance are so predictable you can stake your life on them.

Yet it takes great effort to do this *intentionally*.

The master is one who creates a high level of similarity (what you call "consistency") *intentionally*. A student is one who creates consistency without necessarily intending to.

A person who always reacts the same way to certain circumstances, for instance, will often say, "I couldn't help it."

A master would *never* say that.

Even if a person's reaction produces an admirable behavior—something for which they receive praise—their response will often be "Well, it was nothing. It was automatic, really. Anybody would do it."

A master would never do that, either.

A master, therefore, is a person who—quite literally—*knows what he is doing.*

She also knows *why.*

People not operating at levels of mastery often know neither.

This is why it is so difficult to keep promises?

It is one reason. As I said, until you can predict your future, you cannot promise anything truthfully.

A second reason people find it difficult to keep promises is that they come into conflict with authenticity.

What do You mean?

I mean that their evolving truth about a thing differs from what they *said* their truth would always be. And so, they are deeply conflicted. What to obey—my truth, or my promise?

Advice?

I have given you this advice before:
Betrayal of yourself in order not to betray another is betrayal nonetheless. It is the highest betrayal.

But this would lead to promises being broken all over the place! Nobody's word on *anything* would matter. Nobody could be counted on for anything!

Oh, so you've been counting on others to keep their *word,* have you? No wonder you've been so miserable.

Who says I've been miserable?

You mean this is the way you look and act when you've been *happy?*

All right. Okay. So I've been miserable. Sometimes.

Oh, a great *deal* of the time. Even when you've had every *reason* to be happy, you've allowed yourself to be miserable—worrying about whether you'll be able to *hold onto* your happiness!
And the reason you've even *had* to worry about this is that "holding onto your happiness" has depended to a large degree on other people keeping their word.

You mean I don't have a right to expect—or at least *hope*—that other people will keep their word?

Why would you *want* such a right?

The only reason that anther person would not keep their word to you would be because they didn't want to—or they felt they couldn't, which is the same thing.

And if a person did not want to keep his word to you, or for some reason felt he just couldn't, why on Earth would you want him to?

Do you really want someone to keep an agreement she does not want to keep? Do you really feel people should be forced to do things they don't feel they can do?

Why would you want to force anyone to do anything against his will?

Well, try this for a reason: because to let them get away with *not* doing what they said they were going to do would hurt me—or my family.

So in order to avoid injury, you're willing to inflict injury.

I don't see how it injures another simply to ask him to keep his word.

Yet *he* must see it as injurious, or he would keep it willingly.

So *I* should suffer the injury, or watch my children and family suffer the injury, rather than "injure" the one who made a promise by simply asking that it be kept?

Do you really think that if you force another to keep a promise that you will have escaped injury?

I tell you this: More damage has been done to others by persons leading lives of quiet desperation (that is, doing what they felt they "had" to do) than ever was done by persons freely doing what they wanted to do.

When you give a person freedom, you *remove* danger, you don't increase it.

Yes, letting someone "off the hook" on a promise or commitment made to you may *look* like it will hurt you in the short run, but it will never damage you in the long run, because when you give the other person their freedom, you give *yourself* freedom as well. And so now you are free of the agonies and the sorrows, the attacks on your dignity and your self-worth that inevitably follow when you force another person to keep a promise to you that he or she does not want to keep.

The longer damage will far outweigh the shorter—as nearly everyone who has tried to hold another person to their word has discovered.

Does this same idea hold true in business as well? How could the world do business that way?

Actually it is the only sane way *to* do business.

The problem right now in your whole society is that it is based on force. Legal force (which you call the "force of law") and, too often, physical force (which you call the world's "armed forces").

You have not yet learned to use the art of persuasion.

If not by legal force—the "force of law" through the courts—how would we "persuade" businesses to meet the terms of their contract and keep their agreements?

Given your current cultural ethic, there may not be another way. Yet with a *change* of cultural ethic, the way you are now seeking to keep businesses—and individuals, for that matter—from breaking their agreements will appear very primitive.

Can You explain?

You are now using force to make sure agreements are kept. When your cultural ethic is changed to include an understanding that you are all One, you would never use force, because that would only damage your Self. You would not slap your left hand with your right.

Even if the left hand was strangling you?

That is another thing which would not happen. You would stop strangling your Self. You would stop biting your nose to spite your face. You would stop breaking your agreements. And, of course, your agreements themselves would be much different.

You would not agree to give something of value which you have to another only if they had something of value to give you in exchange. You would never hold back on giving or sharing something until you got what you call a just return.

You would give and share automatically, and so, there would be far fewer contracts to break, because a contract is about the *exchange* of goods and services, whereas your life would be about the *giving* of goods and services, *regardless* of what exchange may or may not take place.

Yet in this kind of one-way giving would your salvation be found, for you would have discovered what God has experienced: that what you give to another, you give to your Self. What goes around, comes around.

All things that proceed from you, return to you.

Sevenfold. So there is no need to worry about what you are going to "get back." There is only a need to worry about what you are going to "give out." Life is about creating the highest quality giving, not the highest quality getting.

You keep forgetting. But life is not "for getting." Life is "for giving," and in order to do that, you need to be forgiving to others—especially those who did not *give you* what you thought you were *going to get!*

This switch will entail a complete shift of your cultural story. Today, what you call "success" in your culture is measured largely by how much you "get," by how much honor and money and power and possessions you amass. In the New Culture "success" will be measured by how much you cause *others* to amass.

The irony will be that the more you cause *others* to amass, the more *you* will amass, effortlessly. With no "contracts," no "agreements," no "bargaining" or "negotiating" or lawsuits or courts which force you to give to each other what was "promised."

In the future economy, you will not do things for personal profit, but for personal growth, which will *be* your profit. Yet "profit" in material terms will come to you as you become a bigger and grander version of Who You Really Are.

In those days and times, using force to coerce someone to give you something because they "said" that they would will seem very primitive to you. If another person does not keep an agreement, you will simply allow them to walk their path, make their choices, and create their own experience of themselves. And whatever they have not given you, you will not miss, for you will know that there is "more where that came from"—and that they are not your source of that, but *you* are.

Whoa. I *got it*. But it feels like we have really gotten off the mark. This whole discussion began with my asking You about love—and if human beings would ever allow themselves to express it without limitation. And that led to a question about open marriage. And suddenly we've gotten way off the mark here.

Not really. Everything we've talked about is pertinent. And this is a perfect lead-in to your questions about so-called enlightened, or more highly evolved, societies. Because in highly evolved societies there is neither "marriage" nor "business"—nor, for that matter, any of the artificial social constructions you have created to hold your society together.

Yes, well, we'll get into that soon. Right now I just want to close down this subject. You've said some intriguing things here. What all of it breaks down to, as I get it, is that most human beings can't keep promises and so, shouldn't make them. That pretty much scuttles the institution of marriage.

I like your use of the word "institution" here. Most people experience that when they are in a marriage, they *are* in an "institution."

Yeah, it's either a mental health institution or a penal institution—or at the very least an institution of higher learning!

Exactly. Precisely. That's how most people experience it.

Well, I was kidding along with You here, but I wouldn't say "most people." There are still millions of people who love the institution of marriage, and want to protect it.

I'll stand by the statement. Most people have a very difficult time with marriage, and do *not* like what it does to them.
Your worldwide divorce statistics prove this.

So are You saying that marriage should go?

I have no preference in the matter, only—

—I know, I know. Observations.

Bravo! You keep wanting to make me a God of preferences, which I am not. Thank you for trying to stop that.

Well, we've not only just scuttled marriage, we've also just scuttled religion!

It is true that religions could not exist if the whole human race understood that God doesn't have preferences, because a religion purports to be a *statement* of God's preferences.

And if You *have* no preferences, then religion must be a lie.

Well, that's a harsh word. I would call it a fiction. It's just something you made up.

Like we made up the fiction that God prefers us to be married?

Yes. I don't prefer anything of the sort. But I notice *you* do.

Why? Why do we prefer marriage if we know that it is so difficult?

Because marriage was the only way you could figure out to bring "foreverness," or eternality, into your experience of love.

It was the only way a female could guarantee her support and survival, and the only way a male could guarantee the constant availability of sex, and companionship.

So a social convention was created. A bargain was struck. You give me this and I'll give you that. In this it *was* very much like a business. A contract was made. And since both parties needed to enforce the contract, it was said to be a "sacred pact" with God—who would punish those who broke it.

Later, when that didn't work, you created man-made laws to enforce it.

But even that hasn't worked.

Neither the so-called laws of God nor the laws of man have been able to keep people from breaking their marriage vows.

How come?

Because those vows as you have them normally constructed run counter to the only law that matters.

Which is?

Natural law.

But it is the nature of things for life to express unity, Oneness. Isn't that what I'm getting from all of this? And marriage is our most beautiful expression of that. You know, "What God has joined together, let no man put asunder," and all that.

Marriage, as most of you have practiced it, is not particularly beautiful. For it violates two of the three aspects of what is true about each human being by nature.

Will You go over it again? I think I'm just starting to pull this together.

Okay. Once more from the top.
Who You Are is love.
What love is, is unlimited, eternal, and free.
Therefore, that is what *you* are. That is the *nature* of Who You Are. You are unlimited, eternal, and free, by nature.
Now, any artificial social, moral, religious, philosophical, economic, or political construction which violates or subordinates your nature is an impingement upon your very Self—and you will rail against it.
What do you suppose gave birth to your own country? Was it not "Give me liberty, or give me death"?
Well, you've given up that liberty in your country, and you've given it up in your lives. And all for the same thing. Security.
You are so afraid to *live*—so afraid of *life itself*—that you've given up *the very nature of your being* in trade for security.

The institution you call marriage is your attempt to create security, as is the institution called government. Actually, they are both forms of the same thing—artificial social constructions designed to *govern each other's behavior.*

Good grief, I never looked at it like that. I always thought that marriage was the ultimate announcement of love.

As you have imagined it, yes, but not as you have constructed it. As you have constructed it, it is the ultimate announcement of fear.

If marriage allowed you to be unlimited, eternal, and free in your love, *then* it would be the ultimate announcement of love.

As things are now, you become married in an effort to lower your love to the level of a *promise* or a *guarantee.*

Marriage is an effort to guarantee that "what is so" now will *always be so.* If you didn't need this guarantee, you would not need marriage. And how do you use this guarantee? First, as a means of creating security (instead of creating security from that which is inside of you), and second, if that security is not forever forthcoming, as a means of punishing each other, for the marriage promise which has been broken can now form the basis of the lawsuit which has been opened.

You have thus found marriage very useful—even if it is for all the wrong reasons.

Marriage is also your attempt to guarantee that the feelings you have for each other, you will never have for another. Or, at least, that you will never *express* them with another in the same way.

Namely, sexually.

Namely, sexually.

Finally, marriage as you have constructed it is a way of saying: "This relationship is special. I hold this relationship above all others."

What's wrong with that?

Nothing. It's not a question of "right" or "wrong." Right and wrong do not exist. It's a question of what serves you. Of what re-creates you in the next grandest image of Who You Really Are.

If Who You Really Are is a being who says, "This one relationship—this single one, right over here—is more special than any other," then your construction of marriage allows you to do that perfectly. Yet you might find it interesting to notice that almost no one who is, or has been, recognized as a spiritual master is married.

Yeah, because masters are celibate. They don't have sex.

No. It's because masters cannot truthfully make the statement that your present construction of marriage seeks to make: that one person is more special to them than another.

This is not a statement that a master makes, and it is *not a statement that God makes.*

The fact is that your marriage vows, as you presently construct them, have you making a very un-Godly statement. It is the height of irony that you feel this is the holiest of holy promises, for it is a promise that God would never make.

Yet, in order to justify your human fears, you have imagined a God who *acts just like you.* Therefore, you speak of God's "promise" to his "Chosen People," and of covenants between God and those God loves, in a special way.

You cannot stand the thought of a God who loves *no one* in a way which is more special than any other, and so you create fictions about a God who only loves certain people for certain reasons. And you call these fictions Religions. I call them blasphemies. For any thought that God loves one more than another is false—and any ritual which asks *you* to make the *same statement* is not a sacrament, but a sacrilege.

223

Oh, my God, stop it. *Stop it!* You're killing every good thought I ever had about marriage! This can't be God writing this. God would never say such things about religion and marriage!

Religion and marriage *the way you have constructed them* is what we are talking about here. You think that this talk is tough? I tell you this: You have bastardized the Word of God in order to justify your fears and rationalize your insane treatment of each other.

You will make God say whatever you need God to say in order to continue limiting each other, hurting each other, and *killing each other* in My name.

Yea, you have invoked My name, and waved My flag, and carried crosses on your battlefields for centuries, all as proof that I love one people more than another, and would *ask you to kill to prove it.*

Yet I tell you this: My love is unlimited and unconditional.

That is the one thing you cannot hear, the one truth you cannot abide, the one statement you cannot accept, for its all-inclusiveness destroys not only the institution of marriage (as you have constructed it), but every one of your religions and governmental institutions as well.

For you have created a culture based on exclusion, and supported it with a cultural myth of a God who excludes.

Yet the culture of God is based on inclusion. In God's love, everyone is included. Into God's Kingdom *everyone* is invited.

And this truth is what *you* call a blasphemy.

And you *must*. Because if it is true, then everything you have created in your life is false. All human conventions and all human constructions are faulty to the degree that they are not unlimited, eternal, and free.

How can anything be "faulty" if there's no such thing as "right" and "wrong"?

A thing is only faulty to the degree that it does not function to suit its purpose. If a door does not open and close, you would not call the door "wrong." You would merely say its installation or operation is faulty—because it does not serve its purpose.

Whatever you construct in your life, in your human society, which does not serve your purpose in becoming human is faulty. It is a faulty construction.

And—just for review—my purpose in becoming human is?

To decide and to declare, to create and to express, to experience and to fulfill, Who You Really Are.

To re-create yourself anew in every moment in the grandest version of the greatest vision ever you had about Who You Really Are.

That is your purpose in becoming human, and that is the purpose of all of life.

So—where does that leave us? We've destroyed religion, we've dissed marriage, we've denounced governments. Where are we, then?

First of all, we've destroyed, dissed, and denounced nothing. If a construction you have created is not working and not producing what you wanted it to produce, to *describe* that condition is not to destroy, diss, or denounce the construction.

Try to remember the difference between judgment and observation.

Well, I'm not going to argue with You here, but a lot of what has just been said has sounded pretty judgmental to *me*.

We are constricted here by the awful limitation of words. There are really so few of them, and so we have to use the same ones over and over again, even when they don't always convey the same meaning, or the same kinds of thoughts.

You say that you "love" banana splits, but you surely don't mean the same thing as when you say you love each other. So you see, you have very few words, really, to describe how you're feeling.

In communicating with you in this way—in the way of words—I've allowed Myself to experience those limitations. And I will concede that, because some of this language has also been used by *you* when *you are being judgmental,* it would be easy to conclude that *I'm* being judgmental when *I* use them.

Let Me assure you here that I am not. Throughout this whole dialogue I have simply been trying to tell you how to get where you say you want to go, and to describe as impactfully as possible what is blocking your way; what is stopping you from going there.

Now, with regard to *religion,* you say where you want to go is to a place where you can truly know God and love God. I am simply observing that your religions do not take you there.

Your religions have made God the Great Mystery, and caused you not to love God, but to fear God.

Religion has done little, as well, to cause you to change your behaviors. You are still killing each other, condemning each other, making each other "wrong." And, in fact, it is your *religions* which have been encouraging you to do so.

So with regard to religion, I merely observe that you say you want it to take you to one place, and it is taking you to another.

Now you say you want *marriage* to take you to the land of eternal bliss, or at least to some reasonable level of peace, security, and happiness. As with religion, your invention called marriage does well with this in the early going, when you are first experiencing it. Yet, as with religion, the longer you reside in the experience, the more it takes you where you say you don't want to go.

Nearly half of the people who become married dissolve their marriage through divorce, and of those who stay married, many are desperately unhappy.

Your "unions of bliss" lead you to bitterness, anger, and regret. Some—and not a small number—take you to a place of outright tragedy.

You say you want your *governments* to ensure peace, freedom, and domestic tranquillity, and I observe that, as you have devised them, they do none of this. Rather, your governments lead you to war, increasing *lack* of freedom, and domestic violence and upheaval.

You haven't been able to solve the basic problems of simply feeding and keeping people healthy and alive, much less meet the challenge of providing them equal opportunity.

Hundreds of you die every day of starvation on a planet where thousands of you throw away each day enough food to feed nations.

You can't handle the simplest task of getting the leftovers from the "Have's" to the "Have Not's"—much less resolve the issue of whether you even *want* to share your resources more equitably.

Now *these are not judgments*. These are things which are *observably* true about your society.

Why? Why is it *like* this? Why have we made so little progress in conducting our own affairs these past many years?

Years? Try *centuries*.

Okay, centuries.

It has to do with the First Human Cultural Myth, and with all the other myths which necessarily follow. Until they change, nothing else will change. For your cultural myths inform your ethics, and your ethics create your behaviors. Yet the problem is that your cultural myth is at variance with your basic instinct.

What do You mean?

227

Your First Cultural Myth is that human beings are inherently evil. This is the myth of original sin. The myth holds that not only is your basic nature evil, you were *born* that way.

The Second Cultural Myth, arising necessarily out of the first, is that it is the "fittest" who survive.

This second myth holds that some of you are strong and some of your are weak, and that to survive, you have to be one of the strong. You will do all that you can to help your fellow man, but if and when it comes down to your own survival, you will take care of yourself first. You will even let others die. Indeed, you will go further than that. If you think you have to, in order for you and yours to survive, you will actually kill others—presumably, the "weak"—thereby defining you as the "fittest."

Some of you say that this is your *basic instinct*. It is called the "survival instinct," and it is this cultural myth that has formed much of your societal ethic, creating many of your group behaviors.

Yet your "basic instinct" is *not* survival, but rather, fairness, oneness, and love. This is the basic instinct of all sentient beings everywhere. It is your cellular memory. It is your *inherent nature*. Thus is exploded your first cultural myth. You are *not* basically evil, you were *not* born in "original sin."

If your "basic instinct" was "survival," and if your basic nature was "evil," you would never move *instinctively* to save a child from falling, a man from drowning, or anyone from anything. And yet, when you act on your basic instincts and display your basic nature, and don't *think about* what you are doing, this is exactly how you behave, *even at your own peril.*

Thus, your "basic" instinct cannot be "survival," and your basic nature is clearly not "evil." Your instinct and your nature is to reflect the essence of Who You Are, which is fairness, oneness, and love.

Looking at the social implications of this, it is important to understand the difference between "fairness" and "equality." It is not a basic instinct of all sentient beings to seek *equality*, or to be *equal*. Indeed, exactly the opposite is true.

The basic instinct of all living things is to express uniqueness, not sameness. Creating a society in which two beings are truly equal is not only impossible, but undesirable. Societal mechanisms seeking to produce true equality—in other words, economic, political, and social "sameness"—work against, not for, the grandest idea and the highest purpose—which is that each being will have the opportunity to produce the outcome of its grandest desire, and thus truly re-create itself anew.

Equality of *opportunity* is what is required for this, not equality *in fact*. This is called *fairness*. Equality in *fact*, produced by exterior forces and laws, would *eliminate*, not *produce*, fairness. It would eliminate the opportunity for true self-re-creation, which is the highest goal of enlightened beings everywhere.

And what would *create* freedom of opportunity? Systems that would allow society to meet the basic survival needs of every individual, freeing all beings to pursue self-development and self-creation, rather than self-survival. In other words, systems that imitate the true system, called life, in which *survival is guaranteed*.

Now, because self-survival is not an issue in *enlightened* societies, these societies would never allow one of its members to suffer if there were enough for all. In these societies self-interest and mutual best interest are identical.

No society created around a myth of "inherent evilness" or "survival of the fittest" could possibly achieve such understanding.

Yes, I see this. And this "cultural myth" question is something I want to explore, along with the behaviors and ethics of more advanced civilizations, later in greater detail. But I'd like to double back one last time and resolve the questions I started out with here.

One of the challenges of talking with You is that Your answers lead us in such interesting directions that I sometimes forget where I began. But in this case I have not. We were discussing marriage. We were discussing love, and its requirements.

Love *has* no requirements. That's what makes it love.

If your love for another carries requirements, then it is not love at all, but some counterfeit version.

That is what I have been trying to tell you here. It is what I have been saying, in a dozen different ways, with every question you've asked here.

Within the context of marriage, for example, there is an exchange of vows that love does not require. Yet *you* require them, because you do not know what love *is*. And so you make each other promise *what love would never ask*.

Then You *are* against marriage!

I am "against" nothing. I am simply describing what I see.

Now you can *change* what I see. You can redesign your social construction called "marriage" so that it does *not* ask what Love would never ask, but rather, declares *what only love could declare*.

In other words, change the marriage vows.

More than that. Change the *expectations* on which the vows are based. These expectations are going to be difficult to change, because they are your cultural heritage. They arise, in turn, from your cultural myths.

Here we go again with the cultural myths routine: What's up with You about this?

I am hoping to point you in the right direction here. I see where you say you want to go with your society, and I am hoping to find human words and human terms that can direct you there.

May I give you an example?

Please.

One of your cultural myths about love is that it's about giving rather than receiving. This has become a cultural imperative. And yet it is driving you crazy, and causing more damage than you could ever imagine.

It gets, and keeps, people in bad marriages, it causes relationships of all kinds to be dysfunctional, yet no one—not your parents, to whom you look for guidance; not your clergy, to whom you look for inspiration; not your psychologists and psychiatrists, to whom you look for clarity; not even your writers and artists, to whom you look for intellectual leadership, will dare to challenge the prevailing cultural myth.

And so, songs are written, stories are told, movies are made, guidance is given, prayers are offered, and parenting is done which perpetuates The Myth. Then you are all *left to live up to it.*

And you can't.

Yet it is not *you* that is the problem, it is The Myth.

Love is *not* about giving rather than receiving?

No.

It *isn't?*

No. It never has been.

But You said Yourself just a moment ago that "Love has no requirements." You said, *that's what makes it love.*

And so it is.

Well, that sure sounds like "giving rather than receiving" to me!

Then you need to reread Chapter Eight of *Book 1.* Everything I'm alluding to here I've explained to you there. This dialogue was meant to be read in sequence, and to be considered as a whole.

I know. But for those who nevertheless came to these words now without having read *Book 1*; could You explain, please, what You're getting at here? Because, frankly, even I could use the review, and I think I now *understand* this stuff!

Okay. Here goes.

Everything you do, you do for yourself.

This is true because you and all others are One.

What you do for another, you therefore do for you. What you fail to do for another, you fail to do for you. What is good for another is good for you, and what is bad for another is bad for you.

This is the most basic truth. Yet it is the truth you most frequently ignore.

Now when you are in a relationship with another, that relationship has only one purpose. It exists as a vehicle for you to decide and to declare, to create and to express, to experience and to fulfill your highest notion of Who You Really Are.

Now if Who You Really Are is a person who is kind and considerate, caring and sharing, compassionate and loving—then, when you are *being* these things with others, you are giving your *Self* the grandest experience for which you came into the body.

This is why you took a body. Because only in the physical realm of the relative could you know yourself as these things. In the realm of the absolute from which you have come, this experience of knowing is impossible.

All these things I've explained to you in far greater detail in *Book 1*.

Now if Who You Really Are is a being who does not love the Self, and who allows the Self to be abused, damaged, and destroyed by others, then you will continue behaviors which allow you to experience that.

Yet if you really *are* a person who is kind and considerate, caring and sharing, compassionate and loving, you will include your *Self* among the people with whom you are *being* these things.

Indeed, you will *start* with yourself. You will *put yourself first* in these matters.

Everything in life depends on what you are seeking to be. If, for instance, you are seeking to be One with all others (that is, if you are seeking to *experience* a conceptualization you already know to be true), you will find yourself behaving in a very specific way—a way which allows you to experience and demonstrate your Oneness. And when you do certain things as a result of this, you will not experience that you are doing something for *someone else,* but rather, that you are doing it *for your Self.*

The same will be true no matter what you are seeking to be. If you are seeking to be love, you will do loving things with others. Not *for* others, but *with* others.

Notice the difference. Catch the nuance. You will be doing loving things *with* others, *for* your *Self*—so that you can actualize and experience your grandest idea about your Self and Who You Really Are.

In this sense, it is impossible to do *anything* for another, for every act of your own volition is literally *just that:* an "act." You are *acting.* That is, creating and playing a role. Except, you are not *pretending.* You are actually *being* it.

You are a human *being.* And what you are being is decided and chosen by you.

Your Shakespeare said it: All the world's a stage, and the people, the players.

He also said, "To be or not to be, that is the question."

And he *also* said: "To thine own Self be true, and it must follow, as the night the day, thou canst not then be false to any man."

When you are true to your Self, when you do not *betray your Self,* then when it "looks like" you are "giving," you will know you are actually "receiving." You are literally giving yourself back to your Self.

You cannot truly "give" to another, for the simple reason that there _is_ no "other." If We are all One, then there is only You.

This sometimes seems like a semantic "trick," a way to change the words around to alter their meaning.

It is not a trick, but it _is magic!_ And it is not about changing words to alter meaning, but changing perceptions to alter experience.

Your experience of everything is based on your perceptions, and your perception is based on your understanding. And your understanding is based on your myths. That is, _on what you have been told._

Now I tell you this: Your present cultural myths have not served you. They have not taken you where you say you want to go.

Either you are lying to yourself about where you say you want to go, or you are blind to the fact that you are not getting there. Not as an individual, not as a country, not as a species or a race.

Are there others species which are?

Oh yes, decidedly.

Okay, I've waited long enough. Tell me about them.

Soon. Very soon. But first I want to tell you about how you can alter your invention called "marriage," so that it takes you closer to where you say you want to go.

Do not destroy it, do not do away with it—_alter it._

Yes, well, I do want to know about that. I do want to know whether there is _any_ way that human beings will ever be allowed to express true love. So I end this section of our dialogue where I began it. What limits shall we—indeed, some would say _must_ we—place on that expression?

None. No limits at all. And that is what *your marriage vows should state.*

That's amazing, because that's exactly what my marriage vows with Nancy *did* state!

I know.

When Nancy and I decided to get married, I suddenly felt inspired to write a whole new set of marriage vows.

I know.

And Nancy joined me. She agreed that we couldn't possibly exchange the vows that had become "traditional" at weddings.

I know.

We sat down and created *new* marriage vows that, well, that "defied the cultural imperative," as You might put it.

Yes, you did. I was very proud.

And as we were writing them, as we put the vows down on paper for the minister to read, I truly believe we were both inspired.

Of course you were!

Do you mean—?

What do you think, I only come to you when you're writing books?

Wow.

Yes, wow.
So why don't you put those marriage vows here?

Huh?

Go ahead. You've got a copy of them. Put them right here.

Well, we didn't create them to share with the world.

When this dialogue began, you didn't think *any* of it would be shared with the world.
Go ahead. Put them in.

It's just that I don't want people to think that I'm saying, "We've written the Perfect Marriage Vows!"

All of a sudden you're worried about what people will think?

C'mon. You know what I mean.

Look, no one says these are the "Perfect Marriage Vows."

Well, okay.

They're just the best anyone on your planet's come up with so far.

Hey—!

Just *kidding.* Let's lighten up here.
Go ahead. Put the vows in. I'll take responsibility for them. And people will love them. It'll give them an idea of what we're talking about here. Why, you may even want to invite others to take these vows—which are not really "vows" at all, but Marriage Statements.

Well, okay. Here's what Nancy and I said to each other when we got married . . . thanks to the "inspiration" we received:

Minister:
Neale and Nancy have not come here tonight to make a solemn promise or to exchange a sacred vow.

236

Nancy and Neale have come here to make *public* their love for each other; to give noticement to their truth; to declare their choice to live and partner and grow together—out loud and in your presence, out of their desire that we will all come to feel a very real and intimate part of their decision, and thus make it even more powerful.

They've also come here tonight in the further hope that their ritual of bonding will help bring us *all* closer together. If you are here tonight with a spouse or a partner, let this ceremony be a reminder—a rededication of your own loving bond.

We'll begin by asking the question: Why get married? Neale and Nancy have answered this question for themselves, and they've told me their answer. Now I want to ask them one more time, so they can be sure of their answer, certain of their understanding, and firm in their commitment to the truth they share.

(Minister gets two red roses from table . . .)

This is the Ceremony of Roses, in which Nancy and Neale share their understandings, and commemorate that sharing.

Now Nancy and Neale, you have told me it is your firm understanding that you are not entering into this marriage for reasons of security . . .

. . . that the only real security is not in owning or possessing, nor in being owned or possessed . . .

. . . not in demanding or expecting, and not even in hoping, that what you think you need in life will be supplied by the other . . .

. . . but rather, in knowing that everything you need in life . . . all the love, all the wisdom, all the insight, all the power, all the knowledge, all the understanding, all the nurturing, all the compassion, and all the strength . . . resides *within* you . . .

. . . and that you are not each marrying the other in hopes of *getting* these things, but in hopes of *giving* these gifts, that the other might have them in even greater abundance.

Is that your firm understanding tonight?

(They say, "It is.")

And Neale and Nancy, you have told me it is your firm understanding you are not entering into this marriage as a means of in any way limiting, controlling, hindering, or restricting each other from any true expression and honest celebration of that which is the highest and best within you—including your love of God, your love of life, your love of people, your love of creativity, your love of work, or _any_ aspect of your being which genuinely represents you, and brings you joy. Is that still your firm understanding tonight?

(They say, "It is.")

Finally, Nancy and Neale, you have said to me that you do not see marriage as producing _obligations,_ but rather as providing _opportunities_ . . .

. . . opportunities for growth, for full Self-expression, for lifting your lives to their highest potential, for healing every false thought or small idea you ever had about yourself, and for ultimate reunion with God through the communion of your two souls . . .

. . . that this is truly a Holy Communion . . . a journey through life with one you love as an equal partner, sharing equally both the authority and the responsibilities inherent in any partnership, bearing equally what burdens there be, basking equally in the glories.

Is that the vision you wish to enter into now?

(They say, "It is.")

I now give you these red roses, symbolizing your individual understandings of these Earthly things; that you both know and agree how life will be with you in bodily form, and within the physical structure called marriage. Give these roses now to each other as a symbol of your _sharing_ of these agreements and understandings with love.

Now, please each of you take this white rose. It is a symbol of your larger understandings, of your spiritual nature and your spiritual truth. It stands for the purity of your Real and Highest Self, and of the purity of God's love, which shines upon you now, and always.

(She gives Nancy the rose with Neale's ring on the stem, and Neale the rose with Nancy's ring on it.)

What symbols do you bring as a reminder of the promises given and received today?

(They each remove the rings from the stems, giving them to the minister, who holds them in her hand as she says . . .)

A circle is the symbol of the Sun, and the Earth, and the universe. It is a symbol of holiness, and of perfection and peace. It is also the symbol of the eternality of spiritual truth, love, and life . . . that which has no beginning and no end. And in this moment, Neale and Nancy choose for it to also be a symbol of unity, but not of possession; of joining, but not of restricting; of encirclement, but not of entrapment. For love cannot be possessed, nor can it be restricted. And the soul can never be entrapped.

Now Neale and Nancy, please take these rings you wish to give, one to the other.

(They take each other's rings.)

Neale, please repeat after me.

I, Neale . . . ask you, Nancy . . . to be my partner, my lover, my friend, and my wife . . . I announce and declare my intention to give you my deepest friendship and love . . . not only when your moments are high . . . but when they are low . . . not only when you remember clearly Who You Are . . . but when you forget . . . not only when you are acting with love . . . but when you are not . . . I further announce . . . before God and those here present . . . that I will seek always to see the Light of Divinity within you . . . and seek always to share . . . the Light of Divinity within me . . . even, and *especially* . . . in whatever moments of darkness may come.

It is my intention to be with you forever . . . in a Holy Partnership of the Soul . . . that we may do together God's work . . . sharing all that is good within us . . . with all those whose lives we touch.

(The minister turns to Nancy.)

Nancy, do you choose to grant Neale's request that you be his wife?

(She answers, "I do.")

Now Nancy, please repeat after me.

I, Nancy . . . ask you, Neale . . . *(She makes the same vow).*

(Minister turns to Neale.)

Neale, do you choose to grant Nancy's request that you be her husband?

(He answers, "I do.")

Please then, both of you, take hold of the rings you would give each other, and repeat after me: With this ring . . . I thee wed . . . I take now the ring you give to me . . . *(they exchange rings)* . . . and give it place upon my hand . . . *(they place the rings on their hands)* . . . that all may see and know . . . of my love for you.

(The Minister closes . . .)

We recognize with full awareness that only a couple can administer the sacrament of marriage to each other, and only a couple can sanctify it. Neither my church, nor any power vested in me by the State, can grant me the authority to declare what only two hearts can declare, and what only two souls can make real.

And so now, inasmuch as *you*, Nancy, and *you*, Neale, have announced the truths that are already written in your hearts, and have witnessed the same in the presence of these, your friends, and the One Living Spirit—we observe joyfully that *you* have declared yourself to be . . . husband and wife.

Let us now join in prayer.

Spirit of Love and Life: out of this whole world, two souls have found each other. Their destinies shall now be woven into one design, and their perils and their joys shall not be known apart.

Neale and Nancy, may your home be a place of happiness for all who enter it; a place where the old and the young are renewed in each other's company, a place for growing and a place for sharing, a place for music and a place for laughter, a place for prayer and a place for love.

May those who are nearest to you be constantly enriched by the beauty and the bounty of your love for one another, may your work be a joy of your life that serves the world, and may your days be good and long upon the Earth.

Amen, and amen

I am so touched by that. I am so honored, so blessed, to have found someone in my life who could say those words with me, and mean them. Dear God, thank You for sending me Nancy.

You are a gift to her, too, you know.

I hope so.

Trust Me.

Do You know what I wish?

No. What?

I wish that all people could make those Marriage Statements. I wish people would cut them out, or copy them, and use them for *their* wedding. I bet we'd see the divorce rate plummet.

Some people would have a very hard time saying those things—and many would have a hard time staying true to them.

I just hope that *we* can stay true to them! I mean, the problem with putting those words in here is that now we have to live up to them.

You were not planning on living up to them?

Of course we were. But we're human, just like everybody else. Yet now if we fail, if we falter, if anything should happen to our relationship, or, good grief, we should ever choose to *end* it in its present form, all kinds of people are going to be disillusioned.

241

Nonsense. They'll know that you are being true to yourself; they'll know that you have made a later choice, a new choice. Remember what I told you in *Book 1*. Do not confuse the length of your relationship with its quality. You are not an icon, and neither is Nancy, and no one should put you there—and you should not put yourself there. Just be human. Just be fully human. If at some later point you and Nancy feel you wish to reform your relationship in a different way, you have a perfect right to do that. *That is the point of this whole dialogue.*

And it was the point of the statements we made!

Exactly. I'm glad that you see that.

Yes, I *like* those Marriage Statements, and I'm glad that we put them in! It's a wonderful new way to begin a life together. No more asking the woman to promise "to love, honor, and obey." It was self-righteous, self-inflated, self-serving men who demanded that.

You're right, of course.

And it was even more self-righteous and self-serving for men to claim that such male preeminence was *God-ordained.*

Again, you are right. I never ordained any such thing.

At last, marriage words which really are inspired by God. Words which make a chattel, personal property, out of *no one.* Words which speak the truth about love. Words which place no limitations, but promise only freedom! Words to which all hearts can *remain true.*

There are those who will say, "Of *course* anyone can keep vows which ask nothing of you!" What will you say to that?

I will say: "It is much more difficult to free someone than to

242

control them. When you control someone, you get what *you* want. When you free someone, they get what *they* want."

You will have spoken wisely.

I have a wonderful idea! I think we should make a little booklet of those Marriage Statements, kind of a little prayer book for people to use on their wedding day.

It could be a small little book, and it would contain not only those words, but a whole ceremony, and key observations about love and relationship from all three books in this dialogue, as well as some special prayers and meditations on marriage—which, it turns out, You're *not* against!

I'm so happy, because it started to sound for a minute as if You were "anti-marriage."

How could I be against marriage? We are *all* married. We are married to *each other*—now, and forevermore. We are united. We are One. Ours is the biggest marriage ceremony ever held. My vow to you is the grandest vow ever made. I will love you forever, and free you for everything. My love will never bind you in any way, and because of this you are "bound" to eventually love Me—for freedom to Be Who You Are is your greatest desire, and My greatest gift.

Do you take Me now to be your lawfully wedded partner and co-creator, according to the highest laws of the universe?

I do.
And do *You* take *me* now as Your partner, and co-creator?

I do, and I always have. Now and through all eternity we are One. Amen.
And amen.

14

I am filled with awe and reverence at the reading of those words. Thank You for being here with me in this way. Thank You for being here with all of us. For millions have read the words in these dialogues, and millions more will yet do so. And we are breathlessly gifted by the coming of You to our hearts.

My dearest beings—I have always been in your hearts. I am only glad you can now actually feel Me there.

I have always been with you. I have never left you. I *am* you, and you are Me, and We shall *never* be separated, *ever*, because that is not *possible*.

Hey, wait a minute! This feels like *déjà vu*. Didn't we just say all of these words before?

Of course! Read the beginning of Chapter 12. Only now they mean even more than they meant the first time.

Wouldn't it be neat if *déjà vu* was real, and that we really *are* sometimes experiencing something "over again" so that we can get more meaning out of it?

What do you think?

I think that's *exactly* what's sometimes happening!

Unless it's not.

Unless it's not!

244

Good. Bravo again. You are moving so rapidly, so quickly, to massive new understandings that it is getting scary.

Yes, *isn't* it—? Now, I have something serious I need to discuss with You.

Yes, I know. Go ahead.

When does the soul join the body?

When do you think?

When it chooses to.

Good.

But people want a more definitive answer. They want to know when life begins. Life as they know it.

I understand.

So what is the signal? Is it the emergence of the body from the womb—the physical birth? Is it the moment of conception, the physical joining of the elements of physical life?

Life has no beginning, because life has no end. Life merely extends; creates new forms.

It must be like that gloppy material in those heated lava lamps that were so popular in the Sixties. The globs would lay in big, soft, round balls at the bottom, then rise from the heat, separating and forming new globs, shaping themselves as they rose, rejoining each other at the top, cascading together to form even larger globs of the all, and starting all over again. There were never any "new" globs in the tube. It was all the *same stuff*, reforming itself into what "looked like" *new* and *different stuff*. The varieties were endless, and it was fascinating to watch the process unfold over and over again.

That's a great metaphor. That's how it is with souls. The One Soul—which is really All There Is—reforms Itself into smaller and smaller parts of Itself. All the "parts" were there at the beginning. There are no "new" parts, merely portions of the All That Always Was, reforming Itself into what "looks like" new and different parts.

There's a brilliant pop song written and performed by Joan Osborne that asks, "What if God was one of us? Just a slob like one of us?" I'm going to have to ask her to change the lyric line to: "What if God was one of us? Just a glob like one of us?"

Ha! That's very good. And you know, her song *was* a brilliant song. It pushed people's buttons all over the place. People couldn't stand the thought that I am no better than one of them.

That reaction is an interesting comment, not so much on God, but on the human race. If we consider it a blasphemy for God to be compared to one of us, what does that say about us?

What, indeed?

Yet You *are* "one of us." That's exactly what You're saying here. So Joan was right.

She certainly was. Profoundly right.

I want to get back to my question. Can You tell us anything about when life as we know it starts? At what point does the soul enter the body?

The soul doesn't enter the body. The body is enveloped by the soul. Remember what I said before? The body does not house the soul. It is the other way around.

Everything is always alive. There is no such thing as "dead." There is no such state of being.

That Which Is Always Alive simply shapes itself into a new form—a new physical form. That form is charged with living energy, the energy of life, always.

Life—if you are calling life the energy that I Am—is always there. It is never *not* there. Life never *ends,* so how can there be a point when life *begins?*

C'mon, help me out here. You know what I'm trying to get at.

Yes, I do. You want Me to enter the abortion debate.

Yes, I do! I admit it! I mean, I've got God here, and I have a chance to ask the monumental question. When does life begin?

And the answer is so monumental, you can't hear it.

Try me again.

It *never* begins. Life *never* "begins," because life never *ends.* You want to get into biological technicalities so that you can make up a "rule" based on what you want to call "God's law" about how people should behave—then punish them if they do not behave that way.

What's wrong with that? That would allow us to kill doctors in the parking lots of clinics with impunity.

Yes, I understand. You have used Me, and what *you* have declared to be *My laws*, as justification for all sorts of things through the years.

Oh, come on! Why won't You just say that terminating a pregnancy is murder!

You cannot kill anyone or anything.

No. But you can end its "individuation"! And in our language, that's *killing.*

You cannot stop the process wherein which a part of Me individually expresses in a certain way without the part of Me that is expressing in that way agreeing.

247

What? What are You saying?

I am saying that nothing happens against the will of God.

Life, and all that is occurring, is an expression of God's will—read that, *your* will—made manifest.

I have said in this dialogue, your will is My will. That is because there is only One of Us.

Life is God's will, *expressing perfectly.* If something was happening *against* God's will, it couldn't happen. By definition of Who and What God Is, it *couldn't happen.* Do you believe that one soul can somehow *decide something* for another? Do you believe that, as individuals, you can affect each other in ways in which the other does not want to be affected? Such a belief would have to be based on the idea that you are separate from each other.

Do you believe that you can somehow affect life in a way in which God does not want life to be affected? Such a belief would have to be based on an idea that you are separate from Me.

Both ideas are false.

It is arrogant beyond measure for you to believe that you can affect the universe in a way with which the universe does not agree.

You are dealing with mighty forces here, and some of you believe that you are mightier than the mightiest force. Yet you are not. Nor are you *less* mighty than the mightiest force.

You *are* the mightiest force. No more, no less. So let the force be with you!

Are You saying that I can't kill anybody without his or her permission? Are You telling me that, at some higher level, everyone who has ever been killed has *agreed* to be killed?

You are looking at things in earthly terms and thinking of things in earthly terms, and none of this is going to make sense to you.

I can't *help* thinking in "earthly terms." I am *here,* right *now,* on the Earth!

I tell you this: You are "in this world, but not of it."

So my earthly reality is not reality at all?

Did you really think it was?

I don't know.

You've never thought, "There's something larger going on here"?

Well, yes, sure I have.

Well *this is what's going on. I'm explaining it to you.*

Okay. I got it. So I guess I can just go out now and kill anybody, because I couldn't have done it anyway if they hadn't agreed!

In fact, the human race acts that way. It's interesting that you're having such a hard time with this, yet you're going around acting as if it were true anyway.

Or, worse yet, you are killing people *against* their will, as if it didn't matter!

Well, of *course* it matters! It's just that what we want matters *more.* Don't You get it? In the moment we humans kill somebody, we are not saying that the fact that we've done that doesn't matter. Why, it would be flippant to think that. It's just that what *we* want matters *more.*

I see. So it's easier for you to accept that it's okay to kill others *against* their will. This you can do with impunity. It's doing it because *it is* their will that you feel is wrong.

I never said that. That's not how humans think.

249

It isn't? Let Me show you how hypocritical some of you are. You say it is okay to kill somebody *against* their will so long as *you* have a good and sufficient *reason* for wanting them dead, as in war, for instance, or an execution—or a doctor in the parking lot of an abortion clinic. Yet if the other person feels *they* have a good and sufficient reason for wanting *themselves* dead, you may not help them die. That would be "assisted suicide," and that would be wrong!

You are making mock of me.

No, *you* are making mock of Me. You are saying that I would *condone* your killing someone *against* his will, and that I would *condemn* your killing someone in *accordance* with his will.

This is insane.

Still, you not only fail to see the insanity, you actually claim that those who *point out the insanity* are the ones who are crazy. *You* are the ones who have your head on straight, and they are just troublemakers.

And this is the kind of tortured logic with which you construct *entire lives* and *complete theologies.*

I've never looked at it quite that way.

I tell you this: The time has come for you to look at things a new way. This is the moment of your rebirth, as an individual and as a society. You must re-create your world now, before you destroy it with your insanities.

Now *listen to Me.*

We are All One.

There is only One of Us.

You are not separate from Me, and you are not separate from each other.

Everything We are doing, We are doing in concert with each other. Our reality is a co-created reality. If you terminate a pregnancy, We terminate a pregnancy. Your will is My will.

No individual aspect of Divinity has power over any other aspect of Divinity. It is not possible for one soul to affect another against its will. There are no victims and there are no villains.

You cannot understand this from your limited perspective; but I am telling you it is so.

There is only one reason to be, do, or have anything—as a direct statement of Who You Are. If Who You Are, as an individual and as a society, is who you choose and desire to be, there is no reason to change anything. If, on the other hand, you believe there is a grander experience waiting to be had—an even greater expression of Divinity than the one currently manifesting—then move into that truth.

Since all of Us are co-creating, it may serve Us to do what we can to show others the way that some parts of Us wish to go. You can be a way-show-er, demonstrating the life that you'd like to create, and inviting others to follow your example. You might even say, "I am the life and the way. Follow me." But be careful. Some people have been crucified for making such statements.

Thank You. I'll heed the warning. I'll keep a low profile.

I can see that you're doing a real good job of that.

Well, when you say you're having a conversation with God, it's not easy to keep a low profile.

As others have discovered.

Which might be a good reason to keep my mouth shut.

It's a little late for that.

Well, whose fault is that?

I see what you mean.

It's okay. I forgive You.

You do?

Yes.

How can you forgive Me?

Because I can understand why You did it. I understand why You came to me, and started this dialogue. And when I understand why something was done, I can forgive all the complications that it may have caused or created.

Hmmm. Now that's interesting. Would that you could think of God as being so magnificent as you.

Touché.

You have an unusual relationship with Me. In some ways you think you could never be as magnificent as Me, and in other ways you think I cannot be as magnificent as you.
Don't you find that interesting?

Fascinating.

It's because you think We are separated. These imaginings would leave you if you thought that We were One.
This is the main difference between your culture—which is a "baby" culture, really; a primitive culture—and the highly evolved cultures of the universe. The most significant difference is that in highly evolved cultures, all sentient beings are clear that there is no separation between themselves and what you call "God."
They are also clear that there is no separation between themselves and others. They know that they are each having an individual experience of the whole.

252

Oh, good. Now You're going to get into the highly evolved societies of the universe. I've been waiting for this.

Yes, I think it's time we explored that.

But before we do, I simply must return one last time to the abortion issue. You're not saying here that, because nothing can happen to the human soul against its will, it's okay to kill people, are You? You're not condoning abortion, or giving us a "way out" on this issue, are You?

I am neither condoning nor condemning abortion, any more than I condone or condemn war.

The people of every country think I condone the war they are fighting, and condemn the war that their opponent is fighting. The people of every nation believe they have "God on their side." Every cause assumes the same thing. Indeed, every *person* feels the same thing—or at least *hopes* it is true whenever any decision or choice is made.

And do you know *why* all creatures believe God is on their side? *Because I am.* And all creatures have an intuitive knowing of this.

This is just another way of saying, "Your will for you is My will for you." And *that* is just another way of saying, I have given you all *free will*.

There is no free will if to exercise it in certain ways produces punishment. That makes a mockery of free will and renders it counterfeit.

So with regard to abortion or war, buying that car or marrying that person, having sex or not having sex, "doing your duty" or not "doing your duty," there is no such thing as right and wrong, and I have no preference in the matter.

You are all in the process of defining yourselves. Every act is an act of self-definition.

If you are pleased with how you have created yourself, if it serves you, you will continue doing so in that way. If you are not, you will stop. This is called evolution.

The process is slow because, as you evolve, you keep changing your ideas about what really serves you; you keep changing your concepts of "pleasure."

Remember what I said earlier. You can tell how highly a person or society has evolved by what that being or society calls "pleasure." And I will add here, by what it declares to serve it.

If it serves you to go to war and kill other beings, you will do so. If it serves you to terminate a pregnancy, you will do so. The only thing that changes as you evolve is your idea of what serves you. And that is based on what you think you are trying to do.

If you are trying to get to Seattle, it will not serve you to head toward San Jose. It is not "morally wrong" to go to San Jose—it simply doesn't serve you.

The question of what you are trying to do, then, becomes a question of _prime importance_. Not just in your life in general, but in every _moment_ of your life specifically. Because it is in the _moments_ of life that a life itself is created.

All of this was covered in great detail in the beginning of our holy dialogue, which you have come to call _Book 1_. I am repeating it here because you seem to need a reminder, or you would never have asked Me your question on abortion.

When you are preparing to have your abortion, therefore, or when you are preparing to smoke that cigarette, or when you are preparing to fry and eat that animal, and when you are preparing to cut that man off in traffic—whether the matter is large or small, whether the choice is major or minor, there is only one question to consider: Is this Who I Really Am? Is this who I now choose to be?

And understand this: _No matter is inconsequential_. There is a consequence to everything. The consequence is who and what you are.

You are in the act of defining your Self right now.

That is your answer to the abortion question. That is your answer to the war question. That is your answer to the smoking question and the meat-eating question and to *every question about behavior you've ever had.*

Every act is an act of self-definition. Everything you think, say, and do declares, "This is Who I Am."

15

I want to tell you, My dearest children, that this matter of Who You Are, and Who You Choose To Be, is of great importance. Not only because it sets the tone of your experience, but because it creates the nature of Mine.

All of your life you have been told that God created you. I come now to tell you this: You are creating God.

That is a massive rearrangement of your understanding, I know. And yet it is a necessary one if you are to go about the true work for which you came.

This is holy work We are up to, you and I. This is sacred ground We walk.

This is The Path.

In every moment God expresses Himself in, as, and through you. You are always at choice as to how God will be created now, and She will never take that choice from you, nor will She punish you for making the "wrong" choice. Yet you are not without guidance in these matters, nor will you ever be. Built *into* you is an internal guidance system that shows you the way home. This is the voice that speaks to you always of your highest choice, that places before you your grandest vision. All you need do is heed that voice, and not abandon the vision.

Throughout your history I have sent you teachers. During every day and time have My messengers brought you glad tidings of great joy.

Holy scriptures have been written, and holy lives have been lived, that you might know of this eternal truth: You and I are One.

Now again I send you scriptures—you are holding one

256

of them in your hands. Now again I send you messengers, seeking to bring you the Word of God.

Will you listen to these words? Will you hear these messengers? Will you *become one of them?*

That is the great question. That is the grand invitation. That is the glorious decision. The world awaits your announcement. And you make that announcement with your life, lived.

The human race has no chance to lift itself from its own lowest thoughts until you lift yourself to your own highest ideas.

Those ideas, expressed through you, *as* you, create the template, set the stage, serve as a model for the next level of human experience.

You are the life and the way. The world will follow you. You are not at choice in this matter. It is the only matter in which you have no free choice. It is simply The Way It Is. Your world will follow your idea about yourself. Ever it has been, ever it will be. First comes your thought about yourself, then follows the outer world of physical manifestation.

What you think, you create. What you create, you become. What you become, you express. What you express, you experience. What you experience, you are. What you are, you think.

The circle is complete.

The holy work in which you are engaged has really just begun, for now, at last, you understand what you are doing.

It is you who have caused yourself to know this, you who have caused yourself to care. And you *do* care now, more than ever before, about Who You Really Are. For now, at last, you see the whole picture.

Who you are, I am.

You are defining God.

I have sent you—a blessed part of Me—into physical form that I might know Myself *experientially* as all that I know Myself to be *conceptually*. Life exists as a tool for God to turn concept into experience. It exists for *you to do the same.* For you *are* God, doing this.

I choose to re-create Myself anew in every single moment. I choose to experience the grandest version of the greatest vision ever I had about Who I Am. I have created you, so that you might re-create Me. This is Our holy work. This is Our greatest joy. This is Our very reason for being.

16

I am filled with awe and reverence at the reading of those words. Thank You for being here with me in this way. Thank You for being here with all of us.

You are welcome. Thank *you* for being here for *Me.*

I have just a few remaining questions, some having to do with those "evolved beings," and then I will allow myself to finish this dialogue.

My Beloved, you will *never* finish this dialogue, nor will you ever have to. Your conversation with God will go on forever. And, now that you are actively engaged in it, that conversation will soon lead to friendship. All good conversations eventually lead to friendship, and soon your conversation with God will produce a *Friendship with God.*

I feel that. I feel that we've actually become *friends.*

And, as happens in all relationships, that friendship, if it is nurtured, kindled, and allowed to grow, will produce, at last, a sense of communion. You will feel and experience your Self as being in *Communion with God.*

This will be a Holy Communion, for then We will speak as One.

And so this dialogue will continue?

Yes, always.

And I won't have to say goodbye at the end of this book?

You never have to say goodbye. You only have to say hello.

You're marvelous, do You know that? You're simply marvelous.

And so are you, My son. And so are you. As are all My children, everywhere.

Do You have children "everywhere"?

Of course.

No, I mean literally, *everywhere.* Is there life on other planets? Are Your children elsewhere in the universe?

Again, of course.

Are these civilizations more advanced?

Some of them, yes.

In what way?

In every way. Technologically. Politically. Socially. Spiritually. Physically. And psychologically.
For instance, your penchant for, your insistence upon, comparisons, and your constant need to characterize something as "better" or "worse," "higher" or "lower," "good" or "bad" demonstrates how far into duality you have fallen; how deeply into separatism you have submerged.

In more advanced civilizations You do not observe these characteristics? And what do You mean by duality?

The level of a society's advancement is reflected, inevitably, in the degree of its duality thinking. Social evolution is demonstrated by movement towards unity, not separatism.

Why? Why is unity such a yardstick?

Because unity is the truth. Separatism is the illusion. As long as a society sees itself as separate—a series or collection of separate units—it lives in the illusion.

All of life on your planet is built on separatism; based in duality.

You imagine yourselves to be separate families or clans, gathered in separate neighborhoods or states, collected in separate nations or countries, comprising a separate world, or planet.

You imagine your world to be the only inhabited world in the universe. You imagine your nation to be the finest nation on earth. You imagine your state to be the best state in the nation, and your family the most wonderful in the state.

Finally, you think that *you* are better than anyone else in your family.

Oh, you claim you *don't* think any of this, but *you act as if you do.*

Your true thoughts are reflected every day in your social decisions, your political conclusions, your religious determinations, your economic choices, and your individual selections of everything from friends to belief systems to your very relationship with God. That is, Me.

You feel so separate from Me that you imagine I won't even talk to you. And so you are required to deny the veracity of your own experience. You *experience* that you and I are One, but you refuse to *believe* it. Thus you are separate not only from each other, but from your own truth.

How can a person be separate from his or her own truth?

By ignoring it. By seeing it and denying it. Or by changing it, twisting it, contorting it to fit a preconceived notion you have about what must be so.

Take the question with which you started off here. You asked, is there life on other planets? I answered, "Of course." I said, "Of *course*" because the evidence is so obvious. It is so obvious that I'm surprised you even asked the question.

Yet this is how a person can be "separate from his own truth": by looking truth in the eye so squarely he can't miss it—and then denying what he sees.

Denial is the mechanism here. And nowhere is denial more insidious than in self-denial.

You've spent a lifetime denying Who and What You Really Are.

It would be sad enough if you limited your denials to less personal things, such as your depletion of the ozone layer, your rape of old-growth forests, your horrible treatment of your young. But you are not content with denying all that you see around you. You won't rest until you deny all that you see *within* you as well.

You see goodness and compassion within you, but you deny it. You see wisdom within you, but you deny it. You see infinite possibility within you, but you deny it. And you see and experience God within you, yet you deny it.

You deny that I am within you—that I *am* you—and in this you deny Me My rightful and obvious place.

I have not, and do not, deny You.

You admit that You are God?

Well, I wouldn't say *that*...

Exactly. And I tell you this: *"Before the cock crows, you will deny Me three times."*

By your very thoughts will you deny Me.

By your very words will you deny Me.

By your very actions will you deny Me.

You *know in your heart* that I am with you, in you; that We are One. Yet you deny Me.

Oh, some of you say I exist all right. But away from you. Way out *there* somewhere. And the further away you imagine Me to be, the further away you step from your own truth.

As with so much else in life—from depletion of your planet's natural resources to the abuse of children in so many of your homes—you see it, but you don't believe it.

But why? *Why?* Why do we see, and yet not believe?

Because you are so caught up in the illusion, you are so deep in the illusion, that you cannot see past it. Indeed, you *must* not for the illusion to continue. This is the Divine Dichotomy.

You *must* deny Me if you are to continue seeking to *become* Me. And that is what you are wanting to do. Yet you cannot become what you already are. So denial is important. It is a useful tool.

Until it is not anymore.

The master knows that denial is for those who are choosing to have the illusion continue. Acceptance is for those who choose now for the illusion to end.

Acceptance, proclamation, demonstration. Those are the *three steps* to God. Acceptance of Who and What You Really Are. Proclamation of it for all the world to hear. And demonstration in every way.

Self-proclamation is *always* followed by demonstration. You will *demonstrate* your Self to be God—even as you now demonstrate what you think of your Self. Your whole life is a demonstration of that.

Yet with this demonstration will come your greatest challenge. For the moment you stop denying your Self, others will deny *you.*

The moment you proclaim your Oneness with God, others will proclaim your partnership with Satan.

The moment you speak the highest truth, others will say you speak the lowest blasphemy.

And, as happens with all masters who gently demonstrate their mastery, you will be both worshipped and reviled, elevated and denigrated, honored and crucified. Because while for you the cycle will be over, those who are still living in the illusion will not know what to make of you.

Yet what will happen to me? I don't understand. I'm confused. I thought You've said, over and over again, that the illusion must go on, that the "game" must continue, in order for there to be any "game" at all?

Yes, I have said that. And it does. The game does go on. Because one or two of you end the cycle of illusion, that does not end the game—not for you, and not for the other players.

The game is not ended until All-in-All becomes One again. Even then it is not ended. For in the moment of divine reunion, All with All, will the bliss be so magnificent, so intense, that I-We-You will literally burst wide open with gladness, exploding with joy—and the cycle will begin all over again.

It will *never* end, My child. The game will *never* end. For the game is life itself, and life is Who We Are.

But what happens to the individual element, or "Part of All," as You call it, which rises to mastery, which achieves all-knowing?

That master knows that only his part of the cycle is complete. She knows that only her experience of the illusion has ended.

Now the master laughs, because the master sees the master plan. The master sees that even with her completion of the cycle, the game goes on; the experience continues. The master then also sees the role he may now play in the experience. The master's role is to lead others to mastery. And so the master continues to play, but in a new way, and with new tools. For seeing the illusion allows the master to step outside of it. This the master will do from time to time when it suits his purpose and pleasure. Thus she proclaims and demonstrates her mastery, and he is called God/Goddess by others.

When all in your race are led to mastery and achieve it, then your race as a whole (for your race *is* a whole) will move easily through time and space (you will have mastered the laws of physics as you understood them) and you will seek to assist those belonging to other races and other civilizations in coming to mastery as well.

Even as those of other races and other civilizations are doing so now, with us?

Exactly. Precisely.

And only when all the races of all the universe have achieved mastery—

—or, as I would put it, only when All of Me has known the Oneness—

—will this part of the cycle end.

You have put it wisely. For the cycle itself will *never* end.

Because the very ending of this part of the cycle is the cycle itself!

Bravo! *Magnifico!*
You have understood!
So yes, there is life on other planets. And yes, much of it is more advanced than your own.

In what way? You never really did answer that question.

Yes I did. I said, in every way. Technologically. Politically. Socially. Spiritually. Physically. Psychologically.

Yes, but give me some examples. Those are statements so broad that they are meaningless to me.

265

You know, I love your truth. It's not everyone who would look God in the eye and announce that what He is saying is meaningless.

So? What are you going to do about it?

Exactly. You have exactly the right attitude. Because, of course, you're right. You can challenge Me, confront Me, and call Me into question as much as you want, and I'm not going to do a damned thing.

I may, however, do a blessed thing, such as I'm doing here, with this dialogue. Is this not a blessed event?

Yes, this is. And many people have been helped by this. Millions of people have been, are being, touched by this.

I know that. It's all part of the "master plan." The plan for how you become masters.

You knew from the beginning that this trilogy would be a massive success, didn't You?

Of course I did. Who do you suppose has made it such a success? Who do you imagine has caused those people who are reading this to have found their way to it?

I tell you this: I know every person who will come to this material. And I know the reason each has been brought.

And so do they.

Now the only question is, will they deny Me again?

Does it matter to You?

Not in the least. All My children will one day come back to Me. It is not a question of whether, but of *when*. And so, it may matter to them. Therefore, let those who have ears to hear, listen.

Yes, well—we were talking about life on other planets, and You were about to give me some examples of how it is so much more advanced than life on Earth.

Technologically, most other civilizations are far ahead of you. There are those which are behind you, so to speak, but not many. Most are far ahead of you.

In what way? *Give me an example.*

Okay, the weather. You don't seem able to control it. (You can't even accurately predict it!) You are, therefore, subject to its whims. Most worlds are not. The beings on most planets can control the local temperature, for example.

They can? I thought temperature on a planet was a product of its distance from its sun, its atmosphere, etc.

Those things establish the parameters. Within those parameters much can be done.

How so? In what way?

By controlling the environment. By creating, or failing to create, certain conditions in the atmosphere.

You see, it is not only a matter of where you are in relationship to a sun, but what you place *between* yourself and that sun.

You have placed the most dangerous things in your atmosphere—and taken out some of the most important. Yet you are in denial about this. That is, most of you will not admit it. Even when the finest minds among you prove beyond doubt the damage you are doing, you will not acknowledge it. You call the finest minds among you crazed, and say that you know better.

Or you say that these wise people only have an ax to grind, a point of view to validate, and their own interests to protect. Yet it is *you* who are grinding an ax. It is _you_ who are seeking to validate a point of view. And it is _you_ who are protecting your special interests.

And your chief interest is yourself. Every evidence, no matter how scientific, no matter how demonstrable or compelling, will be denied if it violates your self-interest.

That's a rather harsh statement, and I'm not sure it's true.

Really? Now you're calling God a liar?

Well, I wouldn't put it that way, exactly . . .

Do you know how long it has taken your nations to agree to simply stop poisoning the atmosphere with fluorocarbons?

Yes . . . Well . . .

Well, nothing. Why do you suppose it took so long? Never mind. I'll tell you. It took so long because to stop the poisoning would cost many major companies a great deal of money. It took so long because it would cost many individual people their conveniences.

It took so long because for years many people and nations chose to deny—_needed_ to deny—the evidence in order to protect their interest in the status quo; in keeping things the way they are.

Only when the rate of skin cancers increased alarmingly, only when the temperatures began rising and the glaciers and snows began melting, and the oceans got warmer and the lakes and rivers began flooding, did more of you begin paying attention.

Only when _your own self-interest_ demanded it, did you see the truth that your finest minds had been placing before you for years.

What's wrong with self-interest? I thought You said in _Book 1_ that self-interest was the place to start.

I did, and it is. Yet in other cultures and other societies on different planets, the definition of "self-interest" is much larger than it is on your world. It is very clear to enlightened creatures that what hurts one hurts the many, and that what benefits the few *must* benefit the many, or, ultimately, it benefits no one.

On your planet it is just the opposite. What hurts one is ignored by the many, and what benefits the few is denied the many.

This is because your definition of self-interest is very narrow, barely reaching past the individual being to his loved ones—and to those only when they do his bidding.

Yes, I said in *Book 1* that in all relationships, do what is in the best interests of the Self. But I also said that when you see what is in your highest self-interest, you will see that it is that which is also in the highest interest of the other—for you and the other are One.

You and all others are One—and this is a level of knowingness that you have not attained.

You're asking about advanced technologies, and I tell you this: You cannot have advanced technologies in any beneficial way without advanced thinking.

Advanced technology without advanced thought creates not advancement, but demise.

You have already experienced that on your planet, and you are very nearly about to experience it again.

What do You mean? What are You talking about?

I am saying that once before on your planet you had reached the heights—beyond the heights, really—to which you now are slowly climbing. You had a civilization on Earth more advanced than the one now existing. And it destroyed itself.

Not only did it destroy itself, it nearly destroyed everything else as well.

It did this because it did not know how to deal with the very technologies it had developed. Its technological evolution was so far ahead of its spiritual evolution

that it wound up making technology its God. The people worshipped technology, and all that it could create and bring. And so they got all that their unbridled technology brought—which was unbridled disaster.
They literally brought their world to an end.

This all happened here, on this Earth?

Yes.

Are You talking about the Lost City of Atlantis?

Some of you have called it that.

And Lemuria? The land of Mu?

That is also part of your mythology.

So then it _is_ true! We did get to that place before!

Oh, beyond it, My friend. Way beyond it.

And we _did_ destroy ourselves!

Why are you surprised? You're doing the same thing now.

I know we are. Will You tell us how we can stop?

There are many other books devoted to this subject. Most people ignore them.

Give us one title, I promise we won't ignore it.

Read _The Last Hours of Ancient Sunlight._

By a man named Thom Hartmann. Yes! I love that book!

Good. This messenger is inspired. Bring this book to the attention of the world.

I will. I will.

It says everything that I would say here, in answer to your last question. There is no need for Me to rewrite that book through you.

It contains a summary of many of the ways in which your Earth home is being damaged, and ways that you can stop the ruination.

So far what the human race has been doing on this planet is not very smart. In fact, throughout this dialogue You have described our species as "primitive." Ever since You first made that remark I've been wondering what it must be like living in a *non*-primitive culture. You say there are many such societies or cultures in the universe.

Yes.

How many?

A great many.

Dozens? Hundreds?

Thousands.

Thousands? There are *thousands* of advanced civilizations?

Yes. And there are other cultures more primitive than yours.

What else marks a society as either "primitive" or "advanced"?

The degree to which it implements its own highest understandings.

This is different from what you believe. You believe that a society should be called primitive or advanced based on how high its understandings *are*. But what good are the highest understandings if you do not implement them?

271

The answer is, they are no good at all. Indeed, they are dangerous.

It is the mark of a primitive society to call regression progress. Your society has moved backward, not forward. Much of your world demonstrated more compassion seventy years ago than it does today.

Some people are going to have a hard time hearing this. You say You are a nonjudgmental God, yet some people may feel judged and made wrong all over the place here.

We've been over this before. If you say you want to go to Seattle and you're actually driving to San Jose, is the person of whom you're asking directions being judgmental if you're told you're heading in a direction that won't get you where you say you want to go?

Calling us "primitive" is not simply giving us directions. The word *primitive* is pejorative.

Really? And yet you say you so admire "primitive" art. And certain music is often savored, for its "primitive" qualities—to say nothing of certain women.

You're using word play now to change things around.

Not at all. I'm merely showing you that "primitive" is not necessarily pejorative. It is your judgment that makes it so. "Primitive" is merely descriptive. It simply says what is true: A certain thing is in the very early stages of development. It says nothing more than that. It says nothing about "right" or "wrong." *You* add those meanings.

I have not "made you wrong" here. I have merely described your culture as primitive. That would only "sounds" wrong to you if you have a judgment about being primitive.

I have no such judgment.

Understand this: An assessment is not a judgment. It is merely an observation of What Is.

272

I want you to know that I love you. I have no judgments about you. I look at you and see only beauty and wonder.

Like that primitive art.

Precisely. I hear your melody and I feel only excitement.

As with primitive music.

You are understanding now. I feel the energy of your race as you would the energy of a man or woman of "primitive sensuality." And, like you, I am aroused.

Now *that* is what is true about you and Me. You do not disgust Me, you do not disturb Me, you do not even disappoint Me.

You *arouse* Me!

I am aroused to new possibilities, to new experiences yet to come. In you I am awakened to new adventures, and to the excitement of movement to new levels of magnificence.

Far from disappointing Me, you *thrill* Me! I am *thrilled* at the wonder of you. You think you are at the pinnacle of human development, and I tell you, *you are just beginning.* You have only just *begun* to experience your splendor!

Your grandest ideas are as yet unexpressed, and your grandest vision unlived.

But wait! Look! Notice! The days of your blossoming are at hand. The stalk has grown strong, and the petals are soon to open. And I tell you this: The beauty and the fragrance of your flowering shall fill the land, and you shall yet have your place in the Garden of the Gods.

17

Now *that's* what I want to hear! *That's* what I came here to experience! *Inspiration,* not degradation.

> You are never degraded unless you think you are.
> You are never judged or "made wrong" by God.

A lot of people don't "get" this idea of a God Who says, "There's no such thing as right and wrong," and Who proclaims that we will never be judged.

> Well, make up your mind! First you say I'm judging you, then you're upset because I'm *not.*

I know, I know. It's all very confusing. We're all very . . . complex. We don't want Your judgments, but we do. We don't want Your punishments, yet we feel lost without them. And when You say, as You did in the other two books, "I will never punish you," we cannot believe that—and some of us almost get mad about that. Because if You're not going to judge, and punish us, what will keep us walking the straight and narrow? And if there's no "justice" in heaven, who will undo all the injustice on Earth?

> Why are you counting on heaven to correct what you call "injustice"? Do not the rains fall from the heavens?

Yes.

> And I tell you this: The rain falls on the just and the unjust alike.

But what about, "Vengeance is Mine, sayeth the Lord"?

I never said that. One of you made that up, and the rest of you believed it.

"Justice" is not something you experience *after* you act a certain way, but *because* you act a certain way. Justice is an *act,* not punishment *for* an act.

I see that the problem with our society is that we seek "justice" after an "injustice" has occurred, rather than "doing justice" in the first place.

Right on the head! You've hit the nail right on the head!

Justice is an action, not a *reaction.*

Do not, therefore, look to Me to somehow "fix everything in the end" by imposing some form of celestial justice in the "afterlife." I tell you this: There *is* no *"afterlife,"* but *only* life. Death does not exist. And the way you experience and create your life, as individuals and as a society, is your demonstration of what you think is just.

And in this You do not see the human race as very evolved, do You? I mean, if the whole of evolution were placed on a football field, where would we be?

On the 12-yard line.

You're kidding.

No.

We're on the *12-yard line* of evolution?

Hey, you've moved from the 6 to the 12 in the past century alone.

Any chance of ever scoring a touchdown?

Of course. If you don't fumble the ball again.

Again?

As I've said, this isn't the first time your civilization has been at this brink. I want to repeat this, because *it is vital that you hear this.*

Once before on your planet the technology you'd developed was far greater than your ability to use it responsibly. You're approaching the same point in human history again.

It's vitally important that you understand this.

Your present technology is threatening to outstrip your ability to use it wisely. Your society is on the verge of becoming a product of your technology, rather than your technology being a product of your society.

When a society becomes a product of its own technology, it destroys itself.

Why is that? Can You explain that?

Yes. The crucial issue is the balance between technology and cosmology—the cosmology of all life.

What do You mean by "the cosmology of all life"?

Simply put, it is the way things work. The System. The Process.

There is a "method to My madness," you know.

I was hoping there was.

And the irony is that once you figure out that method, once you begin to understand more and more of how the universe works, you run a greater risk of causing a breakdown. In this way, ignorance can be bliss.

The universe is itself a technology. It is the *greatest* technology. It works perfectly. On its own. But once you get in there and start messing around with universal principles and universal laws, you run the risk of breaking those laws. And that's a 40-yard penalty.

A major setback for the home team.

Yes.

So, are we out of our league here?

You're getting close. Only you can determine whether you're out of your league. You'll determine that with your actions. For instance, you know enough about atomic energy now to blow yourselves to kingdom come.

Yes, but we're not going to do that. We're smarter than that. We'll stop ourselves.

Really? You keep proliferating your weapons of mass destruction the way you've been doing, and pretty soon they'll get into the hands of somebody who will hold the world hostage to them—or destroy the world trying.

You are giving matches to children, then hoping they won't burn the place down, and you've yet to learn how to *use the matches yourselves.*

The solution to all this is obvious. *Take the matches away from the children.* Then, *throw your own matches away.*

But it's too much to expect a primitive society to disarm itself. And so, nuclear disarmament—our only lasting solution—appears out of the question.

We can't even agree on a halt to nuclear testing. We are a race of beings singularly unable to control ourselves.

And if you don't kill yourselves with your nuclear madness, you'll destroy your world with your environmental suicide. You are dismantling your home planet's ecosystem and you continue to say that you're not.

As if that weren't enough, you're tinkering with the biochemistry of life itself. Cloning and genetically engineering, and not doing so with sufficient care to have this be a boon to your species, but threatening instead to make it the greatest disaster of all time. If you are not careful, you will make the nuclear and environmental threats look like child's play.

By developing medicines to do the work that your bodies were intended to do, you've created viruses so resistant to attack that they stand poised to knock out your entire species.

You're getting me a little scared here. Is all lost, then? Is the game over?

No, but it is fourth-and-ten. It's time to throw a Hail Mary, and the quarterback is looking around for receivers in the clear.

Are you clear? Are you able to receive this?

I'm the quarterback and the last time I looked, you and I were wearing the same color jersey. Are we still on the same team?

I thought there was only one team! Who is on the *other* team?

Every thought which ignores our oneness, every idea which separates us, every action which announces that we are not united. The "other team" is not real, yet it is a part of your reality, for you have made it so.

If you are not careful, your own technology—that which was created to serve you—will kill you.

Right now I can hear some people saying, "But what can one person do?"

They can start by dropping that "what can one person do?" stuff.

I've already told you, there are hundreds of books on this subject. *Stop ignoring them.* Read them. Act on them. Awaken others to them. Start a revolution. Make it an evolution revolution.

Isn't that what has been going on for a long time?

Yes, and no. The process of evolution has been ongoing forever, of course. But now that process is taking a new twist. There's a new turn here. Now you have become *aware* that you are evolving. And not only *that* you are evolving, but *how.* Now you know the *process by which evolution occurs*—and through which *your reality is created.*

Before, you were simply an observer of how your species was evolving. Now you are a conscious participant.

More people than ever before are aware of the power of the mind, their interconnectedness with all things, and their real identity as a spiritual being.

More people than ever before are living from that space, practicing principles that invoke and produce specific results, desired outcomes, and intended experiences.

This truly *is* an evolution revolution, for now larger and larger numbers of you are creating *consciously* the quality of your experience, the direct expression of Who You Really Are, and the rapid manifestation of Who You Choose to Be.

That's what makes this such a critical period. That's why this is the crucial moment. For the first time in your presently recorded history (although not for the first time in human experience), you have both the technology, and the understanding of how to use it, to destroy your entire world. You can actually render yourselves extinct.

These are the exact points made in a book by Barbara Marx Hubbard called *Conscious Evolution.*

Yes, that is so.

It's a document of breathtaking sweep, with wondrous visions of how we can avoid the dire outcomes of previous civilizations, and truly produce heaven on Earth. You probably inspired it!

I think Barbara might say that I had a hand in it. . . .

You said before that You've inspired hundreds of writers—many messengers. Are there other books we should be aware of?

Way too many to list here. Why not conduct your own search? Then, make a list of the ones that have particularly appealed to you, and share that with others.

I have been speaking through authors, poets, and playwrights from the beginning of time. I have placed my truth in the lyrics of songs, and on the faces of paintings, in the shapes of sculptures, and in every beat of the human heart for ages past. And I will for ages to come.

Each person comes to wisdom in a way that is most understandable, along a path that is most familiar. Each messenger of God derives truth from the simplest moments, and shares it with equal simplicity.

You are such a messenger. Go now and tell your people to live together in their highest truth. Share together their wisdom. Experience together their love. For they _can_ exist in peace and harmony.

Then will yours, too, be an elevated society, such as those we have been discussing.

So the main difference between our society and more highly evolved civilizations elsewhere in the universe is this idea we have of separation.

Yes. The first guiding principle of advanced civilization is unity. Acknowledgment of the Oneness, and the sacredness of all life. And so what we find in all elevated societies is that under no circumstances would one being willfully take the life of another of its own species against its will.

No circumstances?

None.

Even if it were being attacked?

Such a circumstance would not occur within that society or species.

Perhaps not within the species, but what about from without?

If a highly evolved species were attacked by another, it is a guarantee that the attacker would be the lesser evolved. Indeed, the attacker would be, essentially, a primitive being. For no evolved being would attack anyone.

I see.

The only reason a species under attack would kill another would be that the attacked being forgot Who It Really Is.

If the first being thought it was its corporal body—its physical *form*—then it might kill its attacker, for it would fear the "end of its own life."

If, on the other hand, the first being understood full well that it was *not* its body, it would never end the corporal existence of another—for it would never have a reason to. It would simply lay down its own corporal body and move into the experience of its noncorporal self.

Like Obi-Wan Kenobi!

Well, exactly. The writers of what you call your "science fiction" are often leading you to greater truth.

I've got to stop here. This seems directly at variance with what was said in *Book 1*.

What was that?

Book 1 said that when someone is abusing you, it does no good to allow the abuse to continue. *Book 1* said that, when acting with love, include *yourself* among those you love. And the book seemed to say, do whatever it takes to stop the attack on you. It even said that *war* was okay as a response to attack—that, and this is a direct quote: ". . . despots cannot be allowed to flourish, but must be stopped in their despotism."

It also says that "choosing to be God-like does not mean you choose to be a martyr. And it certainly does not mean you choose to be a victim."

Now You are saying that highly *evolved* beings would *never* end the corporal life of another. How can these statements stand side by side?

Read the material in *Book 1* again. Closely.

My responses there were all given, and must all be considered, within the context you created; the context of your question.

Read your statement on the bottom of page 127 in *Book 1*. In that statement you allow as to how you are not now operating at a level of mastery. You say that other people's words and actions sometimes hurt you. Given that this is so, you asked how best to respond to these experiences of hurt or damage.

My responses are all to be taken within that context.

I first of all said that the day will come when the words and actions of others will *not* hurt you. Like Obi-Wan Kenobi, you will experience no damage, even when someone is "killing" you.

This is the level of mastery that has been reached by the members of the societies I am now describing. The beings in these societies are very clear Who They Are and who they are not. It is very difficult to cause one of them to experience being "damaged," or "hurt," least of all by placing their corporal *body* in danger. They would simply *exit* their body and leave it for you, if you felt the need to hurt it so much.

The next point I made in My response to you in *Book 1* is that you react the way *you* do to the words and actions of others because you have forgotten Who You Are. But, I say there, that is all right. That is part of the growth process. It is part of evolution.

Then I make a very important statement. All during your growth process "you must work at the level at which you are. The level of understanding, the level of willingness, the level of remembrance."

Everything else I have said there is to be taken within that context.

I have even said, on page 129, "I assume for the purpose of this discussion that you are still . . . seeking to realize (make 'real') Who You Truly Are."

Within the context of a society of beings who do not remember Who They Really Are, the responses I gave you in *Book 1* stand as given. But you didn't ask Me those questions here. You asked Me here to describe the *highly evolved societies of the universe.*

Not only with regard to the subject at hand, but with regard to all the other topics we will cover here, it will be beneficial if you do not see these descriptions of other cultures as criticisms of your own.

There are no judgments here. Nor will there be any condemnation if you do things differently—react differently—than beings who are more evolved.

And so what I have said here is that the highly evolved beings of the universe would never "kill" another sentient being in anger. First they would not *experience* anger. Second, they would not end the corporal experience of any other being without that being's permission. And third—to answer specifically your specific inquiry—they would never feel "attacked," even from outside their own society or species, because to feel "attacked" you have to feel that someone is taking something from you—your life, your loved ones, your freedom, your property, or possessions—*something.* And a highly evolved being would never experience that, because a highly evolved being would simply *give you* whatever you thought you needed so badly that you were prepared to take it by force—even if it cost the evolved being its corporal life—because the evolved being knows she can *create everything all over again*. She would quite naturally give it all away to a lesser being who did not know this.

Highly evolved beings are therefore not martyrs, nor are they victims of anyone's "despotism."

Yet it goes beyond this. Not only is the highly evolved being clear that he can create everything all over again, he is also clear that he *doesn't have to*. He is clear that he needed none of it to be happy, or to survive. He understands that he requires nothing exterior to himself, and that the "himself" which he *is* has nothing to do with anything physical.

Lesser evolved beings and races are not always clear about this.

Finally, the highly evolved being understands that she and her attackers are One. She sees the attackers as a wounded part of her Self. Her function in that circumstance is to heal all wounds, so that the All In One can again know itself as it really is.

Giving away all that she has would be like giving yourself an aspirin.

Whoa. What a concept. What an understanding! But I need to go back to something You said earlier. You said that highly evolved beings—

—Let's abbreviate that as "HEBs" from here on. It's a long name to have to use over and over again.

Good. Well, You said that "HEBs" would never end the corporal experience of another being without the being's permission.

That's right.

284

But why would one being give another being permission to end its physical life?

There could be any number of reasons. It might offer itself as food, for instance. Or to serve some other necessity—like stopping a war.

This must be why, even in our own cultures, there are those who would not kill any animal for food or hides without asking the spirit of that being for permission.

Yes. This is the way of your Native Americans, who would not even pick a flower, an herb, or a plant without having this communication. All of your indigenous cultures do the same. Interestingly, those are the tribes and cultures that *you* call "primitive."

Oh, man, are You telling me I can't even pick a radish without asking if it's okay?

You can do anything you choose to do. You asked Me what "HEBs" would do.

So Native Americans are highly evolved beings?

As with all races and species, some are, and some are not. It is an individual thing. As a culture, though, they have reached a very high level. The cultural myths which inform much of their experience are very elevated. But, you have forced them to mix their cultural myths with your own.

Wait a minute! What are You *saying*? The Red Man was a savage! That's why we had to kill them by the thousands, and put the rest in land-prisons we call reservations! Why, even now we take their sacred sites and put golf courses on them. We *have* to. Otherwise they might *honor* their sacred sites, and *remember* their cultural stories, and *perform* their sacred rituals, and we can't have that.

I get the picture.

No, really. Why, if we hadn't taken over and tried to erase their culture, they might have impacted *ours!* Then how would we have wound up?

We'd be respecting the land and the air, refusing to poison our rivers, and then where would our industry be!

The whole population would probably still be walking around naked, with *no shame,* bathing in the river, living off the land, instead of crowding into high-rises and condominiums and bungalows and going to work in the asphalt jungle.

Why, we'd probably still be listening to ancient wisdom teachings around a campfire instead of watching TV! We would have made *no progress at all.*

Well, fortunately, you know what's good for you.

18

Tell me more about highly evolved civilizations and highly evolved beings. Outside of the fact that they don't kill each other for any reason, what else makes them different from us?

They share.

Hey, *we* share!

No, they share *everything*. With *everyone*. Not a being goes without. All the natural resources of their world, of their environment, are divided equally, and distributed to everyone.

A nation or a group or a culture isn't thought to "own" a natural resource simply because it happens to occupy the physical location where that resource is found.

The planet (or planets) which a group of species calls "home" is understood to belong to everyone—to all the species in that system. Indeed, the planet or group of planets *itself* is understood to be a "system." It is viewed as a whole system, not as a bunch of little parts or elements, any one of which can be eliminated, decimated, or eradicated without damage to the system itself.

The *ecosystem*, as we call it.

Well, it's larger than that. It's not just the ecology—which is the relationship of the planet's natural resources to the planet's inhabitants. It's also the relationship of the *inhabitants* to themselves, to each other, and to the environment.

It's the *interrelationship* of *all the species of life.*

287

The "speciesystem"!

Yes! I like that word! It's a good word! Because what we're talking about is larger than the ecosystem. It's truly the *speciesystem*. Or what your Buckminster Fuller called the *noosphere*.

I like *speciesystem* better. It's easier to understand. I always wondered what in blazes the *noosphere* was!

"Bucky" likes your word, too. He's not attached. He always liked whatever made things simpler or easier.

You're talking to Buckminster Fuller now? You've turned this dialogue into a séance?

Let's just say I have reason to know that the essence which identified itself as Buckminster Fuller is delighted with your new word.

Wow, that's great. I mean, that's so cool—to just be able to know that.

It is "cool." I agree.

So in highly evolved cultures it's the *speciesystem* that matters.

Yes, but it isn't that individual beings *don't* matter. Quite to the contrary. The fact that individual beings *do* matter is reflected in the fact that effect on the *speciesystem* is uppermost when considering any decision.

It is understood that the *speciesystem* supports all life, and *every being*, at the optimum level. Doing nothing that would harm the speciesystem is therefore *a statement that each individual being is important.*

Not only the individual beings with status or influence or money. Not only the individual beings with power or size or the presumption of greater self-awareness. *All* beings, and all species, in the system.

How can that work? How can that be possible? On our planet, the wants and needs of some species *have* to be subordinated to the wants and needs of others, or we couldn't experience life as we know it.

You are moving dangerously close to the time when you will *not* be able to experience "life as you know it" precisely *because* you have insisted on subordinating the needs of most species to the desires of only one.

The human species.

Yes—and not even all *members* of that species, but only a few. Not even the largest number (which might have some logic to it), but by far the *smallest*.

The richest and the most powerful.

You've called it.

Here we go. Another tirade against the rich and the accomplished.

Far from it. Your civilization does not deserve a tirade; any more than a roomful of small children deserves one. Human beings will do what they are doing—to themselves and to each other—until they realize that it is no longer in their best interests. No amount of tirades will change that.

If tirades changed things, your religions would have been far more effective long before now.

Whoa! Zip! Zing! You're getting everyone today, aren't You?

I'm doing nothing of the sort. Are these simple observations stinging you? Look, then, to see why. This much we both know. The truth is often uncomfortable. Yet this book has come to bring the truth. As have others which I have inspired. And movies. And television programs.

I'm not sure I want to encourage people to watch television.

For better or worse, television is now the campfire of your society. It is not the *medium* that is taking you in directions you say you do not wish to go, it is the messages you allow to be placed there. Do not denounce the medium. You may use it one day yourself, to send a different message . . .

Let me get back, if I can . . . can I get back to my original question here? I'm still wanting to know how a *speciesystem* can work with the needs of all species in the system treated equally.

The needs are all treated equally, but the needs themselves are not all equal. It is a question of proportion, and of balance.

Highly evolved beings deeply understand that all living things within what we have chosen here to call the *speciesystem* have needs which must be met if the physical forms that both create and sustain the system are to survive. They also understand that not all these needs are the same, or equal, in terms of the demands they place on the system itself.

Let's use your own *speciesystem* as an example.

Okay . . .

Let's use the two living species you call "trees" and "humans."

I'm with You.

Obviously, trees do not require as much daily "maintenance" as humans. So their needs are not equal. Yet they *are* interrelated. That is, one species depends on the other. You must pay as much attention to the needs of trees as to the needs of humans, but the needs themselves are not as great. Yet if you ignore the needs of one species of living thing, you do so at your peril.

The book I mentioned earlier as being of critical importance—*The Last Hours of Ancient Sunlight*—describes all of this magnificently. It says that trees take carbon dioxide out of your atmosphere, using the carbon portion of this atmospheric gas to make *carbohydrates*—that is, to *grow*.

(Nearly everything of which a plant is made, including roots, stems, leaves—even the nuts and fruits which the tree bears—are carbohydrates.)

Meanwhile, the oxygen portion of this gas is released by the tree. It is the tree's "waste matter."

Human beings, on the other hand, need oxygen to survive. Without trees to convert the carbon dioxide, which is plentiful in your atmosphere, into oxygen—which is *not*—*you* as a species cannot survive.

You, in turn release (breathe *out*) carbon dioxide, which the *tree* needs to survive.

Do you see the balance?

Of course. It is ingenious.

Thank you. Now please quit destroying it.

Oh, come on. We plant two trees for every one we cut down.

Yes, and it will take only 300 years for those trees to grow to the strength and size which will allow them to produce as much oxygen as many of the old-growth trees you are chopping down.

The oxygen manufacturing plant which you call the Amazon rain forest can be replaced in its capacity to balance your planet's atmosphere in, say, two or three thousand years. Not to worry. You're clearing thousands of acres every year, but not to worry.

Why? Why are we doing that?

You clear the land so that you can raise cattle to slaughter and eat. Raising cattle is said to provide more income for the indigenous peoples of the rain forest country. So all this is proclaimed to be about making the land _productive._

In highly evolved civilizations, however, eroding the _speciesystem_ is not looked at as _productive,_ but rather, _destructive._ So HEBs have found a way to balance the _total_ needs of the _speciesystem._ They choose to do this, rather than serve the desires of one small portion of the system, for they realize that no species _within_ the system _can survive_ if the _system itself is destroyed._

Man, that seems so obvious. That seems so painfully obvious.

The "obviousness" of it may be even more painful on Earth in the years ahead if your so-called dominant species doesn't wake up.

I get that. I get it big. And I want to do something about it. But I feel so helpless. I sometimes feel so helpless. What can I do to bring about change?

There's nothing you have to do, but there's a great deal you can be.

Help me with that.

Human beings have been trying to solve problems at the "doingness" level for a long time, without much success. That's because true change is always made at the level of "being," not "doing."

Oh, you've made certain discoveries, all right, and you've advanced your technologies, and so, in some ways, you've made your lives easier—but it's not clear whether you've made them _better._ And on the larger issues of principle, you have made very slow progress.

You are facing many of the same problems of principle that you've faced for centuries on your planet.

Your idea that Earth exists for the exploitation of the dominant species is a good example.

You clearly will not change what you are *doing* around that until you change how you are *being.*

You have to change your idea about who you *are* in relationship to your environment and everything in it before you will ever *act* differently.

It is a matter of consciousness. *And you have to raise consciousness before you can change consciousness.*

How can we do that?

Stop being quiet about all this. Speak up. Raise a ruckus. Raise the issues. You might even raise some collective consciousness.

On just one issue, for instance. Why not grow hemp and use it to make paper? Do you have any idea how many trees it takes just to supply your world with daily newspapers? To say nothing of paper cups, carry-out cartons, and paper towels?

Hemp can be grown inexpensively, and harvested easily, and used not only for making paper, but the strongest rope, and the longest-lasting clothing, and even some of the most effective medicines your planet can provide. In fact, cannabis can be planted *so* inexpensively, and harvested *so* easily, and has *so* many wonderful uses, that there is a huge lobby working against it.

Too many would lose too much to allow the world to turn to this simple plant which can be grown almost anywhere.

This is just one example of how greed replaces common sense in the conduct of human affairs.

So give this book to everyone you know. Not only so that they get *this,* but so that they get everything *else* the book has to say. And there's still a *great deal more.*

Just turn the page . . .

Yeah, but I'm starting to feel depressed, like a lot of people said they felt after _Book 2_. Is this going to be more and more talk about how we're destroying things here, and really blowing it? 'Cause I'm not sure I'm up for this . . .

Are you up for being inspired? Are you up for being excited? Because learning about and exploring what other civilizations—advanced civilizations—are doing should both inspire and excite you!

Think of the possibilities! Think of the opportunities! Think of the golden tomorrows just around the corner!

If we _wake up_.

You _will_ wake up! You _are_ waking up! The paradigm _is_ shifting. The world _is_ changing. It's happening right in front of your eyes.

This book is part of it. You are part of it. Remember, you are in the room to heal the room. You are in the space to heal the space. There is no other reason for you to be here.

Don't give up! Don't give up! The grandest adventure has just begun!

All right. I choose to be inspired by the example and wisdom of highly evolved beings, not discouraged by it.

Good. That is a wise choice, given where you say you want to go as a species. You have much you can remember from observing these beings.

HEBs live in unity, and with a deep sense of interrelatedness. Their behaviors are created by their Sponsoring Thoughts—what you might call the basic guiding principles of their society. Your behaviors, too, are created by your Sponsoring Thoughts—or, the basic guiding principles of _your_ society.

What are the basic guiding principles of a HEB Society?

Their First Guiding Principle is: We Are All One.

Every decision, every choice, all of what you would call "morals" and "ethics," is based upon this principle.

The Second Guiding Principle is: Everything in the One Interrelates.

Under this principle, no one member of a species could, or would, keep something from another simply because "he had it first," or it's his "possession," or it's in "short supply." The mutual dependency of all living things in the *speciesystem* is recognized and honored. The relative needs of every species of living organism within the system are always kept in balance—because they are always kept in *mind*.

Does this Second Guiding Principle mean there is no such thing as personal ownership?

Not as you understand it.

A HEB experiences "personal ownership" in the sense of holding *personal responsibility* for every good thing in his care. The closest word in your language to describe what a highly evolved being feels about what you would call a "prized possession" is *stewardship*. A HEB is a *steward,* not an *owner*.

The word "own," and your concept behind it, are not part of the culture of HEBs. There is no such thing as "possession" in the sense of something being a "personal belonging." HEBs do not *possess,* HEBs *caress*. That is, they hold, embrace, love, and care for things, but they do not own them.

Humans possess, HEBs caress. In your language, this is how the difference could be described.

Earlier in your history humans felt they had the right to personally possess *everything they laid their hands on*. This included wives and children, land, and the riches of the land. "Stuff," and whatever other "stuff" their "stuff" could get them, was also theirs. Much of this belief is still held as truth today in human society.

Humans became obsessed with this concept of

"ownership." HEBs who watched this from a distance called this your "possession obsession."

Now, as you have evolved, you understand more and more that you can really, truly, possess nothing—least of all your spouses and children. Many of you, though, still cling to the notion that you can possess land, and everything on it, under it, and over it. (Yes, you even talk about *"air rights"!*)

The HEBs of the universe, by contrast, deeply understand that the physical planet beneath their feet is not something that can be possessed by any single one of them—although an individual HEB may be granted, through the mechanisms of his or her society, a parcel of land for which to care. If she is a good steward of the land, she may be allowed (asked) to pass stewardship on to her offspring, and they to theirs. Yet if at any time either he or his offspring prove to be poor stewards of the land, the land is no longer kept in their care.

Wow! If that were the guiding principle here, half the industries in the world would have to give up their property!

And the world's ecosystem would dramatically improve overnight.

You see, in a highly evolved culture, a "corporation," as you call it, would never be allowed to despoil the land in order to make a profit, for it would be clearly seen that the quality of the lives of the very people who own or work for the corporation are being irrevocably damaged. What profit is there in that?

Well, the damage might not be felt for many years, whereas the benefits are realized right here, right now. So that would be called Short-Term Profit/Long-Term Loss. But who cares about Long-Term Loss if you're not going to be there to experience it?

Highly evolved beings do. But then, they live a lot longer.

How much longer?

Many times longer. In some HEB societies, beings live forever—or as long as they choose to remain in corporal form. So in HEB societies, individual beings are usually around to experience the long-term consequences of their actions.

How do they manage to stay alive so long?

Of course they are never *not* alive, any more than you are, but I know what you mean. You mean "with the body."

Yes. How do they manage to stay with their bodies for so long? Why is this possible?

Well first, *because* they don't pollute their air, their water, and their land. They do not put chemicals into the ground, for instance, which are then taken up by plants and animals, and brought into the body upon consumption of those plants and animals.

A HEB, in fact, would never consume an animal, much less fill the ground, and the plants which the *animal* eats, with chemicals, then fill the animal *itself* with chemicals, and *then* consume it. A HEB would correctly assess such a practice to be suicidal.

So HEBs do not pollute their environment, their atmosphere, and their own corporal bodies, as humans do. Your bodies are magnificent creations, made to "last" infinitely longer than you allow them to.

HEBs also exhibit different psychological behaviors that equally prolong life.

Such as?

A HEB never worries—and wouldn't even understand the human concept of "worry" or "stress." Neither would a HEB "hate," or feel "rage," or "jealousy," or panic. Therefore, the HEB does not produce biochemical reactions within her own body that eat away at it and destroy it. A HEB would call this "eating itself," and a HEB would no sooner consume itself than it would consume another corporal being.

How does a HEB manage this? Are humans capable of such control over emotions?

First, a HEB understands that all things are perfect, that there is a process in the universe that is working itself out, and that all they have to do is not interfere with it. So a HEB never worries, because a HEB understands the process.

And, to answer your second question: Yes, humans have this control, although some don't believe they have it, and others simply don't choose to exercise it. The few who do make an effort live a great deal longer—assuming chemicals and atmospheric poisons haven't killed them, and also assuming they haven't voluntarily poisoned themselves in other ways.

Wait a minute. We "voluntarily poison ourselves"?

Some of you do, yes.

How?

As I said, you eat poisons. Some of you drink poisons. Some of you even smoke poisons.

A highly evolved being finds such behaviors incomprehensible. He can't imagine why you would deliberately take into your bodies substances that you know can't be doing you any good.

Well, we find eating, drinking, and smoking certain things *enjoyable.*

A HEB finds *life* in the *body* enjoyable, and can't imagine doing anything that she *knows ahead of time* could limit or terminate that, or make it painful.

Some of us don't believe that eating red meat plentifully, drinking alcohol, or smoking plants *will* limit or terminate our lives, or make them painful.

Then your observational skills are very dull. They need sharpening. A HEB would suggest that you simply look around you.

Yes, well . . . what else can You tell me about what life is like in the highly evolved societies of the universe?

There is no shame.

No shame?

Nor any such thing as guilt.

How about when a being proves to be a bad "steward" of the land? You just said they take the land away from him! Doesn't that mean he's been judged and found guilty?

No. It means he's been observed and found unable. In highly evolved cultures, beings would never be asked to do something they've demonstrated an inability to do.

What if they still *wanted* to do it?

They would not "want" to.

Why not?

Their own demonstrated inability would eliminate their desire. This is a natural outcome of their understanding that their inability to do a particular thing could potentially damage another. This they would never do, for to damage the Other is to damage the Self, *and they know this.*

So it is still "self-preservation" that drives the experience! Just like on Earth!

299

Certainly! The only thing that's different is their *definition of "Self."* A human defines Self very narrowly. You speak of *your* Self, *your* family, *your* community. A HEB defines Self quite differently. She speaks of *the* Self, *the* family, *the* community.

As if there were only one.

There *is* only one. That's the whole point.

I understand.

And so, in a highly evolved culture, a being would never, for instance, insist on raising offspring if that being consistently demonstrated to itself *its own inability to do so.*

This is why, in highly evolved cultures, children don't raise children. Offspring are given to elders to raise. This doesn't mean that new offspring are torn from those who gave them life, taken from their arms and given to virtual strangers to raise. It is nothing like that.

In these cultures, elders live closely with the young ones. They are not shuffled off to live by themselves. They are not ignored, and left to work out their own final destinies. They are honored, revered, and held close, as part of a loving, caring, vibrant community.

When a new offspring arrives, the elders are right there, deep within the heart of that community and that family, and their raising of the offspring is as organically correct as it feels in your society to have the parents do this.

The difference is that, though they always know who their "parents" are—the closest term in their language would be "life-givers"—these offspring are not asked to learn about the basics of life from beings who are *still learning about the basics of life themselves.*

In HEB societies, the elders organize and supervise the learning process, as well as housing, feeding, and caring for the children. Offspring are raised in an environment of wisdom and love, great, great patience, and deep understanding.

The young ones who gave them life are usually off somewhere, meeting the challenges and experiencing the joys of their own young lives. They may spend as much time with their offspring as they choose. They may even live in the Dwelling of the Elders with the children, to be right there with them in a "home" environment, and to be experienced by them as part of it.

It is all a very unified, integrated experience. But it is the elders who do the raising, who take the responsibility. And it is an honor, for upon the elders is placed the responsibility for the future of the entire species. And in HEB societies, it is recognized that this is more than should be asked of young ones.

I touched on this earlier, when we talked about how you raise offspring on your planet, and how you might change that.

Yes. And thank You for further explaining this, and how it could work. So, getting back, a HEB does not feel guilt or shame, no matter what he does?

No. Because guilt and shame is something which is imposed on a being from outside of itself. It can then be internalized, no question about that, but it is initially imposed from the outside. *Always.* No divine being (and all beings are divine) *ever* knows itself or anything it is doing to be "shameful" or "guilty" until someone outside of Itself labels it that way.

In your culture, is a baby ashamed of its "bathroom habits"? Of course not. Not until you *tell* it to be. Does a child feel "guilty" for pleasuring itself with its genitals? Of course not. Not until you *tell* it to feel guilty.

The degree to which a culture is evolved is demonstrated by the degree to which it labels a being or an action "shameful" or "guilty."

Are *no* actions to be called shameful? Is a person *never* guilty, no matter what he does?

As I have already told you, there is no such thing as right and wrong.

There are some people who still don't understand that.

To understand what is being said here, this dialogue must be read *in its entirety*. Taking any statement out of context could make it not understandable. *Books 1* and *2* contain detailed explanations of the wisdom above. You are asking Me here to describe the highly evolved cultures of the universe. They already understand this wisdom.

Okay. How else are these cultures different from our own?

In many other ways. They do not compete.

They realize that when one loses, everyone loses. They therefore do not create sports and games which teach children (and perpetuate in adults) the extraordinary thought that someone "winning" while another is "losing" is *entertainment*.

Also, as I said, they share everything. When another is in need, they would never dream of keeping or hoarding something they had, simply because it was in scarce supply. On the contrary, that would be *their very reason for sharing it*.

In your society, the price goes up for that which is rare, if you share it at all. In this way you ensure that, if you *are* going to share something which you "possess," at least you'll *be enriched doing it*.

Highly evolved beings are also enriched by sharing rare things. The only thing that is different between HEBs and humans is how HEBs define "being enriched." A HEB feels "enriched" by sharing everything freely, without needing to "profit." Indeed, this feeling *is* the profit.

There are several guiding principles of your culture, which produce your behaviors. As I said earlier, one of your most basic ones is: *Survival of the Fittest.*

This might be called your Second Guiding Principle. It underlies everything your society has created. Its economics. Its politics. Its religions. Its education. Its social structures.

Yet, to a highly evolved being, the principle itself is an oxymoron. It is self-contradicting. Since the First Guiding Principle of a HEB is We Are All One, the "One" is not "fit" until the "All" is "fit." Survival of the "fittest" is, therefore, impossible—or the *only* thing that is possible (therefore a contradiction)—since the "fittest" is *not* "fit" until it *is.*

Are you following this?

Yes. We call it communism.

On your planet you have rejected out-of-hand any system which does not allow for the advancement of one being at the expense of another.

If a system of governance or economics requires an attempt at equitable distribution, to "all," of the benefits *created* by "all," with the resources *belonging* to "all," you have said that system of governance violates the natural order. Yet in highly evolved cultures, the natural order IS *equitable sharing.*

Even if a person or group has done nothing to deserve it? Even if there has been no contribution to the common good? Even if they are evil?

The common good is *life.* If you are alive, you are contributing to the common good. It is very difficult for a spirit to be in physical form. To agree to take such a form is, in one sense, a great sacrifice—yet one that is necessary, and even enjoyed, if the All is to know itself experientially, and to re-create Itself anew in the next grandest version of the greatest vision it ever held about Who It Is.

It is important to understand why we came here.

We?

The souls which make up the collective.

You're losing me.

As I have already explained, there is only One Soul, One Being, One Essence. Some of you call this "God." This Single Essence "individuates" Itself as Everything In The Universe—in other words, All That Is. This includes all the sentient beings, or what you have chosen to call souls.

So "God" is every soul that "is"?

Every soul that is now, ever was, and ever will be.

So God is a "collective?"

That's the word I chose, because it comes closest in your language to describing how things are.

Not a single awesome being, but a collective?

It doesn't have to be one or the other. Think "outside the box"!

God is *both?* A single Awesome Being which is a collective of individualized parts?

Good! Very good!

And why did the collective come to Earth?

To express itself in physicality. To know itself in its own experience. To be God. As I've already explained in detail in *Book 1*.

You created us to be You?

We did, indeed. That is *exactly* why you were created.

And humans were created by a collective?

Your own Bible said, "Let *Us* create man in *Our image,* and after *Our likeness*" before the translation was changed.

Life is the process through which God creates Itself, and then experiences the creation. This process of creation is ongoing and eternal. It is happening all the "time." Relativity and physicality are the tools with which God works. Pure energy (what you call spirit) is What God Is. This Essence is truly the Holy Spirit.

By a process through which energy becomes matter, spirit is embodied in physicality. This is done by the energy literally slowing itself down—changing its oscillation, or what you would call vibration.

That Which Is All does this in parts. That is, parts of the whole do this. These individuations of spirit are what you have chosen to call souls.

In truth, there is only One Soul, reshaping and reforming Itself. This might be called The Reformation. You are all Gods In Formation. (God's *information!*)

That is your contribution, and it is sufficient unto itself.

To put this simply, by taking physical form *you have already done enough.* I want, I need, nothing more. You *have* contributed to the common good. You have made it possible for that which is common—the One Common Element—to experience that which is good. Even you have written that God created the heavens and the Earth, and the animals who walk upon the land, and the birds of the air, and the fishes of the sea, *and it was very good.*

"Good" does not—cannot—exist experientially without its opposite. Therefore have you also created evil, which is the backward motion, or opposite direction, of good. It is the opposite of life—and so have you created what you call death.

Yet death does not exist in ultimate reality, but is merely a concoction, an invention, an imagined experience, through which life becomes more valued by you. Thus, "evil" is "live" spelled backward! So clever you are with language. You fold into it secret wisdoms that you do not even know are there.

Now when you understand this entire cosmology, you comprehend the great truth. You could then never demand of another being that it give you something in return for your sharing the resources and necessities of physical life.

As beautiful as that is, there are still some people who would call it communism.

If they wish to do so, then so be it. Yet I tell you this: Until your *community of beings* knows about *being in community,* you will never experience Holy Communion, and cannot know Who I Am.

The highly evolved cultures of the universe understand deeply all that I have explained here. In those cultures it would not be possible to fail to share. Nor would it be possible to think of "charging" increasingly exorbitant "prices" the more rare a necessity became. Only extremely primitive societies would do this. Only very primitive beings would see scarcity of that which is commonly needed as an opportunity for greater profits. "Supply and demand" does not drive the HEB system.

This is part of a system that humans claim contributes to their quality of life and to the common good. Yet, from the vantage point of a highly evolved being, your system *violates* the common good, for it does not allow that which is *good* to be experienced *in common.*

Another distinguishing and fascinating feature of highly evolved cultures is that within them there is no word or sound for, nor any way to communicate the meaning of, the concept of "yours" and "mine." Personal possessives do not exist in their language, and, if one were to speak in earthly tongues, one could only use articles to describe things. Employing that convention, "my car" becomes "the car I am now with." "My partner" or "my children" becomes "the partner" or "the children I am now with."

The term "now with," or "in the presence of," is as close as your languages can come to describing what you would call "ownership," or "possession."

That which you are "in the presence of" becomes the Gift. These are the true "presents" of life.

Thus, in the language of highly evolved cultures, one could not even speak in terms of "my life," but could only communicate "the life I am in the presence of."

This is something akin to your speaking of being "in the presence of God."

When you are in the presence of God (which you are, any time you are in the presence of each other), you would never think of keeping from God that which is God's—meaning, any part of That Which Is. You would naturally share, and share equally, that which is God's with any *part* of that which is God.

This is the spiritual understanding which undergirds the entire social, political, economic, and religious structures of all highly evolved cultures. This is the cosmology of all of life, and it is merely failure to observe this cosmology, to understand it and to live within it, which creates all of the discord of your experience on Earth.

307

19

What are the beings like on other planets, physically?

Take your pick. There are as many varieties of beings as there are species of life on your planet.
Actually, more.

Are there beings who look very much like us?

Of course, some look exactly like you—given minor variations.

How do they live? What do they eat? How are they dressed? In what way do they communicate? I want to learn all about E.T.s here. C'mon, out with it!

I understand your curiosity, yet these books are not being given to you to satisfy curiosity. The purpose of our conversation is to bring a message to your world.

Just a few questions. And they're more than curiosities. We may have something to learn here. Or, more accurately, to remember.

That really is more accurate. For you have nothing to learn, but merely to remember Who You Really Are.

You made that wonderfully clear in *Book 1*. Do these beings on other planets remember Who They Are?

As you might expect, all beings elsewhere are in various stages of evolution. But in what you have here termed highly evolved cultures, yes, the beings have remembered.

How do they live? Work? Travel? Communicate?

Travel as you know it in your culture does not exist in highly evolved societies. Technology has advanced far beyond the necessity of using fossil fuels to drive engines embedded in huge machines that move bodies around.

In addition to what has been provided by new physical technologies, understandings of the mind, and of the very nature of physicality itself, have also advanced.

As a result of the combination of these two types of evolutionary advances, it has become possible for HEBs to disassemble and reassemble their bodies at will, allowing most beings in most highly evolved cultures to "be" *wherever* they choose—whenever they choose.

Including light-years across the universe?

Yes. In most cases, yes. Such "long distance" travel across galaxies is done like a stone skipping across water. No attempt is made to go *through* The Matrix which is the universe, but rather, to "skip around" *on* it. That is the best imagery which can be found in your language to explain the physics of it.

As for what you call, in your society, "work"—such a concept does not exist in most HEB cultures. Tasks are performed, and activities are undertaken, based purely on what a being loves to do, and sees as the highest expression of Self.

That's super if one can do it, but how does the menial labor get done?

The concept of "menial labor" does not exist. What you would label as "menial" in your society is often the most highly honored in the world of highly evolved beings. HEBs who do the daily tasks that "must" be done for a society to exist and to function are the most highly rewarded, highly decorated "workers" in the service of All. I put the word "workers" in quotes here because to a HEB this is not considered "work" at all, but the highest form of self-fulfillment.

The ideas and experiences that humans have created around self-expression—which you've called work—are simply not part of the HEB culture. "Drudgery," "overtime," "pressure," and similar self-created experiences are not chosen by highly evolved beings, who, among other things, are not attempting to "get ahead," "rise to the top," or "be successful."

The very concept of "success" as you have defined it is foreign to a HEB, precisely because its opposite—*failure*—does not exist.

Then how do HEBs ever have an experience of accomplishment or achievement?

Not through the construction of an elaborate value system surrounding "competition," "winning," and "losing," as is done in most human societies and activities—even (and especially) in your schools—but rather, through a deep understanding of what real value is in a society, and a true appreciation for it.

Achieving is defined as "doing what brings value," not "doing what brings 'fame' and 'fortune,' whether it is of value or not."

Then HEBs *do* have a "value system"!

Oh, yes. Of course. But one very unlike most humans. HEBs value that which produces benefit to All.

So do we!

Yes, but you define "benefit" so differently. You see greater benefit in throwing a little white sphere at a man with a bat, or taking one's clothes off on a big silver screen, than in leading offspring to remember life's greatest truths, or sourcing a society's spiritual sustenance. So you honor, and pay, ballplayers and movie stars more than you do teachers and ministers. In this you have everything backward, given where you say that you want to go as a society.

You have not developed very keen powers of observation. HEBs always see "what's so," and do "what works." Humans very often do not.

HEBs do not honor those who teach or minister because it is "morally right." They do so because it is "what *works,*" given where they choose for their society to go.

Still, where there is a value structure, there must be "haves" and "have nots." So in HEB societies it's the teachers who are rich and famous, and the ballplayers who are poor.

There are *no* "have nots" in a HEB society. No one lives in the depths of degradation to which you have allowed many humans to fall. And no one dies of starvation, as 400 children an hour, and 30,000 people a day, do on your planet. And there is no such thing as a life of "quiet desperation" as there is in human work cultures.

No. In HEB society there is no such thing as "the destitute" and "the poor."

How have they avoided that? *How?*

By applying two basic principles—

We are all One.

There's enough.

HEBs have an awareness of sufficiency, and a consciousness that creates it. Through the HEB consciousness of the interrelatedness of all things, nothing is wasted or destroyed of the natural resources on a HEB's home planet. This leaves plenty for everyone—hence, "there's enough."

311

The human consciousness of insufficiency—of "not enoughness"—is the root cause of all worry, all pressure, all competition, all jealousy, all anger, all conflict, and, ultimately, all killing on your planet.

This, plus the human insistence on believing in the separation, rather than the unity, of all things is what has created 90 percent of the misery in your lives, the sadness in your history, and the impotence of your previous efforts to make things better for everyone.

If you would change these two elements of your consciousness, everything would shift.

How? I want to do that, but I don't know *how*. Give me a tool, not just platitudes.

Good. That's fair. So here's a tool.

"Act as if."

Act as if you *were* all One. Just start acting that way tomorrow. See everyone as "you," just having a difficult time. See everyone as "you," just wanting a fair chance. See everyone as "you," just having a different experience.

Try it. Just go around tomorrow and try it. See everyone through new eyes.

Then, start acting as if "there's enough." If you had "enough" money, "enough" love, "enough" time, what would you do differently? Would you share more openly, freely, equitably?

That's interesting, because we're doing exactly that with our natural resources, and being criticized by ecologists for it: I mean, we're acting as if "there's enough."

What's really interesting is that you act as if the things which you think *benefit* you are in *short* supply, so you watch your supply of that very carefully—often even hoarding those things. Yet you play fast and loose with your environment, natural resources, and ecology. So it can only be assumed that you do not think the environment, natural resources, and your ecology benefits you.

Or that we're "acting as if" *there's enough.*

But you aren't. If you were, you would share these resources more equitably. Yet right now one-fifth of the world's people are using four-fifths of the world's resources. And you show no signs of changing that equation.

There *is* enough for everybody if you would stop thoughtlessly squandering all of it on the privileged few. If all people used resources wisely, you would use less than you do with a few people using them unwisely.

Use the resources, but don't *abuse* the resources. That's all the ecologists are saying.

Well, I'm depressed again. You keep making me depressed.

You're something, you know that? You're driving down a lonely road, lost and having forgotten how to get where you say you want to go. Someone comes along and *gives you directions.* Eureka! You're ecstatic, right? No. You're depressed.

Amazing.

I'm depressed because *I don't see us taking these directions.* I don't see us even wanting to. I see us marching right into a wall, and *yes,* it depresses me.

You are not using your powers of observation. I see hundreds of thousands of people cheering as they read this. I see millions recognizing the simple truths here. And I see a new force for change growing in intensity on your planet. Entire thought systems are being discarded. Ways of governing yourselves are being abandoned. Economic policies are being revised. Spiritual truths are being reexamined.

Yours is *a race awakening.*

The noticements and observations on these pages need not be a source of discouragement. That you *recognize them as truth* can be tremendously encouraging if you allow this to be *the fuel that drives the engine of change.*

You are the change-agent. You are the one who can *make a difference* in how humans create and experience their lives.

How? What can I do?

Be the difference. *Be* the change. *Embody* the consciousness of "We Are All One," and "There's Enough." Change your Self, change the world.

You have given your Self this book, and all the *Conversations with God* material, so that you might remember once again how it was to live as highly evolved beings.

We lived this way once before, didn't we? You mentioned earlier that we had lived like this once before.

Yes. In what you would call ancient times and ancient civilizations. Most of what I have been describing here has been experienced by your race before.

Now a part of me wants to be even *more* depressed! You mean we got there and then lost it all? What's the point of all this "going around in circles" that we're doing?

Evolution! Evolution is *not a straight line.*

You have a chance now to re-create the best experiences of your ancient civilizations, while avoiding the worst. You don't have to let personal egos and advanced technology destroy your society this time. You can do it differently. You—*you*—can *make a difference.*

That could be very exciting to you, if you allow it to be.

Okay. I get it. And when I allow myself to think of it that way, I *am* excited! And I *will* make a difference! Tell me more! I want to remember as much as I can about how it was with us in our advanced, ancient civilizations, and how it is today with all highly evolved beings. How do they live?

They live in clusters, or what your world would call communities, but for the most part they have abandoned their version of what you call "cities," or "nations."

Why?

Because "cities" became too big, and no longer supported the purpose of clustering, but worked against that purpose. They produced "crowded individuals" instead of a clustered community.

It's the same on this planet! There is more of a sense of "community" in our small towns and villages—even in our wide open rural areas—than there is in most of our big cities.

Yes. There's only one difference, on that score, between your world and the other planets we are now discussing.

Which is?

The inhabitants of those other planets have learned this. They have observed more closely "what works."

We, on the other hand, keep creating larger and larger cities, even though we see that they are destroying our very way of life.

Yes.

We even take *pride* in our rankings! A metropolitan area moves up from number 12 to number 10 on our list of biggest cities and everyone thinks that's a cause for celebration! Chambers of Commerce actually *advertise it!*

It is the mark of a primitive society to view regression as progress.

315

You have said that before. You're getting me depressed again!

More and more of you are no longer doing this. More and more of you are re-creating small "intended" communities.

So, do You think we should abandon our megacities and return to our towns and villages?

I don't have a preference about it one way or the other. I am simply making an observation.

As always. So what is Your observation regarding why we continue to migrate to bigger and bigger cities, even though we see that it is not good for us?

Because many of you do not see that is not good for you. You believe that grouping together in large cities solves problems, when it only creates them.

It is true that in large cities there are services, there are jobs, there are entertainments which are not, and cannot be, found in smaller towns and villages. But your mistake is in calling these things valuable, when, in fact, they are detrimental.

Aha! You *do* have a point of view on this! You just gave yourself away! You said we made a "mistake."

If you're headed toward San Jose—

Here we go again—

Well, you insist on calling observations "judgments," and statements of fact, "preferences," and I know you are seeking greater accuracy in your communications and in your perceptions, so I'm going to call you on this every time.

If you are headed toward San Jose, all the while saying you wish to go to Seattle, is it wrong for the bystander of whom you are asking directions to say that you have "made a mistake"? Is the bystander expressing a "preference"?

I guess not.

You *guess not?*

Okay, he's not.

Then what *is* he doing?

He's merely saying "what's so," given where we say we want to go.

Excellent. You've got it.

But You've made this point before. Repeatedly. Why do I keep reverting to an idea about You as having preferences and judgments?

Because that's the God who's supported by your mythology, and you will throw Me into that category any time you can. Besides, if I *did* have a preference, that would make everything easier for you. Then you wouldn't have to figure things out and come to your *own* conclusions. You'd just have to do as *I* say.

Of course, you'd have no way of knowing *what* it is that I say, since you don't believe I've said anything for thousands of years, so you have no choice but to rely on those who claim to be teaching what I *used* to say during the days when I was actually communicating. But even this is a problem, because there are as many different teachers and teachings as there are hairs on your head. So, you're right back where you started from, having to come to your *own* conclusions.

Is there a way out of this maze—and the cycle of misery it has created for the human race? Will we ever "get it right"?

There *is* a "way out," and you *will* "get it right." You merely have to *increase your observational skills.* You have to better see what serves you. This is called "evolution." Actually, you cannot "not get it right." You cannot fail. It is merely a question of when, not of whether.

But aren't we running out of time on this planet?

Oh, if *that's* your parameter—if you want to "get it right" on *this planet,* that is, while *this particular planet still supports you*—then, within *that* context, you'd better hurry.

How can we go faster? Help us!

I am helping you. What do you suppose this dialogue is about?

Okay, so give us some more help. You said a little bit ago that in highly evolved cultures on other planets, beings also abandoned the concept of "nations." Why did they do that?

Because they saw that a concept such as what you would call "nationalism" works against their First Guiding Principle: WE ARE ALL ONE.

On the other hand, nationalism *supports* our Second Guiding Principle: SURVIVAL OF THE FITTEST.

Exactly.
You separate yourself into nations for reasons of survival and security—and produce just the opposite.
Highly evolved beings refuse to join together in nations. They believe in simply one nation. You might even say they have formed "one nation, under God."

Ah, clever. But do they have "liberty and justice for all"?

Do you?

Touché.

The point is that all races and species are evolving, and evolution—the purpose of observing what serves you, and making behavioral adaptions—seems to keep moving in one direction, and away from another. It keeps moving towards unity, and away from separation.

This is not surprising, since unity is the Ultimate Truth, and "evolution" is just another word for "movement toward truth."

I also notice that "observing what serves you, and making behavioral adaptations" sounds suspiciously like "survival of the fittest"—one of our Guiding Principles!

It does, doesn't it?

So now it's time to "observe" that "survival of the fittest" (that is, evolution of the species) is not achieved, but, indeed, entire species have been doomed—have actually *self-destructed*—by calling a "process" a "principle."

Oops. You lost me.

The *process* is called "evolution." The "principle" which *guides* the process is what directs the course of your evolution.

You are right. Evolution *is* "survival of the fittest." That is the *process*. Yet do not confuse "process" and "principle."

If "evolution" and "survival of the fittest" are synonymous, and if you are claiming "survival of the fittest" as a Guiding Principle, then you are saying, "A Guiding Principle of Evolution *is evolution*."

Yet that is the statement of a race which does not know that it can *control the course of its own evolution*. That is the statement of a species which thinks itself to be relegated to the status of observer of its own evolution. Because most people think that "evolution" is a process

319

which is simply "going on"—not a process which they are *directing,* according to certain *principles.*

And so the species is announcing, "We *evolve* by the principle of . . . well, *evolution.*" But they never say what that principle IS, because they have confused the process and the principle.

The species, on the other hand, which has become clear that evolution is a process—but a process *over which the species has control*—has not confused "process" with "principle," but consciously *chooses* a principle which it *uses to guide and direct its process.*

This is called *conscious evolution,* and your species has just arrived there.

Wow, that's an incredible insight. *That's* why You gave Barbara Marx Hubbard that book! As I said, she actually called it *Conscious Evolution.*

Of course she did. I told her to.

Ah, I love it! So . . . I'd like to get back to our "conversation" about E.T.s. How do these highly evolved beings organize themselves, if not in nations? How do they govern themselves?

They do not use "evolution" as their First Guiding Principle of Evolution, but, rather, they have *created* a principle, based on pure observation. They have simply observed that they are all One, and they have devised political, social, economic, and spiritual mechanisms which *undergird,* rather than *undermine,* that First Principle.

What does that "look like"? In government, for instance?

When there is only one of You, how do you govern yourself?

Come again?

320

When you are the only one there is, how do you govern your behavior? Who governs your behavior? Who, outside of yourself?

No one. When I am all alone—if I were on a deserted island someplace, for instance—no one "outside of myself" would govern or control my behaviors. I would eat, dress, do exactly as I want. I would probably not dress at all. I would eat whenever I was hungry, and whatever felt good and made me feel healthy. I would "do" whatever I felt like doing, and some of that would be determined by what I thought I needed to do to survive.

Well, as usual, you have all the wisdom within you. I've told you before, you have nothing to learn, you have only to remember.

This is how it is in advanced civilizations? They run around naked, picking berries, and carving canoes? Those sound like barbarians!

Who do you think is happier—and closer to God?

We've been through this before.

Yes, we have. It is the mark of a primitive culture to imagine that simplicity is barbarian, and complexity is highly advanced.
Interestingly, those who are highly advanced see it as being just the other way around.

Yet the movement of all cultures—indeed, the process of evolution itself—is toward higher and higher degrees of complexity.

In one sense, yes. Yet here is the greatest Divine Dichotomy:
The greatest complexity is the greatest simplicity.
The more "complex" a system is, the more simple is its design. Indeed, it is utterly elegant in its Simplicity.

The master understands this. That is why a highly evolved being lives in utter simplicity. It is why all highly evolved systems are also utterly simple. Highly evolved systems of governance, highly evolved systems of education, highly evolved systems of economics or religion—all are utterly, elegantly simple.

Highly evolved systems of governance, for instance, involve virtually _no governance at all_, save self-governance.

As if there was only one being participating. As if there was only one being affected.

Which is all there is.

Which highly evolved cultures understand.

Precisely.

I'm starting to put it all together now.

Good. We have not much time left.

You have to go?

This book is getting very long.

20

Wait! Hold it! You can't quit now! I have more questions about E.T.s! Are they someday going to appear on Earth to "save us"? Will they rescue us from our own madness by bringing us new technologies to control the planet's polarities, clean our atmosphere, harness our sun's energy, regulate our weather, cure all disease, and bring us a better quality of life in our own little nirvana?

You may not want that to happen. "HEBs" know this. They know that such an intervention would only subjugate you to *them,* making *them* your gods, rather than the gods to whom you now claim to be subjugated.

The truth is, you are subjugated to *no one,* and this is what the beings from highly advanced cultures would have you understand. If, therefore, they would share with you some technologies, these would be given in a way, and at a rate, which would allow you to recognize your *own* powers and potentials, not those of another.

Similarly, if HEBs were to share with you some teachings, these, too, would be shared in a way, and at a rate, that would allow you to see greater truths, and your *own* powers and potentials, and *not make gods of your teachers.*

Too late. We've already done that.

Yes, I've noticed.

Which brings us to one of our greatest teachers, the man called Jesus. Even those who did *not* make him a god have recognized the greatness of his teachings.

Teachings which have been largely distorted.

Was Jesus one of these "HEBs"—highly evolved beings?

Do *you* think he was highly evolved?

Yes. As was the Buddha, Lord Krishna, Moses, Babaji, Sai Baba, and Paramahansa Yogananda, for that matter.

Indeed. And many others you have not mentioned.

Well, in *Book 2* You "hinted" that Jesus and these other teachers may have come from "outer space," that they may have been visitors here, sharing with us the teachings and wisdoms of highly evolved beings. So it's time to let the other shoe fall. Was Jesus a "spaceman"?

You are all "spacemen."

What does that mean?

You are not natives of this planet you now call home.

We aren't?

No. The "genetic stuff" of which you are made was *placed* on your planet, deliberately. It didn't just "show up" there by accident. The elements that have formed your life didn't combine themselves through some process of *biological serendipity*. There was a plan involved. There is something much larger going on here. Do you imagine that the billion and one biochemical reactions it has taken to cause life as you know it to appear on your planet all occurred haphazardly? Do you see this outcome as simply a fortuitous chain of random events, producing a happy result *by chance?*

No, of course not. I agree that there was a plan. *God's* plan.

324

Good. Because you are right. It was all My idea, and it was all My plan, and My process.

So what, then—are You saying that You are a "spaceman"?

Where have you traditionally looked when you've imagined yourself to be talking to Me?

Up. I've looked up.

Why not down?

I don't know. Everybody always looks up—to the "heavens."

From where I come?

I guess—yes.

Does that make Me a spaceman?

I don't know, does it?

And if I am a spaceman, would that make Me any less a God?

Based on what most of us say You can do, no. I guess not.

And if I am a God, does that make Me any less a spaceman?

It would all depend on our definitions, I guess.

What if I am not a "man" at all, but rather, a Force, an "Energy" in the universe, that IS the universe, and that is, in fact, All That Is. What if I am The Collective?

Well, that is, in fact, what You've said that You are. In this dialogue, You've *said* that.

Indeed, I have. And do you believe it?

Yes, I think I do. At least in the sense that I think God is All That Is.

Good. Now, do you think there are such things as what you call "spacemen"?

You mean, beings from outer space?

Yes.

Yes, I do. I think I've always believed that, and now, here, You've *told me* there are, so I surely believe it.

And are these "beings from outer space" part of "All That Is"?

Well, yes, of course.

And if I am All That Is, wouldn't that make Me a *spaceman?*

Well yes . . . but by that definition, You are also *me.*

Bingo.

Yes, but You've danced away from my question. I asked You if Jesus was a spaceman. And I think You know what I mean. I mean, was he a being from outer space, or was he born here, on Earth?

Your question once again assumes "either/or." Think *outside the box.* Reject "either/or" and consider "both/and."

Are you saying Jesus was born on Earth, but has "spaceman blood," so to speak?

Who was Jesus' father?

Joseph.

Yes, but who is said to have *conceived him?*

Some people believe that it was an immaculate conception. They say that the Virgin Mary was visited by an archangel. Jesus was "conceived by the Holy Ghost, born of the Virgin Mary."

Do you believe this?

I don't know what to believe about that.

Well, if Mary was visited by an archangel, from where do you imagine the angel would have come?

From heaven.

Did you say "from the heavens"?

I said, from *heaven.* From another realm. From God.

I see. And did we not just agree that God is a spaceman?

Not exactly. We agreed that God is *everything,* and that since spacemen are *part* of "everything," God is a spaceman, in the same sense that God is us. All of us. God is Everything. God is the collective.

Good. So this archangel who visited Mary came from another realm. A heavenly realm.

Yes.

A realm deep within your Self, because heaven is within you.

I didn't say that.

Well, then, a realm within the inner space of the universe.

No, I wouldn't say that either, because I don't know what that means.

Then from where? A realm in *outer* space?

(Long pause)

You're playing with words now.

I'm doing the best I can. I'm *using* words, in spite of their awful limitations, to get as close as I can to an idea, a concept of things, which, in truth, cannot be described in the limited vocabulary of your language, or understood within the limitations of your present level of perception.

I am seeking to open you to new perceptions by using your language in a new way.

Okay. So, You're saying that Jesus was fathered by a highly evolved being from some other realm, and thus he was a human, but also a HEB?

There have been many highly evolved beings walking your planet—and there are many today.

You mean there are "aliens among us"?

I can see that your work in newspapers, radio talk shows, and television has served you well.

How do You mean?

You can find a way to sensationalize anything. I didn't call highly evolved beings "aliens," and I didn't call Jesus an "alien."

There is nothing "alien" about God. There are no "aliens" on Earth.

We Are All One. If We Are All One, no individuation of Us is alien to itself.

Some individuation of Us—that is, some individual beings—remember more than others. The process of remembering (re-uniting with God, or becoming, once again, One with the All, with the collective) is a process you call evolution. You are all evolving beings. Some of you are highly evolved. That is, you *re-member more.* You know Who You Really Are. Jesus knew it, and declared it.

Okay, so I get that we're going to do a word dance on the Jesus thing.

Not at all. I will tell you outright. The spirit of that human you call Jesus was not of this Earth. That spirit simply filled a human body, allowed itself to learn as a child, become a man, and self-realized. He was not the only one to have done this. *All spirits* are "not of this Earth." *All souls* come from another realm, then enter the body. Yet not all souls self-realize in a particular "lifetime." Jesus did. He was a highly evolved being. (What some of you have called a god), and he came to you for a purpose, on a mission.

To save our souls.

In a sense, yes. But not from everlasting damnation. There *is* no such thing as you have conceived it. His mission was—is—to save you from not knowing and never experiencing Who You Really Are. His intention was to demonstrate that by showing you what you can become. Indeed, what you *are*—if you will only accept it.

Jesus sought to lead by example. That is why he said, "I am the way and the life. Follow me." He didn't mean "follow me" in the sense that you would all become his "followers," but in the sense that you would all *follow his example* and *become one with God.* He said, "I and

329

the Father are One, and ye are my brethren." He couldn't have put it more plainly.

So, Jesus did not come from God, he came from outer space.

Your mistake is in separating the two. You keep insisting on making a distinction, just as you insist on making a separation and a distinction between humans and God. And I tell you, *there is no distinction.*

Hmmm. Okay. Can You tell me a few final things about beings from other worlds before we end? What do they wear? How do they communicate? And please don't say this is still all about idle curiosity. I think I have demonstrated that there may be something we can learn here.

All right. Briefly, then.

In highly evolved cultures, beings see no need to be clothed, except when some kind of covering is required to protect them from elements or conditions over which they have no control, or when ornaments are used to indicate some "rank" or honor.

A HEB would not understand why you wear total body coverings when you do not have to—she certainly wouldn't understand the concept of "shame" or "modesty"—and could never relate to the idea of coverings to make oneself "prettier." To a HEB, there could be nothing more beautiful than the naked body itself, and so the concept of wearing something on top of it to somehow render it more pleasing or attractive would be utterly incomprehensible.

Equally incomprehensible would be the idea of living—spending most of one's time—in boxes . . . which you call "buildings" and "houses." HEBs live in the natural environment, and would only stay inside a box if their environment became inhospitable—which it rarely does, since highly evolved civilizations create, control, and care for their environments.

HEBs also understand that they are One with their environment, that they share more than space with their environments, but also share a mutually dependent relationship. A HEB could never understand why you would damage or destroy that which is supporting you, and so can only conclude that you do not understand that it is your environment which supports you; that you are beings of very limited observational skills.

As for communication, a HEB uses as his first level of communication the aspect of his being which you would call feelings. HEBs are aware of their feelings and the feelings of others, and no attempt is ever made by anyone to *hide* feelings. HEBs would find it self-defeating, and therefore incomprehensible, to hide feelings, and then complain that no one understands how they feel.

Feelings are the language of the soul, and highly evolved beings understand this. It is the purpose of communication in a society of HEBs to know each other in truth. A HEB, therefore, cannot, and could never, understand your human concept called "lying."

To be successful in getting one's way by communicating an untruth would be for a HEB a victory so hollow as to render it not a victory at all, but a staggering defeat.

HEBs do not "tell" the truth, HEBs *are* the truth. Their whole beingness comes from "what is so," and "what works," and HEBs learned long ago, in a time beyond memory when communication was still accomplished through guttural utterances, that untruth does not work. You have not yet learned this in your society.

On your planet, much of society is based on secrecy. Many of you believe it is what you keep *from* each other, not what you tell *to* each other, that makes life work. Secrecy has thus become your social code, your code of ethics. It is truly your Secret Code.

This is not true of all of you. Your ancient cultures, for instance, and your indigenous people do not live by

331

such a code. And many individuals in your present society have refused to adopt these behaviors.

Yet your government runs by this code, your businesses adopt it, and many of your relationships reflect it. Lying—about things large and small—has become so accepted by so many that they even lie about lying. Thus, you have developed a secret code about your Secret Code. Like the fact that the emperor is wearing no clothes, everybody knows it, but nobody's talking about it. You even try to pretend its not so—and in this you are lying to yourself.

You've made this point before.

I am repeating in this dialogue the essential points, the main points, you must "get" if you truly are to change things, as you say you wish to do.

And so I will say it again: The differences between human cultures and highly evolved cultures is that highly evolved beings:

1. Observe fully
2. Communicate truthfully

They see "what works" and say "what's so." This is another tiny, but profound, change which would immeasurably improve life on your planet.

And this is not, by the way, a question of morals. There are no "moral imperatives" in a HEB society, and that would be a concept equally as puzzling as lying. It is simply a matter of what is functional, of what brings benefit.

HEBs have no morals?

Not as you understand them. The idea of some group devising a set of values by which individual HEBs are called upon to live would violate their understanding of "what works," which is that each individual is the sole and final arbiter of what is, and is not, appropriate behavior for them.

332

The discussion is always around what *works* for a HEB society—what is functional and produces benefit for all—not around what humans would call "right" and "wrong."

But isn't that the same thing? Haven't we simply called what works "right," and what doesn't work for us, "wrong"?

You have attached guilt and shame to those labels—concepts equally foreign to HEBs—and you have labeled an astonishing number of things "wrong," not because they "don't work," but simply because you imagine them to be "inappropriate"—sometimes not even in your eyes, but in the "eyes of God." You have thus constructed artificial definitions of "what works" and what doesn't—definitions having nothing to do with "what's really so."

Honestly expressing one's feelings, for example, is often deemed by human society as "wrong." Such a conclusion could never be arrived at by a HEB, since precise awareness of feelings facilitates *life* in any community or cluster. So, as I said, a HEB would never hide feelings, or find it "socially correct" to do so.

It would be impossible in any event, because a HEB receives "vibes"—actual *vibrations*—from other beings, which make their feelings plain enough. Just as you can sometimes "feel the air" when you walk into a room, a HEB can feel what another HEB is thinking and experiencing.

Actual utterances—what you would call "words"—are rarely, if ever, used. This "telepathic communication" occurs between all highly evolved sentient beings. Indeed, it could be said that the degree to which a species—or a relationship between members of the same species—has evolved is demonstrated by the degree to which beings require the use of "words" to convey feelings, desires, or information.

And before you ask the question, yes, human beings can develop, and some *have* developed, the same

333

capacity. Thousands of years ago, in fact, it was normal. You have since regressed to the use of primal utterances—"noises," actually—to communicate. But many of you are returning to a cleaner form of communication, more accurate and more elegant. This is especially true between loved ones—emphasizing a major truth: *Caring creates communication.*

Where there is deep love, words are virtually unnecessary. The reverse of this axiom is also true: The more words you *have* to use with each other, the less time you must be taking to *care* for each other, because caring creates communication.

Ultimately, all real communication is about truth. And ultimately, the only real truth is love. That is why, when love is present, so is communication. And when communication is difficult, it is a sign that love is not fully present.

That is beautifully put. I might say, beautifully *communicated.*

Thank you. To summarize, then, the model for life in a highly evolved society:

Beings live in clusters, or what you would call small intentional communities. These clusters are not further organized into cities, states, or nations, but each interacts with the others on a co-equal basis.

There are no governments as you would understand them, and no laws. There are councils, or conclaves. Usually of elders. And there are what could best be translated into your language as "mutual agreements." These have been reduced to a Triangular Code: Awareness, Honesty, Responsibility.

Highly evolved beings have decided long ago that this is how they choose to live together. They've made this choice based not on a moral structure or spiritual revelation that some other being or group has brought forth, but, rather, on a simple observation of *what is so,* and *what works.*

And there truly are no wars and/or conflicts?

No, mainly because a highly evolved being shares everything he has, and would give you anything you sought to take by force. He does this out of his awareness that everything belongs to everyone anyway, and that he can always create more of what he "gave away" if he really desires it.

There is no concept of "ownership" or "loss" in a society of HEBs, who understand that they are not physical beings, but beings being physical. They also understand that all beings proceed from the same source, and thus, We Are All One.

I know You said this before . . . but even if someone was threatening a HEB with his life, there would still be no conflict?

There would be no argument. He would simply lay down his body—literally leaving the body there for you. He would then create another body if he chose to, by coming into physicality again as a fully formed being, or by returning as the newly conceived offspring of a loving pair of other beings.

This is by far the preferred method of reentry into physicality, because no one is more honored in highly evolved societies than newly created offspring, and the opportunities for growth are unparalleled.

HEBs have no fear of what your culture calls "death," because HEBs know that they live forever, and it is just a matter of what *form* they are going to take. HEBs can live in a physical body usually indefinitely, because a HEB has learned to take care of the body, and the environment. If for some reason having to do with the physical laws a HEB's body is no longer functional, the HEB simply leaves it, joyfully returning its physical matter to the All of Everything for "recycling." (What you understand as "dust into dust.")

335

Let me go back a bit. I know You said there are no "laws," as such. But what if someone does not behave according to the "Triangular Code"? Then what? _Ka-boom?_

No. No "ka-boom." There is no "trial" or "punishment," just a simple observation of "what's so," and "what works."

It is carefully explained that "what's so"—what the being has done—is now at variance with "what works," and that when something does not work for the group, it ultimately will not work for the individual, because the individual _is_ the group, and the group is the individual. All HEBs "get" this very quickly, usually early in what you would call _youth,_ and so it is extremely rare that a mature HEB is found to act in a way which produces a "what's so" that is _not_ "what works."

But when one does?

He is simply allowed to correct his mistake. Using the Triangular Code, he is first made aware of all the outcomes related to something he has thought or said or done. Then he is allowed to assess and declare his role in producing those outcomes. Finally, he is given an opportunity to take responsibility for those outcomes by putting corrective or remedial or healing measures into place.

What if he refuses to do so?

A highly evolved being would never refuse to do so. It is inconceivable. He would then not be a highly evolved being, and you are now talking about a different level of sentient being altogether.

Where does a HEB learn all this stuff? In school?

There is no "school system" in a HEB society, merely a _process_ of education by which offspring are reminded of "what's so," and "what works." Offspring are raised by elders, not by those who conceive them, though they are not necessarily separated from their "parents" during the process, who may be with them whenever they wish, and spend as much time with them as they choose.

In what you would call "school" (actually, best translated as "learning time"), offspring set their own "curriculum," choosing which skills *they* would like to acquire, rather than being *told* what they are going to *have* to learn. Motivation is thus at its highest level, and life skills are acquired quickly, easily, and joyfully.

The Triangular Code (these are not really codified "rules," but this is the best term one can find in your languages) is not something which is "pounded into" the young HEB, but something which is *acquired*—almost by osmosis—through the behaviors *modeled* for the "child" by "adults."

Unlike your society, in which adults model behaviors *opposite* to those which they want their children to learn, in highly evolved cultures adults understand that children do what they see others doing.

It would never occur to HEBs to place their offspring for many hours in front of a device that shows pictures of behaviors they'd like their offspring to avoid. Such a decision would be, to a HEB, incomprehensible.

It would be equally incomprehensible, if a HEB *did* do this, to then deny that the pictures had anything to do with their offsprings' suddenly aberrant behaviors.

I will say again that the difference between HEB society and human society breaks down to one really very simple element, which we shall call truthful observation.

In HEB societies, beings acknowledge everything they see. In human societies, many deny what they see.

They see television ruining their children, and they ignore it. They see violence and "losing" used as "entertainment," and deny the contradiction. They observe that tobacco harms the body, and pretend it does

337

not. They see a father who is drunken and abusive, and the whole family denies it, letting no one say a word about it.

They observe that over thousands of years their religions have failed utterly to change mass behaviors, and deny this, too. They see clearly that their governments do more to oppress than to assist, and they ignore it.

They see a health-care system that is really a disease-care system, spending one-tenth of its resources on preventing disease, and nine-tenths on managing it, and deny that *profit motive* is what stops any real progress on educating people in how to act and eat and live in a way which promotes good health.

They see that eating the flesh of animals that have been slaughtered after having been force-fed chemical-laden foods is not doing their health any good, yet they deny what they see.

They do more than that. They try to sue talk show hosts who dare even discuss the subject. You know, there's a wonderful book that explores this whole food topic with exquisite insight. It's called *Diet for a New America*, by John Robbins.

People will read that book and deny, deny, *deny* that it makes any sense. And that is the point. Much of your race lives in denial. They deny not just the painfully obvious observations of everyone around them, but the observations of their own eyes. They deny their personal feelings, and, eventually, their own truth.

Highly evolved beings—which some of you are becoming—deny *nothing*. They observe "what's so." They see clearly "what works." Using these simple tools, life becomes simple. "The Process" is honored.

Yes, but how does "The Process" work?

To answer that I have to make a point that I have made before—repeatedly, in fact—in this dialogue.

Everything depends on who you think you are, and what you are trying to do.

If your objective is to live a life of peace, joy, and love, *violence does not work.* This has already been demonstrated.

If your objective is to live a life of good health and great longevity, consuming dead flesh, smoking known carcinogens, and drinking volumes of nerve-deadening, brain-frying liquids *does not work.* This has already been demonstrated.

If your objective is to raise offspring free of violence and rage, putting them directly in front of vivid depictions of violence and rage for years *does not work.* This has *already been demonstrated.*

If your objective is to care for Earth, and wisely husband her resources, acting as if those resources are limitless *does not work.* This has *already been demonstrated.*

If your objective is to discover and cultivate a relationship with a loving God, so that religion *can* make a difference in the affairs of humans, then teaching of a god of punishment and terrible retribution *does not work.* This, *too,* has *already been demonstrated.*

Motive is everything. Objectives determine outcomes. Life proceeds out of your intention. Your true intention is revealed in your actions, and your actions are determined by your true intention. As with everything in life (and life *itself*), it is a circle.

HEBs *see the circle.* Humans do not.

HEBs respond to what is so; humans ignore it.

HEBs tell the truth, *always.* Humans too often lie, to themselves as well as others.

HEBs say one thing, and do what they say. Humans say one thing and do another.

Deep down you *know* that something is wrong—that you intended to "go to Seattle," but you are in "San Jose." You see the contradictions in your behaviors, and you are truly ready now to abandon them. You see clearly both what is *so,* and what *works,* and

339

you are becoming unwilling any further to support divisions between the two.

Yours is *a race awakening*. Your time of fulfillment is at hand.

You need *not* be discouraged by what you have heard here, for the groundwork has been laid for a new experience, a larger reality, and all this was merely preparation for it. You are ready now to step through the door.

This dialogue, in particular, has been intended to throw open that door. First, to point to it. *See? There it is!* For the light of truth will forever show the way. And the light of truth is what you have been given here.

Take this truth now, and live it. Hold this truth now, and share it. Embrace this truth now, and treasure it forever more.

For in these three books—the *Conversations with God* trilogy—have I spoken to you again of *what is so.*

There is no need to go further. There is no need to ask more questions or hear more answers or satisfy more curiosities or provide more examples or offer more observations. All you need in order to create the life you desire, you have found here, in this trilogy as presented so far. There is no need to go further.

Yes, you have more questions. Yes, you have more "but-what-ifs." Yes, you are not "done" yet with this exploration we have enjoyed. Because you are *never done with any exploration.*

It is clear then that this book could go on forever. And it will not. Your *conversation* with God *will,* but this book will not. For the answer to any other question you could ask will be found here, in this now complete trilogy. All we can do now is repeat, re-amplify, return to the same wisdom over and over again. Even this trilogy was an exercise in that. There is nothing new here, but simply ancient wisdom revisited.

It is good to revisit. It is good to become familiar once again. This is the process of remembrance of which I have so often spoken. You have nothing to learn. You have only to remember. . . .

So revisit this trilogy often; turn to its pages time and time again.

When you have a question that you feel has not been answered here, read the pages over again. You will find that your question has been answered. Yet if you really feel it has not, then seek your *own* answers. Have your *own* conversation. Create your *own truth*.

In this will you experience Who You Really Are.

21

I don't want You to go!

I'm not going anywhere. I am always with you. *All ways.*

Please, before we stop, just a few more questions. Some final, closing inquiries.

You do understand, don't you, that you may *go within* at any time, return to the Seat of Eternal Wisdom, and find your answers there?

Yes, I understand that, and I am grateful to the bottom of my heart that it is this way, that life has been created this way, that I have that resource always. But this has been working for me. This dialogue has been a great gift. Can't I just ask a few last questions?

Of course.

Is our world really in danger? Is our species flirting with self-destruction—with actual extinction?

Yes. And unless you consider the very real possibility of that, you cannot avoid it. For what you resist, persists. Only what you hold can disappear.

Remember, also, what I told you about time and events. All the events you could possibly imagine—indeed, have imagined—are taking place right now, in the Eternal Moment. This is the Holy Instant. This is the Moment that precedes your awareness. It is what is happening before the Light gets to you. This is the present moment, sent to you, created by you, before you even know it! You call this the "present." And it IS a "present." It is the greatest gift given to you by God.

You have the ability to choose which, of all the experiences you've ever imagined, you choose to experience *now*.

You've said it, and I am now beginning, even in my limited perception, to understand it. None of this is really "real," is it?

No. You are living an illusion. This is a big magic show. And you are pretending that you don't know the tricks—even though *you are the magician.*

It is important to remember this, otherwise you will make everything very real.

But what I see, feel, smell, touch, *does* seem very real. If that isn't "reality," what is?

Keep in mind that what you are looking at, you are not really "seeing."

Your brain is not the source of your intelligence. It is simply a data processor. It takes in data through receptors called your senses. It interprets this energy in formation according to its *previous data on the subject.* It tells you what it *perceives,* not what *really is.* Based on these perceptions, you *think you know the truth* about something, when, actually, you do not know the half of it. In reality, you are creating the truth that you know.

Including this entire dialogue with You.

Most assuredly.

I'm afraid that will only give fuel to those who are saying, "He's not talking to God. He's making it all up."

Tell them gently that they might try thinking "outside the box." They are thinking "either/or." They might try thinking "both/and."

You cannot comprehend God if you are thinking inside your current values, concepts, and understandings. If you wish to comprehend God, you must be willing to accept that you currently have *limited data,* rather than asserting that you know all there is to know on this subject.

I draw your attention to the words of Werner Erhard, who declared that true clarity can come only when someone is willing to notice:

There is something I do not know, the knowing of which could change everything.

It is just possible that you are both "talking to God" *and* "making it all up."

Indeed, here is the grandest truth: You are making *everything* up.

Life is The Process by which everything is being created. God is the energy—the pure, raw energy—which you call life. By this awareness we come to a new truth.

God is a Process.

I thought You said God was a Collective, that God is The ALL.

I did. And God is. God is also The Process by which All is created, and experiences Itself.

I have revealed this to you before.

Yes. *Yes.* You gave me that wisdom when I was writing a booklet called *Re-creating Yourself.*

Indeed. And now I say it here, for a much larger audience to receive.

God is a Process.

God is not a person, place, or thing. God is exactly what you have always thought—but not understood.

Again?

You have always thought that God is the Supreme Being.

344

Yes.

And you have been right about that. I am exactly that. A BEING. Notice that "being" is not a thing, it is a process.

I am the *Supreme* Being. That is, the Supreme, comma, *being*.

I am not the *result* of a process; I *am* The Process Itself. I am the Creator, and I am The Process *by which I am created.*

Everything you see in the heavens and the earth is Me, *being created.* The Process of Creation is never over. It is never complete. I am never "done." This is another way of saying everything is forever changing. Nothing stands still. Nothing—*nothing*—is without motion. Everything is energy, in motion. In your earthly shorthand, you have called this "E-motion!"

You are God's highest emotion!

When you look at a thing, you are not looking at a static "something" that is "standing there" in time and space. No! You are *witnessing an event.* Because everything is moving, changing, evolving. *Everything.*

It was Buckminster Fuller who said, "I seem to be a verb." *He was right.*

God is an *event.* You have called that event *life.* Life is a Process. That Process is observable, knowable, predictable. The more you observe, the more you know, and the more you can predict.

That's a tough one for me. I always thought that God is the Unchangeable. The One Constant. The Unmoved Mover. It was within this inscrutable absolute truth about God that I found my security.

But that IS the truth! The One Unchanging Truth is that God is always changing. That is the *truth*—and you *can't do anything to change it.* The one thing that *never* changes is that everything is always changing.

Life is change. God is life.

Therefore, God is change.

But I want to believe that the one thing that never changes is God's love for us.

My love for you is *always* changing, because *you* are always changing, and I love you *just the way you are.* For Me to love you just the way you are, My idea of what is "lovable" must change as your idea of Who You Are changes.

You mean You find me lovable even if I decide that Who I Am is a murderer?

We've been through this all before.

I know, but I just can't *get it!*

Nobody does anything inappropriate, given their model of the world. I love you always—all *ways.* There is no "way" you can be that could cause Me not to love you.

But You will punish us, right? You will lovingly punish us. You will send us to everlasting torment, with love in Your heart, and sadness that You had to do it.

No. I have no sadness, *ever,* because there is *nothing* I "have to do." Who would make Me "have to do it"?

I will never punish you, although you may choose to punish yourself in this life or another, until you don't anymore. I will not punish you because I have not been hurt or damaged—nor can you hurt or damage any Part of Me, which *all of you are.*

One of you may choose to *feel* hurt or damaged, yet when you return to the eternal realm, you will see that you have not been damaged in any way. In this moment will you forgive those you imagined to have damaged you, for you will have understood the larger plan.

346

What is the larger plan?

Do you remember the parable of *The Little Soul and the Sun* that I gave you in *Book 1*?

Yes.

There is a second half to that parable. Here it is:

"You may choose to be any Part of God you wish to be," I said to the Little Soul. "You are Absolute Divinity, experiencing Itself. What Aspect of Divinity do you now wish to experience as You?"

"You mean I have a choice?" asked the Little Soul. And I answered, "Yes. You may choose to experience any Aspect of Divinity in, as, and through you."

"Okay," said the Little Soul, "then I choose Forgiveness. I want to experience my Self as that Aspect of God called Complete Forgiveness."

Well, this created a little challenge, as you can imagine.

There was *no one to forgive*. All I have created is Perfection and Love.

"No one to forgive?" asked the Little Soul, somewhat incredulously.

"No one," I repeated. "Look around you. Do you see any souls less perfect, less wonderful than you?"

At this the Little Soul twirled around, and was surprised to see himself surrounded by all the souls in heaven. They had come from far and wide throughout the Kingdom, because they heard that the Little Soul was having an extraordinary *conversation with God.*

"I see none less perfect than I!" the Little Soul exclaimed. "Who, then, shall I have to forgive?"

Just then, another soul stepped forward from the crowd. "You may forgive me," said this Friendly Soul.

"For what?" the Little Soul asked.

"I will come into your next physical lifetime and do something for you to forgive," replied the Friendly Soul.

347

"But what? What could you, a being of such Perfect Light, do to make me want to forgive you?" the Little Soul wanted to know.

"Oh," smiled the Friendly Soul, "I'm sure we can think of something."

"But why would you want to do this?" The Little Soul could not figure out why a being of such perfection would want to slow down its vibration so much that it could actually do something "bad."

"Simple," the Friendly Soul explained, "I would do it because I love you. You want to experience your Self as Forgiving, don't you? Besides, you've done the same for me."

"I have?" asked the Little Soul.

"Of course. Don't you remember? We've been All Of It, you and I. We've been the Up and the Down of it, and the Left and the Right of it. We've been the Here and the There of it, and the Now and the Then of it. We've been the Big and the Small of it, the Male and the Female of it, the Good and the Bad of it. We've *all been the All of It*.

"And we've done it by *agreement,* so that each of us might experience ourselves as The Grandest Part of God. For we have understood that. . . .

"In the absence of that which You Are Not, that Which You ARE, is NOT.

"In the absence of 'cold,' you cannot be 'warm.' In the absence of 'sad,' you cannot be 'happy,' without a thing called 'evil,' the experience you call 'good' cannot exist.

If you choose to *be* a thing, *something or someone opposite to that has to show up somewhere in your universe* to make that possible."

The Friendly Soul then explained that those people are God's Special Angels, and these conditions God's Gifts.

"I ask only one thing in return," the Friendly Soul declared.

"Anything! *Anything,"* the Little Soul cried. He was excited now to know that he could experience every Divine Aspect of God. He understood, now, The Plan.

348

"In the moment that I strike you and smite you," said the Friendly Soul, "in the moment that I do the worst to you that you could ever imagine—in that self-same moment . . . *remember Who I Really Am.*"

"Oh, I won't forget!" promised the Little Soul. "I will see you in the perfection with which I hold you now, and I will remember Who You Are, always."

That is . . . that is an extraordinary story, an incredible parable.

And the promise of the Little Soul is the promise I make to you. *That* is what is unchanging. Yet have you, My Little Soul, kept this promise to others?

No. I'm sad to say I have not.

Do not be sad. Be happy to notice what is true, and be joyous in your decision to live a new truth.

For God is a work in progress, and so are you. And remember this always:

If you saw you as God sees you, you would smile a lot.

So go, now, and see each other as Who You Really Are.

Observe. *Observe. OBSERVE.*

I have told you—the major difference between you and highly evolved beings is that highly evolved beings *observe more.*

If you wish to increase the speed with which you are evolving, *seek to observe more.*

That in itself is a wonderful observation.

And I would have you now observe that *you, too,* are an event. You are a human, comma, *being.* You are a process. And you are, in any given "moment," the product of your process.

You are the Creator and the Created. I am saying these things to you over and over again, in these last few moments we have together. I am repeating them so that you will *hear them*, understand them

Now, this process that you and I are is eternal. It always was, is now, and always will be occurring. It needs no "help" from you in order to occur. It happens "automatically." And, when left alone, it happens *perfectly*.

There is another saying that has been placed into your culture by Werner Erhard—*life resolves itself in the process of life itself.*

This is understood by some spiritual movements as "let go and let God." That is a good understanding.

If you will just *let go*, you will have gotten yourself out of the "way." The "way" is The Process—which is called *life itself*. This is why all masters have said, "I am the life and the way." They have understood what I have said here perfectly. They *are* the life, and they *are* the way—the event in progress, The Process.

All wisdom asks you to do is trust The Process. That is, *trust God*. Or, if you wish, *trust yourself,* for Thou Art God.

Remember, We Are All One.

How can I "trust the process" when the "process"—*life*—keeps bringing me things I don't like?

Like the things life keeps bringing you!

Know and understand that you are bringing it to your Self.

SEE THE PERFECTION.

See it in *everything*, not just in things that *you* call perfect. I have carefully explained to you in this trilogy why things happen the way they happen, and how. You do not need to read that material again here—although it might do you benefit to review it often, until you understand it thoroughly.

Please—just on this one point—a summarizing insight. Please. How can I "see the perfection" of something that I experience as not perfect at all?

> *No one can create your experience of anything.*
> Other beings can, and *do*, co-create the exterior circumstances and events of the life you live in common, but the *one thing* that *no one else can do is cause you to have an experience* of ANYTHING you do not choose to experience.
> In this, you are a Supreme being. And no one—NO ONE—can tell you "how to *be.*"
> The world can present you with circumstances, but only you decide what those circumstances mean.
> Remember the truth I gave you long ago.
> Nothing matters.

Yes. I'm not sure I fully understood it then. That came to me in an out-of-body experience in 1980. I recall it vividly.

> And what do you remember of it?

That I was confused at first. How could "nothing matter"? Where would the world be, where would *I* be, if nothing mattered at all?

> What answer did you find to that very good question?

I "got" that nothing mattered intrinsically, in and of itself, but that I was adding meaning to events, and so, causing them to matter. I got this at a very high metaphysical level as well, giving me a huge insight about the Process of Creation itself.

> And the insight?

I "got" that all is energy, and that energy turns into "matter"—that is, physical "stuff" and "occurrences"—according to how I thought about them. I understood, then, that "nothing matters" means that nothing turns *into* matter except as we

351

choose for it to. Then I forgot that insight for over ten years, until You brought it to me again earlier in this dialogue.

Everything I have brought you in this dialogue you have known before. I have given it to you before, all of it, through others whom I have sent you, or to whose teachings I have brought you. *There is nothing new here*, and you have nothing to learn. You have only to remember.

Your understanding of the wisdom "nothing matters" is rich and deep, and serves you well.

I'm sorry. I cannot let this dialogue end without pointing out a glaring contradiction.

Which is—?

You have taught me over and over again that what we call "evil" exists so that we may have a context within which to experience "good." You have said that What I Am cannot be experienced if there is no such thing as What I Am Not. In other words, no "warm" without "cold," no "up" without "down," and so on.

That's right.

You have even used this to explain to me how I could see every "problem" as a blessing, and every perpetrator as an angel.

Correct again.

Then how come every description of the life of highly evolved beings contains virtually no "evil"? All you've described is *paradise!*

Oh, good. Very good. You are really thinking about all this.

Actually, Nancy pointed this out. She was listening to me read some of the material out loud to her and she said, "I think you need to ask about this before the dialogue is over. How do

HEBs experience themselves as Who They Really Are if they've eliminated all the negative stuff from their lives?" I thought it was a good question. In fact, it stopped me cold. And I know You just said we didn't need any more questions, but I think You need to address this one.

Okay. One for Nancy, then. As it happens, it's one of the best questions in the book.

(Ahem.)

Well, it *is*. . . . I'm surprised you didn't catch this when we were talking about HEBs. I'm surprised you didn't think of it.

I did.

You did?

We are all One, aren't we? Well, the *part of me which is Nancy* thought of it!

Ah, *excellent!* And, of course, *true.*

So, Your answer?

I will return to My original statement.
In the absence of that which you are not, that which you are, is not.
That is, in the absence of cold, you cannot know the experience called warmth. In the absence of up, the idea of "down" is an empty, meaningless concept.
This is a truth of the universe. Indeed, it explains why the universe is the way it *is*, with its cold and its warmth, its ups and downs, and, yes, its "good" and its "evil."
Yet know this: *You are making it all up.* You are *deciding* what is "cold" and what is "warm," what is "up" and what is "down." (Get out in space and watch your definitions disappear!) You are *deciding* what is "good"

and what is "evil." And your ideas about all these things have changed through the years—indeed, even through the _seasons_. On a summer day you would call 42°F "cold." In the middle of winter, however, you would say, "Boy, what a warm day!"

The universe merely provides you with a _field of experience_—what might be called a _range of objective phenomena_. You decide _what to label them_.

The universe is a whole system of such physical phenomena. And the universe is enormous. Vast. Unfathomably huge. _Endless_, in fact.

Now here is a great secret: It is not necessary for an opposite condition to exist _right next to you_ in order to provide a contextual field within which the reality that you choose may be experienced.

The distance between contrasts is irrelevant. The entire universe provides the contextual field within which all contrasting elements exist, and all experiences are thus made possible. That is the _purpose_ of the universe. That is its function.

But if I've never _experienced_ "cold" in person, but merely see that it is "cold" somewhere else, very far away from me, how do I know what "cold" is?

You _have_ experienced "cold." You have experienced _all of it_. If not in this lifetime, then in the last. Or the one before that. Or one of the many others. You _have_ experienced "cold." And "big" and "small" and "up" and "down" and "here" and "there" and every contrasting element that there is. And these are burned into your memory.

You do _not have to experience them again if you don't want to._ You need merely remember them—know that they exist—in order to invoke the universal law of relativity.

All of you. All of you have experienced _everything_. That goes for all beings in the universe, not only humans.

354

You have all not only experienced everything, you *are* everything. You are ALL OF IT.

You are that which you are experiencing. Indeed, you are *causing* the experience.

I'm not sure I fully understand that.

I am about to explain it to you, in mechanical terms. What I want you now to understand is that what you are doing now is simply remembering everything you are, and choosing the portion of that which you prefer to experience in this moment, in this lifetime, on this planet, in this physical form.

My God, you make it sound so simple!

It *is simple*. You have separated your Self from the body of God, from the All, from the Collective, and you are becoming a member of that body once again. This is The Process called "re-membering."

As you re-member, you give your Self once again all the experiences of Who You Are. This is a cycle. You do this over and over again, and call this "evolution." You say that you "evolve." Actually, you RE-volve! Just as the Earth revolves around the sun. Just as the galaxy revolves around its center.

Everything revolves.

Revolution is the basic movement of all of life. Life energy *revolves*. That is what it *does*. You are in a truly *revolutionary movement*.

How do You *do* that? How do You keep finding words that make everything so clear?

It is you who are making it clear. You have done this by clearing up your "receiver." You've tuned out the static. You've entered into a new willingness to know. This new willingness will change everything, for you and for your species. For in your new willingness, you

355

have become a true revolutionary—and your planet's greatest spiritual revolution has just begun.

It had better hurry. We need a new spirituality, _now_. We are creating incredible misery all around us.

That is because, even though all beings have already lived through all contrasting experiences, some _do not know it_. They have forgotten, and have not yet moved into full remembering.

With highly evolved beings this is not so. It is not necessary to have "negativity" right in front of them, in their own world, for them to know how "positive" their civilization is. They are "positively aware" of Who They Are without having to create negativity to prove it. HEBs merely notice who they are _not_ by observing it _elsewhere in the contextual field_.

Your own planet, in fact, is one to which highly evolved beings look if they seek a contrasting field.

As they do so, they are reminded of how it was when _they_ experienced what you are now experiencing, and they thus form an ongoing frame of reference through which they may know and understand what _they_ are now experiencing.

Do you now understand why HEBs do not require "evil" or "negativity" in their own society?

Yes. But then why do we require it in ours?

You _DO NOT_. That is what I have been telling you throughout this whole dialogue.

You _do_ have to live within a contextual field within which That Which You Are Not exists, in order for you to experience That Which You Are. This is the Universal Law, and you cannot avoid it. Yet you _are_ living in such a field, right now. You do not have to create one. The contextual field in which you are living is called _the universe_.

You do not have to create a smaller contextual field in your own backyard.

This means that you can change life on your planet right now, and *eliminate all that you are not,* without endangering in any way your ability to know and experience That Which You Are.

Wow! This is the greatest revelation in the book! What a way to end it! So I *don't* have to keep calling forth the *opposite* in order to create and experience the next grandest version of the greatest vision I've ever had of Who I Am!

That is right. That is what I have been telling you from the very beginning.

But You didn't explain it in this way!

You would not have understood it until now.

You do *not* have to create the opposite of Who You Are and What You Choose in order to experience it. You merely need to observe that it has already been created—elsewhere. You need only remember that it exists. This is the "knowledge of the fruit of the Tree of Good and Evil" which I've already explained to you was not a curse, not the original sin, but what Matthew Fox has called *Original Blessing.*

And to remember that it exists, to remember that *you* have experienced it all before—everything that is—in physical form . . . all you have to do is look up.

You mean "look within."

No, I mean *just what I said.* LOOK UP. Look to the stars. Look to the heavens. OBSERVE THE CONTEXTUAL FIELD.

I have told you before, all you need to do to become highly evolved beings is to increase *your observational skills.* See "what's so," and then do "what works."

So, by looking elsewhere in the universe, I can see how things are in other places, and I can use those contrasting elements to form an understanding of Who I Am right here, right now.

Yes. This is called "remembering."

Well, not exactly. It is called "observing."

What do you think you are observing?

Life on other planets. In other solar systems, other galaxies. I suppose if we gathered sufficient technology, this is what we might observe. This is what I assume the HEBs have the ability to observe right now, given their advanced technology. You said Yourself that they are observing *us*, right here on Earth. So that is what we would be observing.

But what is it, *actually*, that you would be observing?

I don't understand the question.

Then I will give you the answer.
You are observing your own past.

What???

When you look up, you see the stars—as they were hundreds, thousands, millions of light-years ago. What you are seeing is *not actually there*. You are seeing what *was* there. You are seeing the past. And it is a past in which *you participated.*

Say again???

You were *there, experiencing* those things, *doing* those things.

I was?

Have I not told you that you have lived many lives?

358

Yes, but . . . but what if I were to travel to one of these places so many light-years away? What if I had the ability to actually go there? To be there "right now," in the very moment that I am not able to "see" on Earth for hundreds of light-years? What would I see then? Two "me's"? Are You saying that I would then see my Self, existing in *two places at once?*

Of course! And you would discover what I have told you all along—that time does not exist, and that you are not seeing "the past" at all! That is it *all happening NOW.*

You are also, "right now," living lives in what in Earth time, would be your future. It is the distance between your many "Selves" that allows "you" to experience discreet identities, and "moments in time."

Thus, the "past" that you re-member and the future that you would see, is the "now" that simply IS.

Whoa. That's incredible.

Yes, and it is true on another level as well. It is as I have told you before: *there is only One of us.* So when you look up at the stars you are seeing what you would call OUR PAST.

I can't keep up with this!

Hang on. There's one thing more I have to tell you.

You are *always* seeing what by your terms you would define as the "past," even when you are looking at what is right in front of you.

I am?

It is impossible to see The Present. The Present "happens," then turns into a burst of light, formed by energy dispersing, and that light reaches your receptors, your eyes, and *it takes time for it to do that.*

All the while that light is reaching you, life is *going on, moving forward.* The *next event is happening* while the light from *the last event is reaching you.*

The energy burst reaches your eyes, your receptors send that signal to your brain, which interprets the data and tells you what you are seeing. Yet that is not what is now in front of you at all. It is what you *think* you are seeing. That is, you are thinking about what you have seen, telling yourself what it is, and deciding what you are going to call it, while what is happening "now" is preceding your process, and awaiting it.

To put this simply, *I am always one step ahead of you.*

My God, this is *unbelievable.*

Now *listen.* The more *distance* you place between your Self and the physical location of any event, the *further into the "past" that event recedes.* Place yourself a few light-years back, and what you are looking at happened very, very long ago, indeed.

Yet it did *not* happen "long ago." It is merely physical *distance* which has created the illusion of "time," and allowed you to experience your Self as being both "here, now" all the while you are being "there, then"!

One day you will see that what you call time and space are *the same thing.*

Then you will see that *everything is happening right here, right now.*

This is . . . this is . . . *wild.* I mean, I don't know what to make of all this.

When you understand what I have told you, you will understand that *nothing you see is real.* You are seeing the *image* of what was once an event, yet even that image, that energy burst, is something you are interpreting. Your personal interpretation of that image is called your image-ination.

And you can use your imagination to create *any-thing*. Because—and here is the greatest secret of all—your image-ination *works both ways*.

Please?

You not only *interpret* energy, you *create it*. Imagination is a function of your mind, which is one-third of your three-part being. In your mind you image something, and it begins to take physical form. The longer you image it (and the more OF you who image it), the more physical that form becomes, until the increasing energy you have given it literally *bursts into light*, flashing an image of itself into what you call your reality.

You then "see" the image, and once again *decide what it is*. Thus, the cycle continues. This is what I have called The Process.

This is what YOU ARE. You ARE this Process.

This is what God IS. God IS this Process.

This is what I have meant when I have said, you are *both the Creator and the Created*.

I have now brought it all together for you. We are concluding this dialogue, and I have explained to you the mechanics of the universe, the secret of all life.

I'm . . . bowled over. I'm . . . flabbergasted. Now I want to find a way to apply all this in my daily life.

You *are* applying it in your daily life. You cannot *help* but apply it. This is *what is happening*. The only question will be whether you apply it *consciously or unconsciously*, whether you are at the effect of The Process, or are the cause of it. In everything, be *cause*.

Children understand this perfectly. Ask a child, "Why did you do that?" and a child will tell you. "Just because."

That is the only reason to do anything.

This is astounding. This is an astounding rush to an astounding ending to this astounding dialogue.

361

The most significant way in which you may consciously apply your New Understanding is to be the *cause* of your experience, not at the effect of it. And know that you *do not have to create the opposite of Who You Are in your personal space or personal experience* in order to know and experience Who You Really Are, and Who You Choose To Be.

Armed with this knowledge, you can change your life, and you can change your world.

And this is the truth I have come to share with all of you.

Whoa! Wow! I got it. *I got it!*

Good. Now know that there are three basic wisdoms that run through the entire dialogue. These are:

1. We Are All One.
2. There's Enough.
3. There's Nothing We Have To Do.

If you decided that "we are all one," you would cease treating each other the way you do.

If you decided that "there's enough," you would share everything with everyone.

If you decided that "there's nothing we have to do," you would stop trying to use "doingness" to solve your problems, but rather, move to, and come *from*, a state of being which would cause your experience of those "problems" to disappear, and the conditions themselves to thus evaporate.

This is perhaps the most important truth of all for you to understand at this stage in your evolution, and it is a good place to end this dialogue. Remember this always, and make it your mantra:

There's nothing I have to have, there's nothing I have to do, and there's nothing I have to be, except exactly what I'm being right now.

This does not mean that "having" and "doing" will be eliminated from your life. It means that what you experience yourself having or doing will spring *from* your being—not lead you *to it.*

When you come *from* "happiness," you do certain things because you *are* happy—as opposed to the old paradigm in which you did things that you hoped would *make* you happy.

When you come *from* "wisdom," you do certain things because you *are* wise, not because you are trying to *get* to wisdom.

When you come *from* "love," you do certain things because you *are* love, not because you want to *have* love.

Everything changes; everything turns around, when you come *from* "being," rather than seeking to "be." You cannot "do" your way to "being." Whether you are trying to "be" happy, be wise, be love—or be God—you cannot "get there" by doing. And yet, it is true that you *will* be doing wonderful things once you "get there."

Here is the Divine Dichotomy. The way to "get there" is to "be there." Just *be* where you choose to *get!* It's that simple. *There's nothing you have to do.* You want to be happy? *Be happy.* You want to be wise? *Be wise.* You want to be love? *Be love.*

That is Who You Are in any event.

You are My Beloved.

Oh! I just lost my breath! You have such a wondrous way of putting things.

It is the truth that is eloquent. Truth has an elegance that startles the heart to its own reawakening.

That is what these *Conversations with God* have done. They have touched the heart of the human race, and reawakened it.

Now they lead you to a critical question. It is a question all of humanity must ask itself. Can, and will, you create a new cultural story? Can and will you devise a new First Cultural Myth, upon which all other myths are based?

363

Is the human race inherently good, or inherently evil?

This is the crossroads to which you have come. The future of the human race depends on which way you go.

If you and your society believe you are inherently good, you will make decisions and laws that are life affirming and constructive. If you and your society believe that you are inherently evil, you will make decisions and laws that are life denying and destructive.

Laws that are life affirming are laws that allow you to be, do, and have what you wish. Laws that are life denying are laws that stop you from being, doing, and having what you wish.

Those who believe in Original Sin, and that the inherent nature of man is _evil,_ claim that God has created laws which _stop_ you from doing as you wish—and promote human laws (an endless number of them) that seek to do the same.

Those who believe in Original Blessing, and that the inherent nature of man is _good,_ proclaim that God has created natural laws which _allow_ you to do as you wish—and promote human laws that seek to do the same.

What is your viewpoint of the human race? What is your viewpoint of your Self? Left entirely to your own devices, do you see yourself as being able to be trusted? In everything? How about others? How do you view them? Until they reveal themselves to you, one way or the other, what is your basic assumption?

Now, answer this. Do your assumptions further your society in breaking _down,_ or breaking _through?_

I see my Self as trustworthy. I never did before, but now I do. I have _become_ trustworthy, because I have changed my ideas on the kind of person I am. I am also clear now on what God wants, and what God doesn't want. I am clear about You.

These _Conversations with God_ have played a huge role in that change, in making that shift possible. And I now see in society what I see in myself—not something that is breaking down, but something that is breaking through. I see a human culture that is at last awakening to its divine heritage, aware of its divine purpose, and increasingly conscious of its divine Self.

If that is what you see, that is what you will create. Once you were lost, but now you are found. You were blind, but now you see. And this *has* been an amazing grace.

You have sometimes been apart from Me in your heart, but now We are whole again, and We can be forever. For what you have joined together, no one but you can put asunder.

Remember this: You are always a part, because you are never apart. You are always a part OF God, because you are never apart FROM God.

This is the truth of your being. We are whole. So now you know the whole truth.

This truth has been food for the hungry soul. Take, and eat of it. The world has thirsted for this joy. Take, and drink of it. Do this in re-membrance of Me.

For truth is the body, and joy is the blood, of God, who is love.

Truth.

Joy.

Love.

These three are interchangeable. One leads to the other, and it matters not in which order they appear. All lead to Me. All *are* Me.

And so I end this dialogue as it began. As with life itself, it comes full circle. You have been given truth here. You have been given joy. You have been given love. You have been given here the answers to the largest mysteries of life. There is now only one question remaining. It is the question with which we began.

The question is not, to whom do I talk, but who listens?

Thank You. Thank You for talking to *all* of us. We have heard You, and we will listen. I love You. And as this dialogue ends, I *am* filled with truth, joy, and love. I am filled with You. I feel my Oneness with God.

That place of Oneness is heaven.

You are there now.

You are never *not* there, because you are never *not* One with Me.

This is what I would have you know. This is what I would have you take, at last, from this conversation.

And here is My message, the message I would seek to leave with the world:

My Children, who art in Heaven, hallowed is your name. Your kingdom is come, and your will is done, on Earth as it is in Heaven.

You are given this day your daily bread, and you are forgiven your debts, and your trespasses, exactly to the degree that you have forgiven those who trespass against you.

Lead your Self not into temptation, but deliver your Self from the evils you have created.

For thine *is* the Kingdom, and the Power, and the Glory, forever.

Amen.

And amen.

Go now, and change your world. Go now, and be your Highest Self. You understand now all that you need to understand. You know now all that you need to know. You are now all that you need to be.

You never were anything less. You simply did not know this. You did not remember it.

Now you remember. Seek to carry this remembrance with you always. Seek to share it with all those whose lives you touch. For yours is a destiny grander than you might ever have imagined.

You have come to the room to heal the room. You have come to the space to heal the space.

There is no other reason for you to be here.

And know this: I love you. My love is always yours, both now, and even forever more.
I am with you always.
All ways.

Goodbye, God. Thank You for this dialogue. Thank You, thank You, *thank You.*

And you, My wonderful creation. Thank you. For you have given God a voice again—and a place in your heart. And that is all either of Us have ever really wanted.
We are together again. And it is very good.

In Closing . . .

This has been an extraordinary experience for me, as you might imagine. The delivering of this trilogy took six years—four of them consumed by the last volume. I have done my best to stand out of the way and let The Process work its wonders. I believe that for the most part I have succeeded in that, although I readily acknowledge not having been a perfect filter. Some of what has come through me is no doubt distorted. It would, therefore, be a mistake to take this—or any other—writing on spiritual matters and turn it into literal truth. I want to discourage anyone who may have an idea about doing that. Don't make more of it than what is here. On the other hand, *don't make less of it, either.*

What is here is an important message. It is a message which could change the world. Many lives have already been altered by the *CWG* material. Now translated into 24 languages, and on international bestseller lists month after month, it has found its way into the hands of millions of people across the globe. *CWG* study groups have formed spontaneously in over 150 cities, with that number growing each month. At this writing, we are receiving four to six hundred letters a week from people who have been so deeply touched by the insight, the wisdom, and the truth in these writings that they have been moved to contact me personally.

In order to handle this overwhelming response, Nancy and I have formed a non-profit foundation that publishes a monthly newsletter containing answers to readers' questions, and news about lectures, retreats, and other *CWG* teaching materials. If you would like to "stay connected" with the energy of this message, and to help spread it to others, a subscription to this newsletter is a wonderful way to do so. A portion of each subscription fee is placed in our scholarship fund, allowing those would not otherwise be able to afford to do so, an opportunity to attend our programs, or receive our newsletter, free of charge. Send $35 (U.S. $45 for international subscriptions) for one year to:

Newsletter Subscription
c/o **ReCreation**
*The Foundation for Personal Growth
and Spiritual Understanding*
1257 Siskiyou Blvd., #1150
Ashland, OR 97520
Telephone 541-482-8806
e-mail: *recreating@aol.com*

There is more that you can do if you wish to truly become involved in activating the message you have found here. First, you can begin by reading other important material on the subjects covered in this trilogy. Taking a suggestion I was given in this dialogue, I have researched, discovered, and now enthusiastically recommend a brief, but powerful, reading list. I have labeled it Eight Books That Can Change the World.

I do not merely recommend these books, I personally request that you read them. Why? Because I believe that the people of Earth are moving into an extraordinary time. Decisions will be made in the next few years which will set our course and direction for decades to come. The choices now being placed before the human community are enormous, and tomorrow's choices will be even more momentous as our options become increasingly limited.

All of us will play a role in the making of these decisions. They will not be left to someone else. We *are* the someone else. The decisions I am talking about cannot, or will not, be made by any political power structure, the influential elite, or corporate giants. They will be made in the hearts and in the homes of individuals and families around the world.

What shall we teach our children? Where shall we spend our money? Which of our dreams and aspirations, wants, and desires shall be our highest goals, our top priorities? How shall we treat our environment? What is the best way to stay healthy, and how shall we improve our diet? What shall we ask of our leaders—and what shall we demand? How shall we judge when life is going well? What shall be our measure of success? How shall we learn to love? The aggregate impact of these very personal choices will create what scientist and author Rupert Sheldrake calls a "morphic field"—a "resonance" that sets the tone for life on a worldwide scale.

So it is important—crucial, in fact—that each individual's role be a *conscious* one. Our choices cannot be made in a vacuum. And as well informed as many of us believe we are (and, frankly, because some of us are not), I believe there will be profound benefit in reading these books, or I would not take this time to point them out to you.

I know that there are many wonderful titles, and obviously this list could be much longer. These are my own personal choices, some written by people I have come to know, others by people I have never met, but every book very powerful, meaningful, and important. I hope you will read these Eight Books That Can Change the World:

1. *The Healing of America*, by Marianne Williamson. A fiery book filled with searing insights and brave solutions, it provides rich nourishment for anyone thinking seriously about where we are and where we want to go, as individuals, as a nation, and as a species. The latest work from a woman of uncommon courage and social commitment, this book cries out to those who would seek a newer world.

2. *The Last Hours of Ancient Sunlight*, by Thom Hartmann. A book that will shock and awaken you . . . and may even anger you. What it will not do is leave you untouched. You will be unable to experience your life, and life on this planet, in the same way again—and that will be good for you *and* the planet. A "shaker-upper." Easy to read, urgent and powerful.

3. *Conscious Evolution—Awakening the Power of Our Social Potential*, by Barbara Marx Hubbard. A document of breathtaking scope and vision—eloquent, compelling, and wise in its description of where we have been and where we are heading as *homo sapiens*—it sweeps us to a new level of awareness of our possibilities. An inspiring call to our highest selves as we move into the time of co-creating the new millennium.

4. *Reworking Success*, by Robert Theobald, who has been called one of the ten most important and influential futurists of our time. A small book with a huge message: unless we rechoose what we call "winning" in this culture, the culture itself will not be around much longer. Our old ideas of what is "good" for us are killing us.

5. _The Celestine Vision,_ from James Redfield. Offers a road map into a new and possible future, a path to a wonderful tomorrow, if we will but take it. The simplest truths and the most profound, they are placed right before us to use as tools in the creation of the life of which we have all for so long dreamed. Suddenly, the dream is within reach.

6. _The Politics of Meaning,_ by Michael Lerner. Down to earth and yet wonderfully uplifting, this is an eloquent plea for sanity, compassion, and simple, human love in our politics, in our economics, and in our corporate world. Contains striking ideas and marvelous visions of how the world could work, if we could only get the power structure to truly care—with suggestions on how we might cause that to happen.

7. _The Future of Love,_ by Daphne Rose Kingma. A dazzling exploration of a new way to love each other—a way that acknowledges the power of the soul in intimate relationships. Deeply insightful and daringly fresh, this book takes a breathtaking step away from tradition and into the possibility of saying yes to the true and grandest desire of our being: to love fully.

8. _Diet for a New America,_ by John Robbins. A highly impactful treatment of a simple subject: food. It is a revelation. The poisons we eat, and the poor quality of our nutrients, is explored in a way that will change forever how you look at what you put into your body. This book challenges the assumption that it is good to consume the flesh of dead animals, and presents startling evidence of the economic and health benefits of no longer eating meat.

All of these books offer a blueprint for tomorrow. The similarities in their articulations are often startling. It is difficult to believe that these writers didn't sit down with each other and agree on what they were going to say, and how they were going to say it. That didn't happen, of course, and so the astonishment here is the level of syncronicity.

The vision of these eight authors is so clear, so exciting, and offers a view of civilized society so outrageously better than our present day-to-day reality, that your heart will sing with exaltation, and you will immediately want to know what you can do to help move things along. Fortunately for all of us, Marianne, Thom, Barbara, Robert, James, Michael, Daphne, and John have provided specific and solid suggestions on where to go from here. The books, all of them, are chock full of ideas on what *you can do, now,* to make things better, and to create long-term change in our world.

I also would like to make you aware of three organizations which are, at this very moment, actively and vigorously engaged in the work to which the *Conversations with God* trilogy calls us, and one grass-roots citizen campaign which seeks to uplift the world. You may wish to explore these groups further, to see if you agree with their philosophies, and if they may have already put into place a mechanism through which your own visions and choices can be realized.

In the area of spirituality: *The Emissaries.*

This is an association of people in many countries whose primary interest is to coordinate accurately with the way life works in all aspects of daily experience and to seek to reveal the character of God in practical living. The group believes that when this is done consistently and in concert with others, the resulting collective revelation of divine character sounds a tone in humanity, calling forth awakening and a return to true identity.

The descriptive term "emissary of divine light" refers to anyone who consistently expresses a stable, true, and loving spirit. Implicit in this is the acceptance of responsibility to face and let go of attitudes and assumptions that limit the release of inherent spiritual potential.

Of course, there are thousands of people, never having heard of The Emissaries, whose presence where they are is genuinely radiant and uplifting. To that extent they are emissaries of divine light, and their lives carry authority and power. Through the means of deliberate association and activities such as correspondence courses, seminars, attunement, and regular weekly meetings, The Emissaries provide an ongoing context for shared spiritual and creative work. They may be reached at:

The Emissaries
5569 North County Road, #29
Loveland, Colorado 80538
Telephone 970-679-4200
e-mail: *sunrise@emnet.org*

In the area of politics: _The Natural Law Party._

Founded in 1992 to fill a void in the political structure of the United States, the Natural Law Party has now established itself in many countries of the world. The party believes that to continue human progress and to flourish as a planetary community, we must bolster our alliance with "natural law," which is described as "the laws of nature—orderly principles governing life throughout the physical universe."

The candidate for president of the Natural Law Party in the United States in the last election, physicist John Hagelin, says, "It is unfortunately true that many of our institutions, modern technologies, and patterns of behavior increasingly violate the laws of nature. Our medicines with their dangerous side effects, chemical pesticides, fertilizers and genetically engineered crops, and even some of our financial institutions, are sowing the seeds of future epidemics, class warfare, and environmental disasters." Of course, _Conversations with God_ makes the same points, over and over again.

The Natural Law Party offers a political platform from which to address these issues. It may be contacted in the United States at:

The Natural Law Party
1946 Mansion Drive
P. O. Box 1900
Fairfield, IA 52556
Telephone 515-472-2040
online at: _www.natural-law.org_

In the area of spiritual-political activism in the United States: _The American Renaissance Alliance._

This is an organization which I am personally partnering in co-creating with author, lecturer, and visionary, Marianne Williamson, who observes that "as the power of the spirit rises within us, so does our desire to be of service to the world. The processes of democracy can facilitate such service, giving every citizen the opportunity to express our spiritual values in the political domain."

Love, mercy, peace, and justice will dwell at the forefront of our global political landscape when enough people decide to place them there. In the U.S., the American Renaissance Alliance provides an organized context for philosophical inquiry and political action, bringing together like-minded people in the service of a common good. Our purpose is to harness the spiritual power at the core of American democracy, in powerful witness to the love of God within us all.

Marianne and I envision that in cities throughout the United States, two or more will gather to pray for peace and work for justice. As Marianne writes for our brochure, "Dedicated to the idea that soul force is more powerful than brute force, the Alliance actively proclaims a vision of an America delivered from the clutches of greed, grounded in peace, and evolving toward even more love. We believe this is our destiny as a global species, as well, and will support similar organizations which create themselves worldwide.

"The American Renaissance Alliance is not a traditionally issue-oriented political organization. We feel that *the issues are not the issue.* The vast majority of America's problems stem from an underlying source: the disengagement of average people from their country's political process. The same is true around the world."

I believe the message in *Conversations with God* contains not only an explicit invitation, but a call to action. I hope it will be heard by people everywhere. In the United States, where I live, Marianne Williamson and I hope that our American Renaissance Alliance will provide a model that can be duplicated worldwide. Again, as Marianne says, it is "A model of a non-partisan organization affirming the political importance of high-minded conservative, as well as high-minded liberal, values. Our desire is not to limit, but rather to release, the political power of every individual according to his or her own conscience, and in support of his or her own beliefs. In short, we seek to assist people in bringing their souls to bear on the world around them."

If you are interested in more information about the work Marianne and I are doing around holistic politics and its principles in action, and would like to join with us, please contact:

The American Renaissance Alliance
P. O. Box 15712
Washington, D.C. 20003
Telephone 202-544-1219
online at: *www.renaissancealliance.org*

Finally, you could not have missed the repeated references in this third installment of the *CWG* trilogy to "what works." The point was made a number of times in the dialogue that highly evolved beings consistently observe "what's so" and "what works."

There are now cropping up in our society several efforts to take a closer look at programs and undertakings which are already addressing many of the problems we face. One of which I am personally aware is the Campaign for Positive Solutions, an initiative to help build a new civilization based on what is already working.

The campaign's purpose is to scan for, map, connect, and communicate these breakthroughs, and encourage their replication. When these breakthroughs are adapted and adopted more widely, we will save billions of dollars and improve the quality of life for millions of people. I am working closely with this campaign, and through it I hope to build support for people to bring the best of what works to their community, and to create projects which contribute to healing and evolving our world.

The director of the Campaign for Positive Solutions is Eleanor Mulloney LeCain, working with futurist Barbara Marx Hubbard, Nancy Carroll, and Patricia Ellsberg. The Campaign is a project of Barbara's non-profit foundation. Individuals, groups, organizations, and institutions are invited to place projects that are working into its website, providing a way to share what you know, and to learn from the successes of others. You may visit the website at http://www.cocreation.org.

You may also form a small group in your community, church, organization, or among your friends and begin the process of synergy and co-creation. Ask yourselves these questions: 1) What is my passion to create right now? Where is the "juice" for me? 2) What are my needs? Where do I feel blocked in taking my next step? 3) What resources do I want to share freely with others? 4) What do I know that is already working, in my own life, in my work, and in the world? Then, place your projects, and others that you know are working, on the web site.

Further information on this initiative may be had by contacting:

The Foundation for Conscious Evolution
P.O. Box 6397
San Rafael, CA 94903-0397
Telephone 415-454-8191
e-mail: *fce@peaceroom.org*

I hope that some of this information has served you. My object here has been to offer you a jump-start, if you choose it, in activating the message of *CWG*. I know that not all of you will agree with all of the authors or organizations I have mentioned here. That's okay. If they do nothing but cause us all to stop and think, they will have provided a wonderful service.

Now, as we end this three-book dialogue, I want to say thank you. Thank you for extending me the tolerance of allowing the free flow of the ideas which have come through me. I am sure that not every one of you has agreed with everything that has been written here. Again, that's okay. In fact, it's *preferable*. I am not comfortable with anything which is swallowed whole. And the largest message of *Conversations with God* is that we may, each of us, conduct our own dialogue with Deity, contact our own inner wisdom, and find our own inner truth. That is where the freedom is. That is where the opportunity lies. That is where the ultimate purpose of life is fulfilled.

We have a chance now, you and I, to recreate ourselves anew in the next grandest version of the greatest vision we ever held about Who We Are. We have a chance to change our lives, and to truly change the world.

I am told that it was George Bernard Shaw who first said, "There are those who see the world as it is, and ask, *Why?* And there are those who see the world as it could be, and ask, *Why not?*" Today, as you and I finish this journey through the *CWG* trilogy together, I invite you to embrace your highest vision of yourself and the world, and to ask, *Why not?*

Blessed be.

Neale Donald Walsch

Index

A

abortion, 247, 250, 254
abuse, tolerating, 282, 338
acceptance, as prerequisite for change, 150
action, to initiate internal change, 14–16
afterlife. *See* life after death
age, wisdom and, 28–29, 34–35
aliens. *See* life, on other planets; spacemen
altruism, 17. *See also* giving; selfishness
American Renaissance Alliance, 374–375
anger, 24, 283, 312
  allowing children to express, 26
  based on sexual shame, 32–33
  healthy, natural, 25
  repression of, 26, 40
animals, 134, 297
  killing, 285
approval, need for, 4
arrogance, 261
art, primitive, 272, 273
Atlantis, Lost City of, 270
attack. *See also* force; killing
  experience of, 281, 283
aura, 173, 174, 177
avoidance, ineffectiveness of, 110, 150. *See also* denial
awareness, 164, 182, 292–293, 334. *See also* God; love, and awareness
  vs. guilt, 5
  total, 83, 84, 161–162, 164–165

B

Babaji, Mahavatar, 95, 324
"bad child," 46
Bain, Barnet, 73
Be-Do-Have paradigm, 14–15, 17
being, 21, 331, 362
belief(s). *See also* values
  awareness as key to, 83
  as determining experience, 82, 86
  influenced by behavior, 13
  levels of, 82, 83
Bible, 73, 94, 208, 274, 305
birth, 201
bliss. *See* Oneness
body, physical, 170–174, 177, 246, 281, 330
books, recommended, 185, 270, 279, 370–373
brain, 170
breathing, 163
Buddha, 144, 188, 324

C

Campaign for Positive Solutions, 376
cannabis, 293
Carroll, Nancy, 376
caution
  vs. fear, 5, 26
  as love of Self, 26
celebration, 110
Celestine Vision (Redfield), 372
celibacy. *See* sexual abstinence
chakras, 54, 151, 152, 154–157, 162, 171

379

About the Artists

Louis Jones is a native of Tidewater, Virginia. His egg temperas, watercolors, and drawings reflect his love of nature and his love for people—capturing, as he describes, "the moving skies, the fluid landscapes . . . the discarded homes and faded dreams of rural America." Jones's work has been shown in galleries throughout the United States and Europe, and he was one of the select few American artists to display at the Contemporary Art Exhibit in Bath, England. He has been included in *American Artists of Renown.*

Elizabeth Hinshaw is a self-taught portrait artist who specializes in charcoal and pastel pencils. For fifteen years she has been showing her art and accepting commissions from corporate and private clients around the world. Elizabeth may be reached at P.O. Box 585, Ashland, OR 97520.

For a limited edition reprint of the original cover painting by Louis Jones, please write to:

The Louis & Susan Jones Art Gallery
Dominion Tower
999 Waterside Drive
Norfolk, VA 23510

Or call (757) 625-6505 for further information.

Hampton Roads Publishing Company
publishes and distributes books on a variety of subjects,
including metaphysics, health, alternative/complementary medicine,
visionary fiction, and other related topics.

To order or receive a copy of our latest catalog, call toll-free,
(800) 766-8009, or send your name and address to:

Hampton Roads Publishing Company, Inc.
134 Burgess Lane
Charlottesville, VA 22902

Internet: www.hrpub.com
e-mail: hrpc@hrpub.com